C000257461

RF

ISBN 185414 138 4

Published by Capital Transport Publishing
38 Long Elmes, Harrow Weald, Middlesex

Printed by Winchmore Press Ltd
Fowler Road, Hainault, Ilford, Essex

© Ken Glazier 1991

RF

KEN GLAZIER

WALTON-ON-THE-HILL
80A Sutton
Belmont

PAY AS YOU ENTER
PLEASE

MXX 284

Capital Transport

Left **Private Hire RF 6 at Wembley Stadium in the early 1960s.** Fred Ivey

Opposite **BEA 4RF4 coaches in the original and second liveries at Heathrow Airport in 1965.** B.J. Davis

RFW 6 alongside RFs 129 and 77 at London Airport (Heathrow) in May 1957. Bruce Jenkins

RF 126 in experimental light green livery passes K1 trolleybus 1114 at Shepherds Bush in 1961. Fred Ivey

CHAPTERS

APPENDICES

Top left **Modernised Green Line RF 201 at Hampton Court in October 1966**. G.A. Rixon

Centre left **RF 69 at Luton in the 'light National green' livery which was the first departure by London Country from London Transport's Lincoln green**. John Boylett

Left **RF 183 in Staines High Street in the light National green livery as applied to modernised Green Line coaches converted to buses**. John Boylett

Above **RF 312 in NBC corporate livery at Harlow in June 1973**. Capital Transport

RF 221, one of the last survivors with LCBS, seen at work at Hampton Court in May 1978. G.A. Rixon

RF 79, converted for use as a breakdown vehicle by LCBS, is seen at the Green Line 50th anniversary rally at Brent Cross in 1980. Stephen Fennell

Former RF 633 with the west London company of Valliant in 1974. Colin Brown

PASSENGER TRANSPORT

Vol. 102. No. 2595.   APRIL 12th, 1950   30/- Yearly, Post Free. Single Copies 1/6.

REGISTERED AT THE G.P.O. AS A NEWSPAPER.

AEC
SOUTHALL

'REGAL' mark IV
UNDERFLOOR
ENGINE CHASSIS

A.C.V. SALES LTD., 49, BERKELEY SQUARE, LONDON, W.1.
BUILDERS OF LONDON'S BUSES.

THE MOST ADVANCED
PASSENGER CHASSIS
DESIGN OF TO-DAY

WRITE FOR DETAILS

AUTHOR'S NOTE

The London RF shares with the RT family a special distinction, both having represented the pinnacle of achievement in their respective fields and both destined to serve London well beyond their planned operational lives. The Regal IV was itself the culmination of a long series of developments dating back to the earliest days of motor bus manufacture and, when I was asked to write this book, I decided that it was appropriate to set the RF in its true historical context. In doing so I was honoured to receive the help of Alan Townsin, who was responsible for the original text of the two chapters on the history and technical development of the model. I am most grateful to Alan, not only for this but also for the considerable help and guidance he was able to give, for which his wealth of experience and knowledge of the industry was invaluable. My particular thanks must also go to Lawrie Bowles for his unstinted efforts on the detailed research, and to Ken Blacker, Martin Elms, Malcolm Papes and Colin Stannard for supplying invaluable information which has helped me to enrich the text and make it as accurate as I can.

London, August 1991   KEN GLAZIER

NEW QUIET GREEN LINE COACH MAKES LONDON TRIP No. 1

London Transport's new Green Line coach made its first trip on the streets of London to-day. It ran through the West End on route 704 from Windsor to Tunbridge Wells, and is the first of a fleet of over 260 super-comfort vehicles of a new design.

They are to replace all present coaches on the Green Line routes during the next nine months.

London Transport officials say the "RF" is the smoothest riding vehicle which they have ever put on the road. Luxury-car type springing has been achieved by putting the engine under the floor, which has enabled the suspension to be "softened."

The coach will be very quiet, because "pilot injection," which almost eliminates noise, has been introduced into the engine. Hitherto London Transport has only used pilot injection experimentally on a few buses.

The new coach has a distinctive blunt-nosed front, with deep windows, which resembles the cab of a modern tube train.

Above Evening Standard 1st October 1951.

Above Left **An April 1950 advert for the new Regal IV with an illustration of the vehicle that entered trial service with London Transport the following month.**

Below **At the start of its long career, RF 26 turns from Eccleston Bridge into Buckingham Palace Road when both were two-way streets.** LT Museum 15047

The Central Area
version of the Q
adopted the entrance
position ahead of the
front wheels, a
layout which was to
be used for the RFs
fifteen years later.
The thirty-seven seat
bodywork was
supplied by Park
Royal Coachworks
Ltd, whose factory
forms the
background to this
maker's photograph
of Q 107.
Alan Townsin
Collection

1 THE PATHFINDERS

Opposite Top Q 1 in its original condition at AEC's Southall works in the spring of 1932, before its remarkably modern looking LGOC built Chiswick body had been modified for service. The absence of partitions behind the driver's seat and the entrance doorway can be seen clearly in this view.

Opposite Centre Left The interior of Q 1 after it had been modified before entering service. Bulkheads have now been added behind the driver and to the rear of the entrance steps. The wooden framed seats, with their straight sides, add a dated stamp to otherwise cleanly finished modern styling, the curved tops to the window frames being particularly notable. LT Museum U11334

Opposite Centre Right The interior of a BRCW body of a 4Q4 when new. The stanchion of the transverse seat for two alongside the driver's cab incorporates a partial bulkhead above cantrail level, presumably to shield the cab from the saloon lighting. The treatment of the windows, with window cappings semi-circular in section and fully rounded corners, was the first application of a style which was not to appear on production double-deckers for another five years and remained in use up to and including the RF class.
Alan Townsin Collection

Opposite Bottom Left The interior of the 5Q5 established the basic finish which was to remain standard until the RF era. Tubular aluminium framed seats were adopted generally by London Transport from the beginning of 1936 and the treatment of the windows and other interior finishes continued the styling started by the 4Q4s. Opening windows were operated by a winding mechanism for the first time on these vehicles.
Alan Townsin Collection

Opposite Bottom Right Although similar in most respects to the 5Q5, the coach specification for the thirty-two seat Park Royal bodywork of the 6Q6 introduced the full width driving cab at the production stage and included overhead parcel racks, deeper seat cushions, moquette coverings on the seat backs, a saloon heater and ash trays.
Alan Townsin Collection

As the initials indicate, the London Transport RF class of single-decker was a 'flat' engined contemporary of the RT double-decker and its principal mechanical feature was the use of a horizontal underfloor engine. Yet not only London Transport and its predecessors but the industry as a whole had been considering where best to put the engine long before the first RF models appeared on the road in May 1951.

Possibly influenced by experiments in the United States in the 1920s, the Associated Equipment Company, under the firm guidance of the renowned George Rackham, developed a remarkably innovative side-engined model known as the 'Q' in the early 1930s. A six-cylinder petrol engine, of basically similar design to that then in use on the conventional 'Regent' and other models, was mounted behind the offside front wheel, the transmission running down the chassis along that side to the rear axle. Setting the axle much nearer the rear of the vehicle than usual allowed the weight it carried to be reduced sufficiently to permit the use of single rear tyres. With the differential offset as far to the right as possible, the propellor shaft was angled only slightly.

The prototype single-decker (Q 1) entered service with the LGOC in September 1932 but immediate subsequent development concentrated on the double-deck version, which was eventually not pursued because it gave no advantage over conventional types. For a single-decker, however, the pros and cons stacked up differently. In London a relatively spacious seating layout tended to be favoured in the interests of easy circulation of boarding and alighting passengers. Even the thirty-foot long LT type Renown single-deckers of 1931 seated only thirty-five. Yet limited seating capacity had obvious economic disadvantages

on routes where bridges or other obstacles made double-deck operation impossible but where traffic was relatively heavy and more seats per vehicle were desirable.

Even so, it came as something of a surprise when the newly formed London Passenger Transport Board placed an order for 100 AEC 'Q' type single-deckers, for use in the country area, late in 1934. This was the Board's first order for full size single-deckers and made a dramatic contrast to the double-deck policy based on the STL class 'Regent' model. Moreover, the model had hardly been a success from the sales point of view, despite extensive publicity.

The original design of the 100 LPTB single-deckers delivered in the spring of 1935 was that they were to seat thirty-eight passengers. The first vehicles were built in this form but were reduced to thirty-seven before entering service. This batch, of which the general LPTB classification was 4Q4, had bodywork built by the Birmingham Railway Carriage and Wagon Company of basically similar layout to the prototype, with the entrance just behind the front axle. With hindsight, it seems surprising that the standard Q single-deck chassis had insufficient front overhang to permit the positioning of the entrance ahead of the front axle. The 4Q4 class vehicles had bodywork with a longitudinal seat for two passengers to the left of the driver but this was soon found to be unsatisfactory and removed, allowing a full width partition to be fitted but reducing the seating capacity to thirty-five, barely more than would have been possible with a reasonably spacious layout on a conventional front-engined 'Regal' chassis. Indeed only a few years later thirty-four seat bodies were to be built on conventional 'Regal' chassis for the Green Line coach services.

Meanwhile, however, the idea of a single-decker with entrance ahead of the front axle had been taken up by the Northern General Transport Co. Ltd, many of whose routes were quite busy but could not be operated by double-deckers because of low bridges. The first prototype, built in 1933, seated forty-five, effectively the maximum attainable on a thirty-foot long single-decker with normal seating. Such a vehicle length was only permissible at that date by adopting a three-axle layout and the earlier NGT buses were all six-wheelers, using an engine position and transmission layout very similar to that of the AEC 'Q'. However, there was a fundamental difference for, by using the side valve-engine, it was possible to take advantage of its reduced height and arrange forward facing seats directly above it, something not possible on the diesel-engined 'Q' unless a very high floor was adopted.

The prototype NGT SE6 had the entrance behind the front wheels but five further buses built in 1934 adopted the set-back front axle and entrance directly to the left of the driver. Seating capacity was forty-four, arranged in eleven rows, all facing forward. NGT, well pleased with these vehicles, decided to build thirty-one for its 1935 programme but could not cope with the chassis assembly in its own shops and gave the job to AEC. Doubtless both AEC and LT were aware of the NGT vehicles in any case but the assembly of these chassis at Southall must have underlined the possibilities.

London Transport had decided to standardise on oil-engined vehicles and since the oil engine had of necessity to be of the overhead valve layout, the NGT 'low-built engine' idea could not have been applied. However, it is significant that the batch of eighty 'Q's built mainly for Central Area duties in 1936 (coded 5Q5) adopted the entrance ahead of the front axle. The wheelbase was reduced from the unusually long 18ft 6ins of the standard model by two feet, and the floor level was slightly higher than the 4Q4, but even so the thirty-seven seat capacity in the Park Royal built bodies included longitudinal seats over both front wheel arches as well as the engine.

Meanwhile, there had been further developments elsewhere. In 1935 the Birmingham and Midland Motor Omnibus Company, better known as 'Midland Red', built a prototype rear-engined bus with the power unit mounted transversely at the nearside of an engine compartment running across the rear of the bus. This and three further similar chassis built in 1936 were petrol-engined. These REC models were admired but never put into production.

Among manufacturers, Leyland experimented with a rear-engined single-decker, completed in January 1936, but this was also not put into production. However, at about the end of that year it was Leyland that became involved with London Transport in what proved to be something of a landmark in British bus development as well as what could be regarded as a direct precursor of the RF. This was the construction of a single-decker with horizontal underfloor engine. Such a layout could not be claimed as entirely new, for Büssing had introduced its Trambus model with similar engine configuration in Germany in 1930 and, in America, White had put a

Northern General's prototype SE6 when new in July 1933, posed, judging by the architecture, somewhere in the Medway Towns before making its journey north from the Short Bros factory in Rochester. Unlike subsequent models, No.586 (CN5674) as it became, did not have its entrance ahead of the front axle. The American built Hercules side-valve engine was low enough to enable forty-five seats to be accommodated in the thirty-foot long body, all facing forwards. *Alan Townsin Collection*

model with a twelve-cylinder horizontal petrol engine into production following its announcement in 1932. Significantly, perhaps, official Leyland pictures dated May 1937 exist of the installation of a Leyland T-type six-cylinder engine in horizontal form under a White bus. It is not possible to distinguish from the photographs whether it was petrol or oil but from a design viewpoint this is not in itself very important, as Leyland's T-type engine, of which the original had been designed under G.J. Rackham's chief engineering for the Titan TD1, was the company's standard engine in both forms in the 1930s.

The Leyland underfloor-engined model for the LPTB was designated FEC, presumably signifying 'flat-engined coach', by its makers and given the usual model name 'Tiger' then applied to the standard front-engined six-cylinder single-deck model of the time. In fact it had precious little in common with the contemporary TS8 standard 'Tiger' model which had just been introduced by the time the FEC

prototype was first licensed in September 1937, beyond the basic design of the 8.6 litre T-type oil engine and, of course, even this was turned on its side. The model was far better known by its London Transport designation TF and it seems clear that the input to its design came as strongly from Chiswick as from Leyland's own drawing office.

The TF was intended primarily as a Green Line coach and as such the LPTB did not at that stage require the entrance to be ahead of the front axle. The final batch of AEC 'Q'-type single-deckers for the Board, fifty vehicles with Park Royal bodywork, also for Green Line duty, built in the winter of 1936-37, had reverted to the standard wheelbase and full-width cab, albeit rather shallower on the nearside than on the offside where the driver sat. These 6Q6 coaches had seats for thirty-two passengers and the use of longitudinal seats tended to be wasteful of space as well as undesirable in themselves for the longer journeys of most Green Line passengers.

Parallel development of both underfloor and rear engined single-deckers was taking place in the late 1930s, both by Leyland Motors Ltd and London Transport. The family resemblance between twenty-seat one-man bus CR 1B and experimental Green Line coach TF 1C is well illustrated in this view at Chiswick when both were new. The more conventional frontal appearance of the CR closely resembles that eventually adopted for the TF. *Dennis Odd Collection*

The first TF had a very unusual style of body which can perhaps best be described as looking like a contemporary normal-control coach onto which had been grafted something akin to a small greenhouse, just big enough to accommodate the driver. To be more precise the 'greenhouse' enclosed the steering column and controls, the driver's seat and rear part of the cab being within the body shell. The slim glazing bars ahead of the driver must have given exceptional angles of vision, virtually equivalent to an unbodied chassis but the appearance was evidently a bit too controversial even for the self-confident London Transport, so often a styling leader in that period.

The TF broke new ground in other respects. The chassis frame was straight and higher than usual at that date. In the immediate vicinity of the engine, this was necessary to allow sufficient height for the cylinder block to fit below the sidemember but it was also reasoned that a relatively high floor was desirable to allow all seats to face forward. Straight frames had, of course, been usual on early bus designs but since the mid-1920s a 'proper' passenger chassis was apt to be identified as one with low sidemembers cranked up over the front and rear axles. Similarly, the traditional way of building bodywork was for a body underframe to be constructed to mount on top of the chassis frame. In the TF, however, what was sometimes called 'outrigger' construction was adopted, with the body floor mounted directly on the chassis. Substantial outrigger brackets projecting from the sidemembers connected directly to the body pillars.

This form of construction, though retaining a separate chassis, produced a structure when completed that was virtually equivalent to integral construction. London Transport was interested in this subject and, at the same period, was involved in developing what were then called 'chassisless' trolleybus designs, one of which, produced by the Metropolitan-Cammell concern, was put into production.

It was probably also trolleybus influence which led London Transport to adopt air-pressure brake operation for motor buses. They could offer better performance in relation to driver effort and a further logical development was air-pressure operation of the preselective Wilson type of epicyclic gearbox. The manually-operated preselective gearbox had been adopted as standard for London buses from 1934, again after experiments which had begun in LGOC days. However, the gearchange pedal action was quite heavy and by using air pressure to operate the gearbox, this could be reduced.

The TF incorporated an AEC-built preselective gearbox, much as used in other London buses of the time but with an external air cylinder to lighten the pedal action. The first vehicle, TF 1, was therefore a pointer to what was to follow, for the air-operated preselective gearbox with internal air cylinder, standardised in the AEC RT-type double-decker, did not appear even in the prototype form until the first chassis was built in 1938. A production batch of a further eighty-seven TF vehicles, mainly for Green Line work but including twelve Park Royal bodied coaches for sightseeing duties, was completed in 1939. The front end, though still half-cab, was more orthodox than that of TF 1.

Park Royal supplied the bodywork for the first production batch of twelve TFs, thirty-three seat private hire and tours coaches, which entered service at Old Kent Road garage in the spring of 1939. The livery was dark and light green. By some quirk of fate the vehicle chosen for the Board's official photographs, TF 9C was destined to be the only survivor of the sub-class, the rest of which perished in the blitz at Bull Yard Peckham in 1940. The oval white plate on the lower rear panel was the Metropolitan Stage Carriage number, then carried by all buses, but this requirement ceased soon after the delivery of the first TFs. LT Museum U29511

The arrangement of the interior of the TF3s was basically the same as TF 1, except that the sliding door to the driver's cab was replaced by a hinged slam door. The light and airy effect given by the cant glass panels, which could be made even better by opening the sliding centre section of the roof, is well illustrated in this view of TF 9. Special features of the Private Hire version were the clock in the front bulkhead, the lampshades in contemporary styling, patterned moquette on the seat backs, two ash trays to each seat and pockets for passengers' bits and pieces. LT Museum U29513

There is a marvellous air of self confidence in this design, reflecting LT's feelings, not afraid to be unorthodox and yet full of practicality in both concept and detail. TF 16C numerically the third of the main production run classified 2TF2, was for Green Line work. All seventy-five vehicles went to Romford (London Road) during 1939. LT Museum U29233

When production of the 'Q'-type ended in 1936 — the last deliveries being made early in 1937 — AEC listed no model with other than a front-engined layout. However, a particularly interesting prototype chassis was built for Canada in the autumn of 1939. Not only did this have an amidships-mounted underfloor engine but it was also arranged with long front overhang to suit the, by then, usual transatlantic type of entrance ahead of the front axle. The engine is believed to have been a 9.6-litre unit and a torque converter transmission system was fitted, again in line with North American practice. It was bodied by Weymann and shipped to Canada in 1940, giving five years service and thus building up useful operational experience of such a vehicle. In some ways this could be regarded as the prototype of the Regal IV.

The 1939-45 war stopped development of the TF. AEC also built no further underfloor-engined chassis for the time being. However, it did not stop engineers from thinking about the future and in some cases trying out the results of their thoughts. In particular, the appointment of Donald M. Sinclair as Chief Engineer of the Midland Red concern in 1940 was to prove crucial, not only for that firm but for the British bus industry as a whole. He had been Assistant Chief Engineer of Northern General, under another famous engineer G.W. Hayter, when the side-engined buses were being developed.

By the time he arrived at Midland Red, Sinclair was forming the view that the future lay with the underfloor engine. The Midland Red rear-engine prototypes were thus, one-by-one, taken in hand and rebuilt, using a horizontal version of the company's own K-type engine, mounted under the frame amidships. The body on the first one, BHA1, dating originally from 1935, was rebuilt, gaining more than a little resemblance to the final NGT design. It reappeared in its new form in 1941 and the other three chassis were similarly treated and their bodies more extensively rebuilt or replaced by new in 1942-1944. As rebuilt, they received designations S1, S2 and so on and, after a further prototype, a production form was arrived at, this being the S6, offering a forty-seat capacity in its 27ft 6ins length.

Top TF 16 with its front panels removed or open to reveal its inner secrets. On the nearside the radiator filler cap is placed centrally alongside the cooling system and, on the right, the horn. On the nearside, the steering column and box can be seen behind the pipework. LT Museum U29237

Upper Centre The offside of the TF with the engine side panels removed, showing the engine suspended on the underframe. LT Museum 18438

Lower Centre The chassis of the 'Canadian' underfloor engined prototype, photographed at Southall, according to the negative, on 24th October 1939. Alan Townsin Collection

Left The specification is understood to have included a 9.6-litre engine, torque converter transmission, though with a gear lever to engage forward or reverse, and air brakes. The AEC monogram is upside down, presumably because the same 'part' as for the vertical version has been used. Alan Townsin Collection

Midland Red, under Sinclair's lively influence, decided that the S6 was what was wanted for post-war additions to the fleet and one hundred were put in hand, the chassis built in usual fashion in the company's Carlyle Works and the bodies, also to BMMO design, by Brush or Metro-Cammell. As Midland Red put its 100 S6 models into service in 1946-47, some other fleets had to be content with models that would not have been accepted in 1939. Among them was London Transport, which would certainly not have considered purchasing fifty AEC Regal and 131 Leyland Tiger single-deck buses with crash gearboxes in 1946-1948 had there not been an acute shortage of modern single-deckers in the fleet.

The immense demand for bus travel, both for journeys to and from work and for other purposes, in the immediate post-war years meant that operators were not only glad of every vehicle they could put on the road but were increasingly conscious of the need for greater seating capacity. The Government had been approached in wartime with a request for longer as well as wider maximum dimensions for buses but until 1950 no action was taken on this, apart from limited permission, from 1946, to operate vehicles of 8ft rather than 7ft 6ins width on routes which had to be individually approved. Many operators found the inability to run such buses wherever they seemed most useful unacceptable and so the take-up of the idea was limited. Typical front-engined single-deckers of the period seated 32-35 in company fleets, though often slightly less in municipal or London Transport service and the prospect of up to forty in an underfloor-engined model was attractive.

There was also the export market and manufacturers were increasingly conscious of the need to compete with vehicles from other sources. The effect of the war on the British economy meant that there was also strong Government pressure to increase exports and indeed availability of steel and other scarce materials was sometimes conditional on export orders being sufficiently large. Yet it was difficult to divert attention from simply getting urgently needed vehicles of existing types built and at the 1948 Commercial Motor Show, the only complete underfloor-engined bus on display was a Sentinel-Beadle. Even so, it was widely known that both AEC and Leyland were working on such projects and some operators whose circumstances allowed, tended to hold back from placing orders for single-deck buses, concentrating on modernisation of coach fleets. Examples of this were the Ribble and Southdown companies among the BET Group.

Outwardly, it seemed that a relatively small firm, or pair of firms, had stolen a march on the big guns of the business. Beadle, basically a bodybuilding concern, had introduced a very light form of integral construction, early examples, using units from such chassis as Leyland Cub, Commer, Bedford or Dennis Ace models of the pre-war period, having been built for various Tilling Group companies since 1945. All these had front-mounted engines but the Show vehicle used the then recently introduced Sentinel underfloor four-cylinder oil engine. The Show vehicle was for a Tilling company, Southern National, but the only major user was a BET company, Ribble Motor Services Ltd, which had six of the four-cylinder version, followed in 1951 by fourteen of the larger six-cylinder model which had been developed by then, built purely by Sentinel.

In fact, the engineering departments of both AEC and Leyland were busy and may well have had prototypes running by the time of the 1948 Show. In the case of Leyland, the first model to be announced was an integral single-decker, the 'Olympic' of which the body structure was built by the MCW organisation and, although this was not revealed publicly until the end of 1949, the chassis number of the first to be completed was issued in the early months of 1948. At AEC, as will be seen in Chapter Three, the first prototype of its new Regal IV model was bodied in January 1949 though both AEC and Leyland, then fiercely competitive with each other, chose not to announce their new models until December of that year.

Below Left **Midland Red 1551 (BHA1) had its original petrol rear engine replaced in 1941 by a horizontal underfloor version of BMMO's own 8-litre K type. The rebuilt body brought in some Northern General-like features, similar to the 1938 batch of SE4s, particularly in the outline of the front end. It remained in this form until 1952 when the front end was again rebuilt. In this 1950 rear view it is parked behind one of West Bromwich Corporation's tram replacement Metro-Cammell bodied Daimler COG6s. Below Right The old New Street station in Birmingham broods over the Navigation Street stand, where Midland Red's pioneering experimental chassisless underfloor engined single-decker prepares for a trip to Stourbridge. Classified S5, 2579 had a forty-seat Metro-Cammell body and was new in 1946. Behind the S5 is a wartime austerity Bedford OB. Bottom Left The eight-foot wide version of the standard early post-war BMMO S6 single-decker was classified S8, 100 of which entered service in 1948/49. The 27ft 6in long Metro-Cammell forty-seat bodywork was mounted on conventional underfloor engined BMMO chassis. All were lengthened to 29ft 3ins and their seating increased to forty-four between 1951 and 1953. Bottom Right The Brush bodied version of the S8 was called S9 but this one, 3441, was extensively modified by Carlyle Works when it was new in March 1950 with what was called the American front. The more upright front, with recessed windscreens, designed to incorporate glider entrance doors, set the standard for subsequent production and could well have influenced the Metro-Cammell design adopted on the RF. Alan Townsin Collection/Dennis Odd Collection**

2 AFTER WORLD WAR TWO

It is perhaps idle but nevertheless interesting to speculate on what might have happened had the war not intervened and put a stop to further development for six years. On the day before Green Line services were abruptly withdrawn, apart from the almost new fleet of 10T10s and TFs, there were still thirty-four 9T9s, forty-nine 6Q6s, a solitary 7T7 and a 4Q4 scheduled for coach service and these may well have been ripe for replacement as coaches within a couple of years. There was therefore potential for perhaps another one hundred coaches (after adding engineering spares) but there was also a quantity of life-expired buses of the T (171) and single-deck LT (201) classes, which in the ordinary course of events would have been replaced in the early 1940s. After allowing for the displaced coaches, there was a possible immediate market for over 270 new vehicles, followed by perhaps another 100 when the Qs and 9T9s became life-expired in the mid-forties. London Transport and its predecessors had sometimes used manufacturers other than AEC for experimental work and then turned to the Southall company for the production model. They might have done so in this case, perhaps by use of the work done on the Canadian prototype (see chapter one), and London might then have seen the RF ten years earlier than it did. The TF order was an exceptionally large one in proportion to the size of the single-deck fleet for an experimental

Top **Thirty-seat 10T10 T 606 at the northern extremity of Green Line route 717, Welwyn Garden City, a town redolent of the 1930s from which the vehicle and the network both dated.** G.W. Morant

Above **The oldest single-deckers in service after the war were the 1T1s, such as T 43 at Epping Forest, Wake Arms.** D.A. Thompson

The Marshall rebuilds retained their basic body shape but were substantially cleaned up by the removal of external beading. LT 1186 was new in December 1931 and was destined to survive until March 1952, when it was scrapped. Wrong route number displays are clearly not a modern invention; LT 1186 is on route 218 but shows 213 on its nearside stencil. F.G. Reynolds

batch, however, and it could have been intended to be the basis of a new standard model, in which case the class might have reached a total of 500 and we might never have seen the RF.

The war not only stopped all this, it also had the effect of thinning out the number of buses owned, so that by 1945 the single-deck fleet had shrunk by 119, mostly through enemy action or by government requisition. The postwar Green Line network was also slimmer and the number of coaches needed for scheduled service was some one hundred fewer than it had been in 1939. Including the Green Line coaches which had yet to be recovered from the American Red Cross and the Home Office, the single-deck fleet in 1945 comprised: eighty-one T (1T1, 3T3 and 7T7 dating from 1930-32); forty-nine 9T9 (1936); 254 10T10 (1938-39); thirty-one 11T11 (chassis 1930-32; bodies 1935); 189 LT (classified LTL — 1931-32); 102 4Q4 (1935-36); eighty 5Q5 (1936); forty-nine 6Q6 (1936-37); twenty-four LTC (1937-38); and seventy-six TF (1939), giving a total of 935. Of these, by pre-war standards, at least 270 (301 if the hybrid 11T11s are included) were life-expired and, in normal circumstances, the rest would have been due for replacement by 1949.

The earliest post-war planning made allowance for the withdrawal of these 270 life-expired vehicles between 1948 and 1950 but

not by purchasing new single-deckers. The plan was to change over the whole of the Green Line operation to double-deckers, using a new design whose development was authorised in October 1947. The intention was to purchase 386 of these, of which 100 were earmarked for increased services and new routes. The experimental vehicle, which materialised as RTC 1, did not enter service until April 1949 and in anticipation of this delay, the Board had planned to use standard RTs, fitted with platform doors and saloon heaters, between 1948 and 1951, after which they were to have been replaced by the production version of the RTC. The RTs would then have reverted to bus operation, their platform doors and, probably, their heaters removed for the purpose. Had this programme been fulfilled, the single-deck fleet would have been reduced in size to just over 700.

The vehicles displaced from the Green Line would have been downgraded to bus duties and used as replacements for the LTs and older Ts. Presumably this would have been done by re-allocating the whole of the 10T10 sub-class, as this would have been virtually the right total but this can only be speculation. None of these interesting possibilities came to anything because there was a serious slippage in deliveries of the RT family right from the start of the programme (which should have been in 1946), which led to a change of plan.

The double-deck fleet suffered from similar problems of ageing but the scale was much larger and the proportion of buses overdue for withdrawal substantially greater than in the single-deck fleet. There was also an even more elderly tram fleet awaiting replacement by double-deck motor buses. London Transport therefore decided to concentrate its immediate efforts on renewing the double-deck fleet, leaving the single-deckers for attention later. By the time orders for the coaches were being placed at the end of 1950, the experiment with RTC 1 had been completed and deemed a failure. Single-deckers remained in favour for coach operation and large scale operation of double-deckers had to await the superior suspension and ride characteristics of the Routemaster a decade later.

In the immediate aftermath of the war, nevertheless, London Transport was only too happy to accept whatever crumbs were allowed to fall from the tables of the Ministries of Supply and War Transport and it was through the medium of their strict system of control and allocation that London's first post-war single-deckers were supplied. These were a batch of fifty AEC Regal 0662s with 35-seat bodywork to Weymann's then standard design, delivered during 1946. These were followed immediately by another thirty-one buses with identical bodywork but this time mounted on Leyland Tiger PS1 chassis. All

Bearing a strong family resemblance to the 11T11s, the first post-war single-deckers (the 14T12s) also had Weymann bodies. The deep radiator and the extension of the wings to cover the dumbirons were features which gave this model a particularly 'provincial' flavour. Uxbridge was the first garage to receive the class in April 1946. J.F. Higham Collection

Carrying identical bodywork to the 14T12s, the first Tiger PS1s entered service at Muswell Hill at the end of 1946. A less dated appearance than given by the Ts was achieved by the straight line of the bottom of the windscreen. TD 14 is in Park Road, at 'The Victoria', Alexandra Park on route 212, the home of all thirty-one of the class until replaced by RFs in 1953. G.W. Morant

London's last vertical engined Regals had Mann Egerton thirty-one seat bodywork which derived its handsomeness from simplicity of line and unfussy detail. They were the last to be painted in the green and white colour scheme introduced during the war, surprisingly as contemporary RTs were in green and cream. T 791, new in July 1948, was one of twelve allocated to Watford Leavesden Road. Behind it, at Uxbridge, is one of the other Watford garage's 18STL20 double-deckers. Alan B. Cross

eighty-one buses went to Central Buses, where the largest accumulation of elderly buses was to be found and were used to enlarge the fleet, no older vehicles being withdrawn at that time. One of the uses to which the displaced buses was put was to operate on double-deck routes to cover vehicle shortages and on these duties they were joined by five 7T7s and six 9T9s on loan from the country department.

Despite this injection of resources, the general lack of any sustained intake of new buses during the ensuing four or five years was to create a persistent problem for the two departments in trying to cover their scheduled requirements. An interesting illustration of this came in the spring of 1947 when the Country department was planning its summer programme, for which it needed additional single-deckers. It recalled the eleven Ts on loan to the Central Area but this was not enough. At that time thirty vehicles had still to be returned from wartime activities and only seven of these were due to come back in time. Curiously, the Private Hire LTC Renown coaches had all been released from ambulance duties while a number of the Ts and TFs were still being withheld and a serious proposal was therefore made that they should be operated on Green Line route 703. A test was carried out, the result of which was that the LTC was found to be 'most unsuitable for normal Green Line operation'. The reason for this conclusion is not known but, apart from prejudice, there are at least three possible explanations. One is that the fuel consumption of these petrol-engined vehicles must have been phenomenally high, which would have had a disastrous effect on the finances of any service to which they were allocated and might have presented practical difficulties in ensuring that they did not run out of fuel on the very high mileage coach duties. Another possibility is that the design and layout of the seats, which were to full coach standard and arranged in staggered pairs, slowed down the movement of passengers inside the vehicle at stops. Finally, the LTC was a low-geared vehicle as built and this may have made them too slow. It is certainly unlikely that the standard of comfort could have been in question since the combination of petrol engine and fluid flywheel made these exceptionally quiet and smooth running vehicles.

The solution to the immediate dilemma was to agree to the use of the Renowns for coach duplication, spread around the fleet, though why this was more acceptable is not clear. Despite all these doubts, they were nevertheless sometimes used on scheduled Green Line duties, presumably to cover when other types were not available and are reported to have had no trouble in keeping time. The use of these precious resources in this way was to prove a thorn in the side of the Private Hire department right up to the arrival of the RFs, because any easement in the needs of the Country Bus department was always matched by a need for help in the Central Bus fleet.

Q 10 was one of fifteen of the class transferred into Kingston in 1950 which retained their green livery until withdrawn. The open door, required by Metropolitan Police regulation, is probably not too welcome by passengers as it makes its way through Esher on a bright, probably cold, winter's day. G.W. Morant

Keeping the Central Bus fleet going until the main replacement programme could get under way was a major pre-occupation for Chiswick during these five or six years. The 270 1T1s, 3T3s, 7T7s and LTs were the biggest headache because of their great age and the bold decision was taken to select eighteen of the Regals and fifty-nine Renowns for major rebuilding by Marshalls of Cambridge. The need to do more was avoided by a surprisingly large injection of 130 new vehicles during 1948 and 1949. At its meeting on 3rd April 1947, the LPTB was presented with a report which argued that there was an immediate necessity to introduce thirty single-deckers because traffic conditions in certain parts of the Country Area required the immediate strengthening and development of services. Of the eight bodybuilders who were approached, seven were unable to offer delivery before late 1948, whereas Mann Egerton of Norwich were able to offer a delivery six months after the order was placed. AEC was able to match this with the appropriate chassis.

The vehicles which resulted were thirty AEC Regal MkIIIs (T 769-798), with Mann Egerton bodywork seating thirty-one, costing £3,000 each. Classified 15T13, these were the closest that LT got to having a single-deck version of the RT. In the event, they were delivered between March and September 1948, about five months later than promised.

In the meantime, the Board had reviewed the increasing difficulties in the Central Area single-deck fleet. In the fleet as a whole, 62% of it was then twelve or more years old and 45% between sixteen and eighteen years old. Apart from the urgent need to replace many of these over-age vehicles, there was also an increasing need to put on new services and strengthen existing ones. The slippage in the delivery of the double-deck fleet was already so severe that it was clear that no immediate relief was to be forthcoming from that source. On 9th October 1947, the Board therefore approved the purchase of no fewer than one-hundred Mann Egerton bodied Leyland Tiger PS1s at a cost of £3,140 each.

These became TD 32-131 (classified 1/1TD2) and had the same Mann Egerton bodywork as the Regal IIIs, (although without platform doors). The choice of chassis may have been influenced by the Ministry of Transport, despite their formal control over such matters having been discontinued in January 1946, or may have been dictated by the ability of Leyland to deliver more quickly than AEC. It is unlikely that the Central Bus department would have settled happily for manual transmission unless it was imposed on them.

The delivery of these vehicles during 1948 and 1949 provided the temporary scope for the enlargement of the fleet to enable the rebuilding of the Ts and LTs to go ahead without causing shortages. Even so, it was still necessary for buses to be borrowed by Central from Country Buses and in the summer of 1948 eleven 4Q4 (for route 233 at West Green) and fourteen 5Q5 (for Cricklewood and Sidcup) were transferred. The 4Q4s ran into immediate trouble with drivers who were not happy with the poor nearside visibility when running through the grounds of Alexandra Palace, so these were exchanged with 5Q5s from Dalston, on which the nearside visibility was improved by having the doorless entrance alongside the driver. Meanwhile the ageing 7T7s in the Country fleet were becoming increasingly unpopular and the department asked for them to be scrapped. This was not at first allowed, as there was still a shortage in the Central Area. However, the Central Bus department was not prepared to accept the 7T7s to cover that shortage, not surprisingly bearing in mind how much younger the average age of the green fleet was. In the end, they were forced to do so and eleven were transferred at the end of 1949.

All this was happening after the delivery of the TDs and was being caused by the need to scrap significant numbers of Ts and LTs which had become unfit and beyond repair. An offer of ten more 4Q4s was turned down at first because of the problem that had arisen at West Green but a further eight 9T9s were accepted. The option of scrapping perfectly roadworthy Qs was not acceptable, however, and the decision was eventually made to put fourteen of them into Kingston, painted red, for use on the 215 and 219. With these various borrowings, the refurbishment programme and the delivery of the new Tigers, the fleet was now at the point where it awaited only the arrival of the new generation of underfloor engined vehicles.

Harrow Weald was one of nine garages which shared the Mann Egerton Leylands. TD 67, new in February 1949, serves idyllic suburbia in Headstone Lane on route 221, ultimately replaced by double-deck 98B and never to receive RFs.
Peter G. Mitchell

3 DEVELOPMENT OF THE REGAL IV

Above **Prototype Regal IV UMP227 in 1949 before entering service with London Transport** AEC

Right **Interior view showing the London Transport style window finishing and the smart treatment of the entrance and cab areas.** PRV

From AEC's point of view, the switch to the underfloor-engined layout for the firm's principal single-deck model was a logical step. With hindsight it might be asked why it was not done earlier but foundations of the new design were being laid almost as soon as the war ended. While the emphasis in terms of production was at first on sheer volume of more

conventional buses to begin to meet the pent-up demand, the first design decisions on the new model were being taken in the summer of 1946. Doubtless Rackham's memories of the 'Q' episode, when his vision of the way forward was rejected by the operating industry, gave rise to a certain caution or perhaps a particularly thorough appraisal of the market.

Even so, the technical know-how was already there, for the 1939 Canadian proto-type was a clear basis for further development and Rackham's knowledge of the transit bus, as understood in North America, gave him renewed confidence to go ahead. It would have been interesting to be a fly on the wall of the AEC boardroom around that first summer of

Above **The Chiswick influenced rear end can be seen in this picture taken in 1949 prior to a series of visits to potential customers outside London.** PRV

Left **Looking towards the rear inside, UMP227 has very much the appearance of a London Transport vehicle, apart from the lampshades, including the famous standard bus moquette of the time which looks less happy on the design of seat back used on the prototype.** PRV

the post-war period but it seems unlikely that any discussion would have been long or contentious. The influential factors could be summed up as follows:

(1) The home market climate was changing. In particular, Midland Red's success with its underfloor-engined models was being followed with interest by the British Electric Traction group, to which it belonged, and indeed the whole industry. Although some operators had ordered front-engined single-deckers which would be delivered in the next two years or so, there was a growing tendency to hold back from placing further orders until underfloor-engined models were available.

(2) Exports to some countries seemed likely to be promising. The rear- or underfloor-engined layout was more widely accepted abroad, although this varied from country to country and the idea of a large single-decker, often designed to carry a high proportion of standing passengers, was one which could be linked logically to a model with minimum use of floor space for anything other than passenger accommodation.

(3) London Transport's clearly-expressed wish to pick up the threads of the advanced thinking it had displayed in the 1930s. In addition to the Q and TF, there had been the CR class of rear-engined Leyland Cub models which, even though smaller than the type of vehicle needed for the renewal of the bulk of the fleet, again showed acceptance of radical thinking in the 1938-39 period.

Of these, the London Transport factor was the clearest cut. Despite the financial divorce of AEC from the operating side of London's main bus provider which occurred on the formation of the LPTB in 1933, the practical links and in particular technical liaison remained remarkably close. To some extent, this could be regarded as inevitable when it is remembered that the output of many of AEC's most popular models was devoted to London's needs more than all other operators put together. There had been an agreement that AEC would be the principal supplier to the LPTB on its formation and, after some soul-searching, this was renewed in 1944 to cover the post-war vehicle replacement programme. The continuity of contact was indicated by the way in which the most minute alteration to any item used on a passenger model was duly reported to Chiswick, at least to the mid-1950s.

More important, there was frequent contact, formal and informal, between the managements of both organisations. AEC directors would have quite an accurate picture both of the thinking of the LPTB and its successor the London Transport Executive, which took over on 1st January 1948, and of the undertaking's probable needs. A simple list of the existing single-deck fleet and its age gave the clue to a requirement for replacement of most of its composition within the life-span of a new model. Equally, it was virtually certain that the basic concept of a generously-sized engine, an air-operated preselective gearbox and air pressure brake system that was proving so successful with the RT double-decker, would be the favoured choice for a new generation of single-deckers too.

Indeed, it is rather interesting to ponder on why a single-deck direct equivalent of the RT was not developed for London Transport, to go into production alongside the double-deck model. From AEC's point of view, it would only have taken a small amount of drawing office time to produce a version of the Regal III with the RT pattern of front end and virtually no new parts would have been needed beyond those already in production. Yet, clearly, London Transport was not interested in any large quantity of such a model and the batch of thirty Regal III buses which formed the 15T13 type was too small for any departure from AEC's 'provincial' standard when supplied in 1948.

But with a potential market within LT alone of something not too far short of 1,000 single-deckers, there doubtless seemed plenty of scope. Admittedly, there were 211 front-engined single-deck models that had entered service since 1946 or were in progress of delivery, but of these only the 15T13 batch conformed to LT's ideas on transmission and brakes and it seemed likely that the remainder might be regarded as sub-standard and hence likely to be sold off early.

In fact, a more detailed study of the numbers of single-deckers needed was carried out by LTE in 1949, but meanwhile there was enough information to justify the design and construction of the prototypes. Clearly, an underfloor-engined equivalent to the Regent III, in its preferred 9.6-litre fluid transmission and air-braked form, was what was wanted both as a logical counterpart to the London Transport RT and the equivalent 'provincial' and export models.

Above **What might have been? . . . One of the Leyland-MCW Olympic HR40 pre-production prototypes built in 1948/1949 with Metro-Cammell bodywork rather than Weymann, which was the usual manufacturer for the home market (HR = Home Range). The use of Green Line livery was a sign of Leyland's hope that they could break into the London market, but the use of a constant-mesh gearbox and dry-plate clutch, rather than the required pre-selective transmission, ruled it out of London Transport's reckoning.** Alan Townsin Collection

Opposite **History in the making. The solitary survivor of the pioneering underfloor engined Private Hire fleet of 1939, TF 9, shares a Private Hire outing with RF 19, one of the first production batch of Regal IVs from twelve years later.** Lens of Sutton

At that date, the 27ft 6in overall length limit that had been in force since January 1932 was still current and there was little expectation that the increase sought during the war would be granted. London always tended to be more conservative on such matters and, in any case, the original standard home-market version of the new model was designed as a 27ft 6in by 7ft 6in vehicle. The wheelbase was appreciably shorter than the 1936 Central Area Qs, which also had the entrance ahead of the front wheels, at 15ft 8ins compared with 16ft 6ins. This was made possible by having twin tyres at the rear, allowing the rear overhang to be longer. It also allowed enough length for the horizontal version of the 9.6-litre engine and separate pre-selective gearbox to be accommodated between the axles, though propellor shaft lengths on this version of the model were decidedly short. The export version, with 17ft 6in wheelbase, was intended for a length of about thirty-five feet and was to be available in both right- and left-hand forms.

By 1948, it was being taken for granted that an underfloor-engined model intended for bus work would have a sufficiently long front overhang to permit a front entrance directly opposite the driver, even though operators were still divided on the merits of this layout. Coach operators tended to favour either a true centre entrance for such a vehicle, or at any rate one other than at the extreme front, while municipalities and even some company fleets were sometimes still wedded to the rear entrance. It must be remembered that driver-only operation of a bus in Britain was still restricted to vehicles with not more than twenty-six seats.

In overall specification and many aspects of detail design, AEC's new Regal Mark IV underfloor-engined chassis was closely related to the Regal Mark III in its standard 9.6-litre preselective form. The change in engine position clearly implied a different frame design but Rackham did not favour the completely straight relatively high frame adopted by some makers and as used on the Leyland-built TF. The level of the side-members between the axles had to be sufficiently high to accommodate the engine beneath them but there was still a slight 'kick-up' over both the front and rear axles.

However, when considering floor heights on a completed vehicle, the method of body construction is an important factor and there are also other considerations, such as the relative desirability of an unobstructed floor level and whether most or all of the seats should face forward. As a chassis manufacturer catering for widely varying markets, AEC had to design to suit a variety of needs. In one sense, the typical underfloor-engined model, with appreciable overhang at both front and rear, presents less severe stress problems than a front-engined chassis and hence the frame can be shallower in the mid-section. However, the model had to cater for anything between an overseas style 'standee' model with passenger loading liable to be as high as could be crammed into the vehicle, and a relatively low seating-capacity coach.

Modern metal-framed bodywork could contribute much to the vehicle's overall strength and, from the beginning, the Regal IV was designed so that the chassis and body framing could be united via outrigger brackets projecting from the side-members and intended to be attached directly to the body side-framing. In some locations, these were fitted to all versions of the chassis but it was also possible to fit a full set, thus making it possible to produce what was sometimes described as a semi-integral form of construction. This was one of the features chosen for the London Transport version of the design and thus picking up the threads in design terms from the TF. It was perhaps the most obvious distinction between the LTE-specification version of the chassis, for which AEC chose the model designation 9821LT, and the 'provincial' version 9821E, though there were numerous detail differences.

It would be more accurate to describe 9821LT as the equivalent, in Regal IV terms, of the 0961 designation which, by that date, was being used only on Regent III chassis built to London Transport RT specification, as opposed to the 'provincial' Regent which by then was type 9612E if of the 9.6 litre preselective form. All the chassis built for the RF class vehicles retained the 9821LT designation and the original form of outrigger frame, with the shallow style of side-member of nominal eight inches depth, although later home-market 'provincial' models graduated to a revised design with deeper (10⅛ inch) side-members, which suited most coachbuilders better, these being designated 9822E. While referring to chassis designations, it is convenient to mention the versions with synchro-mesh gearbox, introduced to suit the preferences of some 'provincial' operators from about 1951, designated 9821S or 9822S according to frame type, though London Transport was not a customer for either of these.

The differences between 'provincial' and London-style chassis were less obvious on the Regal IV than the Regent III, there being no external radiator and bonnet assembly on the former, but there were many even so and AEC found it convenient to keep the two versions distinct from a manufacturing viewpoint. Some items were quite small — for example, the 'mushroom' type of accelerator pedal which had been dropped in favour of the organ-pedal type on other AEC models, was specified, just as it was on the RT.

The designs of most chassis units were almost directly equivalent to those used on the Mark III passenger range, but many items were revised to suit the different layout. The engine went rather beyond this for, although the A219 unit was in essentials equivalent to an A218, as used in the 'provincial' Regent III, laid over on its side, there were further changes. Clearly it was essential to redesign the lubrication and cooling systems to suit this. Avoiding circulation troubles is always most difficult in a cooling system lacking the height given by a traditional type of upright radiator. The Regal IV had the usual squat type of radiator found on an underfloor-engined model and, on the prototypes there was a shallow header tank near the engine, with the filler above; but a taller front-mounted tank was adopted subsequently.

The lubrication system adopted was of the so-called dry-sump type, as used on aircraft, in which the oil which escapes from bearings etc. is drawn away from the crankcase by a suction pump, to a reservoir from which it is recirculated in the normal way. A further difference from contemporary upright AEC engines was the use of a monobloc cylinder block and crankcase casting, instead of the separate items then still generally favoured.

The 120mm by 142mm cylinder dimensions and the toroidal-cavity pistons were as on the vertical engine. At first, the nominal power output claimed was also the same, 125bhp at 1,800rpm but in fact it was found that the horizontal engine developed slightly less due to the quirk of the layout of the fuel injection system. The injection pump was mounted at the front of the engine to allow convenient access from the offside of the vehicle, rather than requiring a floor-trap to be lifted with the likelihood that the interior would become soiled by mechanics' hands or clothing. It was found that the unequal lengths of the injector pipes slightly reduced the maximum power and later this was quoted as 120bhp, though London Transport derated its engines in the manner then usual to prolong life, in this case to 110bhp. It was planned that the Regal IV would have a special injection system which had been tested on some RT-type buses and which gave quieter running. It was of Swedish origin and was known as Atlas pilot injection. Unfortunately, it proved unreliable and, apart from the London RFs, all of which were fitted with the system, production vehicles reverted to the conventional system with more audible effects similar to those on most oil engines.

Even so, the Regal IV was quiet running. The engine mounting system was intended to give a similar degree of insulation from vibration as on the Regent III and at the front there was a similar ring-shaped rubber bush. At the rear, however, the different layout dictated the use of a vee-shaped mounting and this was carried on a cross-tube known within the works as the 'hockey stick' because it was of much the same size and shape. In typical AEC fashion, ease of maintenance was regarded as important. It was claimed that an engine could be removed in fifteen minutes

and another fitted in half-an-hour, there being a small hoist built into the chassis to facilitate lowering and raising the complete engine once the various connections and mountings were released. No doubt this was so in the case of new units with all the right tools ready to hand and such a time would be inadequate in more normal circumstances, but even so the idea of simplifying such tasks was logical as a counter to operators' doubts as to ease of maintenance compared with previous types of vehicle.

The separate gearbox mounting simplified work on that unit or on the fluid flywheel and these items and the rear axle were fundamentally very similar to those used on the Mark III models, though the rear axle had the differential casing off-set to the right rather than the left. It was also of the underslung worm-drive type, again as on the Mark III, unlike the general practice on underfloor-engined models of using bevel-drive axles.

The air-pressure system for both brake and gearbox operation was very similar to that of the corresponding front-engined models, though the prototype examples had an unusual system of mounting the compressor directly on the engine crankcase, with operation from an eccentric on the crankshaft. A conventional belt-driven unit was chosen for production vehicles.

Believed to be the second right-hand drive example built, Regal IV prototype U137523 was given a Park Royal thirty-eight seat body for use as a demonstrator. It is seen here at Southall in the colours of Douglas Corporation, to whom it was sold in June 1951. Its Middlesex registration VMK271 was altered to NMN255 a few hours after this photograph was taken. The tall chimneys in the background are from the AEC engine test house. E.J. Smith/Alan Townsin Collection

In most other respects the chassis followed typical AEC practice. The steering was by worm-and-nut gear, the low gearing favoured helping to give quite light action without power assistance, then in its infancy. However, in moving the steering column further forward than usual, an unusual instance of a design fault was introduced. The geometry of the linkage between the steering box and the axle introduced a slight 'kick' effect when travelling over uneven ground — something which was corrected on the later 'Reliance' underfloor-engined model.

There was an interesting reminder of the 'Q' type chassis in the front springs. The model used conventional leaf springs, of course, but quite a good standard of comfort was achieved. This was partly by rather more generous spring deflection than had been usual and partly because of the way in which the proportion of weight taken by each axle varied less between an empty and fully-laden vehicle than it did with a front-mounted engine. However, because most of the engine weight was carried on the offside front spring, it had a greater number of leaves than the nearside unit, just as had been so with the 'Q'. An odd effect of this was that the chassis had a slight lean to the right before bodying, the springs being set so that the completed vehicle would stand level with a medium load, though a full load would cause a very slight lean to the left.

UMP227 in trial service on route 355 in St Peter's Street, St Albans. The forty-seat Park Royal bodywork was rather like an up-to-date version of their pre-war models on the Qs, the likeness being underlined by the short rear overhang, a product of the 27ft 6in length.

The first prototype chassis was sent to Park Royal for bodying, that concern's records showing it to have been completed in January 1949. The chassis had been built in AEC's experimental department and, as usual at the time, received a chassis number in the U series issued for any item designed there and one more usually intended for part numbers, in this case U135974. At that stage, there was still no expectation that the home market length limit would be increased beyond the 27ft 6ins applicable to two-axle vehicles, so it was of that length as well as the 7ft 6in width and had seating for forty passengers. It had a distinct resemblance to contemporary Midland Red practice in layout and such details as the recessed windscreen, though there were also echoes of London Transport practice in such items as winding half-drop windows and the interior trim as well as the approximation to Country Area livery in which it was painted. Its existence was kept fairly quiet at first but later in the year it began visiting potential customers, having been registered UMP227.

In London the trials were carried out on Country Bus route 355. This was operated by St Albans garage, which had been chosen for the trials because a new design of pit specially designed for servicing underfloor-engined vehicles had recently been installed there. When it entered service in May 1950, its seating capacity had been reduced to thirty-six, in line with London Transport's normal policy of spacious seating layouts. It continued to operate on the 355, with occasional periods away on AEC business, until September 1951, when it was returned to Southall for the last time. UMP227 was retained by AEC as a 'hack' vehicle both for minor testing of components and as a sort of van, most seats having been removed. For many years, it could be seen

parked alongside the playing fields opposite the experimental shop at AEC's Southall factory. At first it remained in green livery, becoming more and more shabby, but was repainted flat grey in about 1954 and finally, in about 1959, into the yellow and blue used for AEC/PRV service vans.

Meanwhile, LTE had carried out a more detailed survey of its single-decker requirements in the summer of 1949, which resulted in an estimate of 779 as the number of new vehicles to be added to the post-war buses already received. The question of dimensions was still a problem, however. Renewed pressure to increase the maximum length dimension for two-axle single-deckers, partly on the ground that this would allow greater standardisation with exports, was countered by a combination of opposition from Trade Unions and those nervous about the suitability of larger vehicles in the narrow and often twisting streets of Britain's older towns and cities. London, with its tradition of Police control over bus operation, was more conservative than some provincial cities.

The Ministry of Transport belatedly indicated that it would be prepared to allow the maximum length of all single-deckers to be thirty feet in the forthcoming revision of Regulations early in 1950, but this allowed very little time as the new limits came into effect on 1st June. Eight foot width was no longer subject to specific route approval outside London from the same date. London Transport's response to this situation is described in more detail in chapter four.

By early 1951 it had been settled that 700 vehicles were to be ordered, all except the private hire coaches being thirty feet long, which by then was the standard production length for home-market models. For this, a

wheelbase length of 16ft 4ins had been adopted and, in the event, the only production versions of the Regal IV built to the shorter 27ft 6in length were the LTE Private Hire batch (RF 1-25), which were also the first in the numerical series, being 9821LT001-025, in a sequence which also included the 9821E (home and right-hand overseas) and, later the 9821S, 9822E and 9822S variants. Examples built for the 1950 Commercial Motor Show and related demonstrators took the numbers 9821E026-031. The 30ft by 8ft chassis for London Transport, numbered RFW 1-15, were 9821E318-332.

The earlier plan of building buses for both Central and Country fleets next had given way to updating the Green Line fleet and the hope was that production would follow almost immediatley after the private hire batch. AEC's standard practice was to allocate chassis numbers on receipt of a firm order and in the circumstances of the time was apt to be quite far removed from the actual order of build. The first batch of thirty-foot 9821LT chassis was given the serial numbers 032-166, totalling 135 vehicles. At first they duly became RF 26 upwards in numerical order but it seems that a degree of the same congestion of stored chassis as had been experienced with the RT gave rise to bodying out of sequence after the first twenty had gone onto Metro-Cammell's shop floor. All this batch of chassis did become Green Line coaches and, in a broad fashion, covered the vehicles numbered up to about 160. However, 9821LT069 became RF 282, near the end of the complete Green Line batch which finished at RF 288, making a total of 263 such vehicles, a total oddly reminiscent of the 266 of the 10T10 batch which was the largest group they were to replace. Another less noticeable out-of-batch vehicle was RF 162, built on 9821LT106.

The next and largest batch of chassis, 490 vehicles, were numbered 9821LT646-1135. Rather curiously, continuation of Green Line RF body manufacture was on 9821LT1008 upwards, that chassis becoming RF 159 and the sequence of chassis and fleet numbers, though not exact, was roughly in step to 9821LT1122, which became RF 278. From then until the end of this chassis batch at 9821LT1135, Green Line and Central Area buses were intermingled, the first bus numerically, RF 289, being on 9821LT1124. Only then did the lower chassis numbers in this batch begin to appear, 9821LT646-672 also being a mixed sequence of high-numbered Green Line coaches (the last, RF 288, being on 9821LT660) and Central buses.

The changeover to red bus delivery took place in September 1952 and went more rapidly, for the most part roughly — sometimes quite roughly — in step in terms of chassis and fleet number. The switch to green buses for the Country Area came in March 1953 at RF 514. In terms of chassis, RF 514 was quite an early number, 9821LT780, and the general changeover was nearer to a hundred or so chassis later, with RF 513, the last red straggler at 9821LT917. When the rest of that chassis batch was completed, RF chassis output switched to the numbers 9821LT1320-1369 and these became the last fifty green buses, RF 651-700, though not in strict order, delivery being completed in December 1953.

Above **Windsor's RF 212 typifies the Green Line version of the class.**
John Fozard

Left **Central Area RF 290 edges its way through the pinchpoint created by the Old Toll House at Spaniards Inn, Hampstead Heath, closely followed by an even more famous contemporary, a Morris Minor, soon after entering service on route 210.**
J. Wyndham

RF 528 on route 447, looking little different from its Central Bus counterpart, represents the Country department's version, which had power-operated doors. Surfleet Transport Photographs

The 4RF4 airport coaches were more closely related to the RT double-decker in styling than the other London Regal IVs as this view of MLL748 at Waterloo Air terminal illustrates. F.G. Reynolds

Meanwhile, there was another RF variant, in terms of London Transport specification for British European Airways. The 30ft by 8ft chassis were nominally of type 9822E but, as with chassis for the RFW coaches, there were quite a number of London Transport features in the specification. Curiously enough, there was another divergence beween AEC and LTE in terms of batches. It seems that the initial order was for forty and AEC's in initial chassis batch was of that number, 9822E1175-1214. However, this was increased to fifty and there was a second revision when a further fifteen was added to the requirement. AEC allocated a further twenty-five chassis, 9822E1485-1509. Delivery of the BEA vehicles was spread between April 1952 and September 1953.

By that date, the writing was on the wall for the Regal IV, at least as a home market model. A prototype, lighter underfloor-engined chassis had been built by AEC in the early months of 1953, this later being given the model name 'Reliance'. A prototype integral-construction version of the same general design was tried by London Transport and in due course this 'Monocoach' model and the far more important 'Reliance' went into production. Sales to British operators did continue on a small scale into 1955 but, to all intents and purposes, the Regal IV was obsolete so far as the home market was concerned from the introduction of the production 'Monocoach' and 'Reliance' models in 1954. There was a new consciousness of the influence of weight on fuel economy and the Regal IV was often heavier than contemporary double-deckers, as was the case in London, where the typical RF was 7tons 15cwt, compared to the RT at 7tons 10cwt.

The total of 780 Regal IV models built for London Transport and BEA outnumbered the total of approximately 675 for other British operators. Of these, the majority were coaches sold in ones and twos, largely to independent operators. The largest fleet went to Scottish Omnibuses, part of which was diverted to Western SMT, and these two operated seventy-four, largely on their services between Edinburgh or Glasgow and London. Relatively few received bus bodywork, notable among these being twenty for Western Welsh and a total of fifteen for Rochdale Corporation, this latter modest total being the largest municipal fleet of the model.

Output of the Regal IV continued until 1960 for export, many of these being of the left-hand 9831E and subsequent types, as well as long-wheelbase versions of the 9821E etc. Figures issued by AEC in 1965 quote a total of 1,170 right-hand and 752 of the left-hand types, excluding the 9821LT version (of which the total quoted is, unaccountably, 668 rather than the true 700) and it seems very probable that both the former figures refer to export sales.

Left The integrally built AEC/Park Royal Monocoach prototype took the registration NLP635 immediately ahead of the second series of BEA coaches, underlining the writing on the wall for the Regal IV. It ran experimentally for London Transport during 1953, while the last of the RFs were still being delivered, and is seen at Redhill. F.G. Reynolds

4 COMPLETING THE OPERATIONAL PLAN

While the prototype Regal IV (UMP227) was being built and then running in experimental service at St Albans and Reigate, things were beginning to move on the RF project. Work had been going on behind the scenes to plan for the ordering and delivery of the new generation vehicles but even at this late stage the project was fraught with many uncertainties. High on the list of questions awaiting answers was the matter of vehicle dimensions. As indicated in the previous chapter, it was known that the government was contemplating increasing the permitted length of two-axle single-deckers from 27ft 6ins to 30ft and of double-deckers form 26ft to 27ft but it was not known when this would become law. More importantly for London Transport, the attitude of the Metropolitan Police and the Licensing Authority for the Metropolitan Area was still an unknown quantity. The law already allowed buses to be built to a width of 8 feet, subject to specific approval being obtained for each route, but the traffic authorities were wary of allowing such monsters loose on the streets of London; a similar attitude could be expected towards longer vehicles.

In August 1949, it was necessary to start thinking seriously about what orders could be placed with the manufacturers. Despite its acceptance of so many non-standard saloons between 1945 and 1948, London Transport was still committed to a high degree of stan-dardisation and wanted to base its orders on such needs as could be foreseen through at least the first half of the life of the new class. With this in mind, an assessment was made of the expected service requirements for the ten years from 1950 to 1959. This involved some fairly heroic assumptions, made it needs to be remembered at a time when demand for bus travel was at record levels and the general mood in the industry was of great optimism. The allowance made for service developments was nevertheless cautiously confined to the period 1950-1955 and examined in two categories: increasing service levels on existing routes, which would need twelve buses in the Central Area and twenty-three in the Country Area; and new or extended routes, for which Central Buses would require thirty and Country Buses five. Offset against this was the intention to put double-deck buses on certain routes when the availability of double-deckers made it possible and if the traffic authorities approved. This reduced the number of saloons by fifteen. Another fourteen for new routes in the Country Area were identified but omitted form the final total as they would not be required until after 1955.

The review also considered the position of the Private Hire fleet, which comprised twenty-five vehicles, all effectively life-expired for the type of work they did and severely diminished in size by comparison with the pre-war fleet of thirty-six. In deciding what to do the Executive had to bear in mind that fuel was still rationed and the amount available for pleasure party contract work strictly limited by Government decree. On the other hand, the Festival of Britain, planned for 1951, would generate a great deal of contract work and the London Transport fleet by now compared very unfavourably with its competitors in this field, who had been able to indulge in at least some fleet renewal since 1945. Again it was decided to adopt a cautious approach. Replacement of the LTCs and TF 9 by twenty-five new coaches would be included in the programme but any additional needs for the Festival season would be met by retaining the pre-war vehicles. The LTCs were to be 'upgraded' by having their petrol engines replaced by 8.8-litre diesels, a step which many thought, on the contrary, to be retrograde, given the refinement of ride given by the combination of fluid flywheel and petrol engine.

Above **The early post-war green and white colour scheme lent a slight air of ordinariness to the Weymann bodies of the Renown coaches in their last years, although they were always kept in smart condition. LTC 20, new in January 1938, still had its petrol engine when photographed eleven years later on tour at Windsor. It was one of the class which was fitted with cant glass panels.**
D.W.K. Jones

Finally, the need for spare vehicles was critically examined. Greater reliability was confidently expected from the new model and it was therefore considered reasonable to reduce the allowance for engineering spares from fourteen percent to ten percent. This was still larger than the seven percent planned for the double-deck fleet, mainly because single-deckers were dispersed in smaller quantities. In the Country Area twenty coaches and two buses were added for 'traffic spares', a concept which allowed for the fact that garages in the Country Area were far apart and therefore unable so readily to lend each other vehicles at short notice, that the routes were generally on wide headways and therefore needed greater protection from the effect of late running and, perhaps most to the point, gave a small margin of vehicles for unscheduled duplication. (In the event, the split between bus and coach was more evenly arranged as ten and twelve but the total was unchanged.)

The conclusions are summarised in Table 1.

As there were already 211 post-war buses in the fleet, the total of new vehicles needed was 779, of which 248 would be Central Area buses, 235 Country buses, 271 Green Line coaches and 25 Private Hire coaches for the Central Area.

Having established four basic operational classes of vehicle, it was possible that these could be further sub-divided into short (27ft 6ins) and long (30ft), narrow (7ft 6ins) and wide (8ft), with a potential for up to thirteen sub-classes, assuming that the Private Hire vehicles would all be the same. To the engineers, this loss of standardisation was very alarming but, short of adopting the smallest vehicle as the standard, inevitable as things stood at the time. Nevertheless, knowing the strength of feeling on the part of the Metropolitan Police against the extra width, the operating departments judged that approval was not likely to be forthcoming for any significant number of routes to be operated by eight-footers and it was therefore decided from the outset to adopt the 7ft 6in width as standard.

The same approach was not acceptable for the length because the additional passenger capacity gained by the longer vehicle was vital to improving the cost-effectiveness of the single-deck fleet. Informal route surveys were therefore carried out which established that as many as 635 of the new vehicles could be thirty-footers, leaving 159 of the shorter vehicle. Table 2 shows the estimated split of types but does not add up to the same total as the earlier summary, because for this purpose the Country department appears to have restored the allowance for new routes and added one for luck!

Of these, it was possible to be very confident about the 204 Central buses as these were for routes already approved for the LT single-deckers, whose three-axle arrangement allowed them to be thirty-feet long under existing regulations. The rest would depend on the attitude of the police. This could not be tested formally until the Minister had at least announced his intentions about the legislation but there was a healthy scepticism about the likelihood of getting approval for such a large number of routes. A prudent attitude to specifying the dimensions of vehicles was therefore adopted.

Table 1

	1948 Schedule	Augmentation	New Routes	Conversion to D/D	Spares	Total
Central Area						
Buses	363	+12	+30	–15	39 (10%)	429
Private Hire	25	—	—	—	—	25
Country Area						
Buses	214	+23	+5	–3	26 (11%)	265
Coach	228	—	—	—	43 (19%)	271
Total	830	+35	+35	–18	108 (13%)	990

Table 2

	New Vehicles			T/TD	Ultimate Fleet		
	27'6"	30'	Total	27'6"	27'6"	30'	Total
Central	44	204	248	181	225	204	429
Country	90	168	258	30	120	168	288
Green Line	—	263	263	—	—	263	263
Private Hire	25	—	—	—	25	—	25
TOTAL	159	635	794	211	370	635	1005

The result of this review was that the Executive agreed to seek authority for the purchase of 779 new single-deckers, this being the difference between the 990 which they expected to need by 1954, less the 211 post-war Ts and TDs. The balance of fourteen (or fifteen, depending on which estimate you use) for new and strengthened routes in the Country Area would have been added to the order nearer the end, when requirements were clearer. This total was greater than had been included in the purchasing programme submitted to the Executive in December 1948 because it had by now been decided that the coaches would be replaced by new single-deckers and not double-deckers. The Executive was more or less forced into this decision by the delays in the delivery of double-deckers but had in any case drawn some fairly quick conclusions about the performance of RTC 1, which was not delivering the standard of ride required from the new generation vehicles. It is therefore likely that the use of double-deckers would have been postponed anyway.

The December 1948 programme had also assumed that, apart from the Private Hire coaches which were required for the summer season in 1951, deliveries would start in December 1952 and be completed in mid-1955. This timetable was drastically altered by the terms of a contract adjustment which was negotiated with Metro-Cammell during 1948 and ratified early in 1949.

It had been agreed that 700 vehicles would be bodied by Metro-Cammell, which was somewhat surprising to those familiar with previous London choices for the construction of its single-deck body requirements. Historically, Weymann or possibly Park Royal might have been expected to get the work but both were heavily engaged on RT family double-deckers and doubtless hard pressed to maintain reasonable delivery times for their other regular customers. Metro-Cammell had been a major supplier of trolleybuses to London in the late 'thirties and it had been planned that it was to contribute 1,000 bodies for the Leyland RTL chassis, originally to the same closely-controlled design as built by Park Royal and Weymann, allowing complete interchangeability of components. This idea was abandoned to give more rapid delivery, Metro-Cammell using its own construction, despite external conformity to the standard RT outline. Its share of the RTL order was cut to 450 and the order for 700 single-deck bodies was allocated to compensate for the lost 550 double-deckers.

Under the terms of this agreement, which was ratified by the Executive on 28th February 1949, Metro-Cammell were guaranteed continuity of production after the completion of their double-deck contract. The delivery programme for the new single-deckers was therefore brought forward by eighteen months, to commence in the spring of 1951. 'Accidental' though it may have been, this was to prove a happy choice. Metro-Cammell's bodywork had an excellent reputation for durability and its experience with integral construction was doubtless also useful.

It is significant that both Metro-Cammell and Weymann were involved at the time with the Leyland-MCW Olympic integral-construction single-decker which interested LTE because of certain of its 'novel features'. Both the prototype Regal IV and the 'Olympic' were therefore inspected during April 1949 as part of the review of requirements for the Private Hire fleet. This was followed by a formal demonstration of both vehicles during July. The AEC won the contest, the Leyland presumably being disqualified because it had synchromesh transmission and no epicyclic alternative. (Leyland's involvement with Self-Changing Gears was not to occur until 1953.) A proposal was submitted to the Executive recommending the purchase of two prototypes for trial purposes but this came to nothing and the trials were made instead with the manufacturer's demonstrator (UMP227).

Although the Executive had not yet formally approved a purchasing programme for the RFs, during October 1949 the Chief Mechanical Engineer used the authority of the vehicle replacement programme approved in August that year to issue instructions to AEC and Metro-Cammell to go ahead with the twenty-five Private Hire coaches. An immediate decision had been needed if they were to be ready in time for the start of the Festival of Britain in May 1951. A firm order, was therefore placed specifying the shorter length. As the Country Bus department had the potential for the largest number of short vehicles, it was also decided at this time to allocate the first main production batch after the Private Hire vehicles to them and again to specify the shorter length. No fewer than 200 were intended ultimately to be allocated to this order, which looks surprisingly large when compared with the figures shown in the table but this reflected again a high level of caution about the actual number of thirty-footers likely to be approved. This total was also considered to be 'safe' because, if the number proved too many, later deliveries could be switched to Central buses simply by the omission of the doors and giving them the different livery. Nothing would have been wasted by this approach, as the door gear would have been used on the later, longer vehicles instead. These decisions on the first 225 covered the expected delivery programme for 1951 and enabled further decisions to be delayed until September 1950 while firmer commitments could be obtained from the traffic authorities.

The Minister of Transport announced his decision on 9th February 1950 that the operation of single-deckers with a maximum length of thirty feet would be permitted from June 1950. At the end of February, the Chief Mechanical Engineer gave authority for the manufacture of a further 125 vehicles of 27ft 6ins length, bringing the total to 150, roughly in line with the number that the preliminary surveys had shown might be needed but some fifty short of the number previously thought appropriate.

In March 1950, the Executive approved the ten-year forward plan for single-deck vehicles, which phased the delivery of the RF class over three years, 217 in 1951, 400 in 1952 and 177 in 1953. Chassis deliveries were scheduled to start in 1950 (25), followed by 240 in 1951, 400 in 1952 and 129 in 1953. At the same time it gave its formal authority for firm orders to be placed for 217 single-deckers as part of its Rolling Stock programme for 1951, subject to formal approval of the total project by the British Transport Commission. The commitment to Metro-Cammell was not enlarged beyond the 700 required by the Agreement.

The authority that was sought from the BTC was for a total of 779 but even as early as October 1949 the Executive seems to have realised that it would need only 700, since an internal memorandum refers to the balance of 675 (after delivery of the twenty-five Private Hire coaches) not being needed until 1951-1953 and that the design of these had not yet been settled. It was not until much later that the BTC was informed that the full authorisation would not be required. In the meantime, the Commission gave authority in August 1950 for the purchase of 217 complete vehicles

and a further forty-eight chassis; the balance of 537 bodies and 489 chassis was authorised in May 1951. The orders actually placed with AEC were for quantities of 160, 490 and 50 (see chapter three). The amount of money authorised for this project showed that the RF was by no means a cheap bus, coming out at an average price of £4,149 for each vehicle, only £50 less than a Park Royal bodied RT! The expensive element was the chassis, which at £2,218 cost £459 more than a contemporary AEC Regent 3RT chassis (itself not cheap), whilst the body cost £576 less than the Park Royal version for the RT. The final cost of the vehicles was higher than this because of inflation.

By the autumn of 1950, circumstances had changed substantially. The Motor Vehicles (Construction and Use) Amendment Regulations, which authorised the use of 30ft-long single-deckers, had come into force on June 6th and the pessimism of the operators had proved to be unfounded. Against all expectations, approval had been obtained for thirty-footers on all routes for which application had been made. The relatively few routes where shorter vehicles would be needed could be served by the post-war T and TD buses for the foreseeable future. The instructions to AEC and Metro-Cammell were immediately amended so that, after the first twenty-five, all vehicles in the order would be built to the new maximum permitted length.

The only problem which remained unsolved was that of the weight limit on Walton Bridge. The only buses which were light enough to cross the bridge were the pre-war 1T1s, which, although recently thoroughly refurbished, were by this time twenty years old and the engineers were prepared to forecast only that they could be kept running until 1953 and no longer. The Executive had been trying to solve this problem since 1946, when an application was first made to Middlesex County Council for a weight dispensation, at that time with the idea of running double-deckers, but without success. The application was renewed in 1948 when it was hoped to put some of the new TDs on the 218 and a planned new route 264. This time extra evidence was rolled out in the form of proof that the bridge had been used regularly during the war by heavy military vehicles. A tougher line was also taken with a threat that the service would have to be withdrawn in 1949 if the new vehicles could not be used, but this also failed to soften the corporate heart of the county council. The county did have plans to erect a temporary bridge and then to build an entirely new structure but nobody was sure when this would happen. As things turned out, the temporary bridge was provided in the nick of time and the 1T1s were replaced by heavier vehicles at the end of January 1953.

The main programme of 7ft 6in wide machines (the RF class) was to comprise twenty-five Private Hire Coaches (the only 27ft 6in long examples), 263 Green Line, 225 Central Bus and 187 Country Bus versions, but there was an unexpected addition in the form of fifteen 'long distance coaches', as they were described in official documents, the purchase of which was authorised by the Executive in August 1950.

This surprising change of heart compared with the findings of the August 1949 review

had its origin in a decision of the British Transport Commission, on 23rd May 1950, to issue a 'direction' to the London Transport Executive to enable them to operate contract carriages outside the statutorily defined London Transport Area. Without this direction, LT was prohibited by statute from operating outside the boundaries of that area, except on certain defined lengths of road. The 'direction' was followed immediately by a 'request' from the Commission to the Executive to provide, as their agents, contract carriage services originating within the London Passenger Transport Area and operating within a radius of one hundred miles of 55 Broadway. These decisions were the culmination of a long and hard fought review of the BTC's policy on contract carriage, there being a strong body of opinion that it should be discouraged as being wastefully competitive with the railways. What appears to have swayed the Commission eventually was the existence of many private operators, over whom they had no control, competing with Commission-owned companies.

As an indirect consequence, the Road Passenger Transport Executive of the BTC offered to transfer to London Transport an order for five coaches on AEC chassis which had been placed by "a Tilling Group company" who had agreed to take Bristols instead. The company concerned was not identified but the expression 'Tilling Group' seems to have been used fairly loosely to include all BTC-owned provincial companies and could include, for example, Midland General, traditionally an AEC operator. While gratefully accepting the offer, London Transport had come to the conclusion, independently, that it would need fifteen coaches to meet its new commitments and therefore sought to order an additional ten identical machines. The Commission approved the order on 5th September 1950 at a cost of roundly £4,000 for each complete vehicle. The final cost was to be substantially greater, inflation having taken its toll. This relatively expensive price, by 1950 standards, was governed not only by the cost of the special features, such as glass roof panels, the public address sytem and sliding roofs but also because the urgent need to take delivery before the Festival of Britain meant that many parts which, given time, would have been manufactured in production tooling, had to be made by hand. The cost of the RF coaches was similarly inflated.

These vehicles (the RFW class) were to be the 'flagships' for the Festival of Britain season but were intended ultimately for the longer coach tours and longer distance private hire work. To most people's surprise, the new vehicles, London's first to be built to the maximum permitted dimensions on two axles of 8ft wide and 30ft long, were to be bodied by Eastern Coach Works, then a wholly owned subsidiary of the British Transport Commission and as such restricted by statute to supplying bodies to the nationalised sector. The choice of the Lowestoft manufacturer for this batch of vehicles was directly related to this fact. The Commission had been worried about the fall in the level of trade for the Lowestoft factory which had resulted from the loss of all the business from the non-nationalised sector when the factory passed into public ownership, along with the Tilling

Group. The Government had therefore instructed all Government-owned undertakings to place their bodybuilding requirements with ECW, unless there were good reasons for not doing so. London Transport had been able to plead exclusion from this edict for the supply of the bulk of its post-war fleet because ECW did not have the capacity to build in the quantities which the Executive required. The Regal IV coaches were the first example of a small non-standard class for which an order could be placed under these rules and the offer of the first five from the Road Passenger Transport Executive may well have been intended as an incentive to the Executive to use ECW more.

The order of replacement of the pre-war fleet was more complicated than was the case for double-deckers because the distribution between the two operating departments was much more uneven. By far the greatest proportion of the oldest vehicles, dating from 1929-31 were in the Central Bus fleet, while the bulk of those dating from the late 1930s were on Green Line services run by the Country department, the bulk of whose buses dated from the mid-thirties. Now that the Green Line and service bus RFs were all to be the same length, the original idea of renewing the Green Line fleet first was restored. Only then would the red bus fleet receive attention, leaving the Country buses until last. As this would mean that the youngest vehicles would be replaced first, a five phase programme of withdrawals and redeployment was worked out:

I   Thirty-seven 30-seat 10T10s displaced from Green Line and transferred to Central Buses, replacing twenty-three 11T11 and fourteen 9T9 buses for scrap.

II   Thirty-two 6Q6 Green Line coaches to be scrapped.

III Seventy-two 30-seat 10T10 coaches to be re-allocated to the Country area to replace eight 11T11 and thirty-five 9T9 buses; and the Central area to replace twenty-six 1T1 and three 4Q4 buses.

IV   Fifty-two 34-seat 10T10/1 coaches to be re-allocated within the Country area to replace thirty-three 30-seat 10T10s, seventeen 6Q6 (coaches in use as buses) and two 4Q4.

V   The seventy TF coaches would be re-allocated within the Country department to replace a like number of 4Q4 buses.

This plan was intended to eliminate the 1T1 (26 buses), 9T9 (49), 11T11 (31), and 6Q6 (49 coaches) and to start the replacement of the 4Q4 (75) and 10T10 (33 buses) classes. The seeming premature withdrawal of the 6Q6 sub-class, dating from 1936, caused some raised eyebrows, particularly in Trade Union circles and this was to become an interesting issue later. At the planning stage, however, the decision was made on the basis that the Q was not a universally popular vehicle and it might have been difficult to find a garage where the staff were prepared to take it on as a new type.

Like all plans, this one was to suffer from deviation as will be seen in later chapters, but its basic principles were to see the programme through its first year or so without too many hitches.

Already nearly twenty years old, eighteen 1T1s were rebuilt by Marshalls of Cambridge in 1949 into this slightly 'cleaned-up' appearance. T 2, which started life at Hornchurch in October 1930, leads an early 1950s-style traffic queue through Esher on its way to the troublesome Walton Bridge and Staines. The bulkhead slip board announces that there is a minimum fare of 3d on buses leaving Kingston. G.W. Morant

Weymann built these attractive thirty-seat bodies on the 9T9 sub-class for Green Line service in 1936, in June of which year T 405 started work at Watford (Leavesden Road). After the war it went to Uxbridge and received this Country bus version of the post-war livery. Because of their narrow gangways they were as unpopular for local bus work with conductors as with drivers. Alan B. Cross

The Central bus 11T11s had priority for withdrawal in the first phase of the replacement programme. The Buckinghamshire registration of T 359, at Alexandra Palace in 1949, gives a clue to its origins as a thirty-two seat Strachan bodied coach bought by Amersham and District in January 1932. This Weymann body was transferred from R 26 in November 1938. D.W.K. Jones

Some 10T10s were always used for bus work in post-war years, their handsome Chiswick-built bodies and comfortable seats adding a touch of style to local journeys on routes like the 390 for which the southern aspect of Hertford Bus Station was home territory. G.W. Morant

5 THE PRIVATE HIRE FLEET

RF 1-25. The first production chassis for the new RF class, numbered 9821LT001 was delivered to Metro-Cammell's works at Elmdon, Birmingham, on 17th November 1950. It was over a month ahead of the second delivery, which took place on 19th December, after which chassis were arriving at Elmdon at the rate of three or four a week until early February. RF 1, being the pilot vehicle for the run, was not returned as a complete vehicle to Chiswick Works until 14th April 1951 but it was then closely followed at three or four day intervals by the remaining twenty-four, all of which had arrived by 1st June. The first to be licensed was RF 2, which was delivered to Camberwell garage on 25th April, where it was immediately put to use for driver and courier training. Three more were licensed on 2nd May (RFs 1, 3 and 4), followed by RF 5 on the 4th, so that the Executive could mark the start of the Festival of Britain that day with five of the new coaches. The batch was

given the registrations LUC201-225, coming between Weymann-bodied RT 4041, delivered two months earlier and the start of a batch of Park Royal bodied vehicles (RT 2000) as far back as November 1950. The near-matching of registrations to fleet numbers was unusual at the time and had no immediate significance but is interesting because it was to be during the run of RF deliveries that the policy was to change.

The chassis specification was the same as for UMP227 (described in chapter three) and London Transport made much in its publicity of the features which were designed to give quietness and smoothness of ride. Anti-vibration engine mountings were, by now, a common feature in the London fleet but the Regals were also fitted, as a standard component, with the Atlas Pilot Injection system which was claimed to reduce diesel 'knock' and had been tried experimentally on some RTs at Turnham Green. The Chiswick development

Above **The choice of RF 24 for the official photographs was probably driven by the desire not to delay the earlier deliveries from entering service. The simple outline of the Metro-Cammell bodywork is well matched by the inspired choice of Lincoln green and grey for the main body colours. The vertical black line which can be seen behind the entrance doors was the semaphore signalling arm, a feature not otherwise in general use on the LT fleet.** LT Museum LTE/134/1

Facing Page **The rear view reveals the characteristic Chiswick hinged Emergency Exit door placed centrally at the rear. Also evident, immediately above the registration plate, is the two-headed arrow for indicating turns, which proved to be confusing in operation because the whole display was on the offside of the vehicle. Although 'R' garage plates were fitted for these photographs, RF 24 actually went to Upton Park.** LT Museum LTE/134/5

engineers apparently wished to persevere with this system, despite the fact that AEC had become disenchanted and did not plan to use it in the provincial models. Southall's opinion was the one which eventually prevailed, as the system gave much poorer fuel consumption and all RFs were eventually converted to standard injection during their first overhaul.

The stressed inner-skin type all-metal body-work employed Metro-Cammell's standard methods of construction whilst honouring the detailed specification laid down by Chiswick's design staff. The main structure comprised nickel steel floor cross-bearers in deep hot-pressed channel section. These were connected at their outer ends to mild steel crib angles by lubricated steel brackets and, by rivets, to vertical pillars of Metro-Cammell's patented solid drawn tubular section. These pillars were riveted to channel section waistrails and 'Z'-section cantrails, which ran all round the body. Bracing for the body framing was provided by high tensile, 16-gauge, aluminium alloy truss panels, which were secured by counter-sunk rivets. The lap-jointed external panels, which were made of 18-gauge hard aluminium, were pop-riveted to the main structure. The roof was built with 10-gauge aluminium sheets riveted to the aluminium alloy internal car-lines; these were attached to the body side pillars and cantrails with fabricated steel brackets.

The general outline of the bodywork, which was to set the pattern for the whole of the class, marked a move away from the curvacious styles popular in the 1930s and still then evident in contemporary double-deckers and also a departure from the tradition that Chiswick designed single-deckers had always been an obvious development from one to another. The reason for this was that the RF was the first London Transport body design for which they engaged an external consultant from the outset. (Although external expertise was used for the RTC, the scope for originality was limited by the already existing body shell.) Rather as the Routemaster was to do three years later (under the same designer's influence), the RF allied a severely upright front end with a more relaxed curved rear. This had the happy effect of incorporating the front indicator box within the dome, without recourse to projections, giving a virtually uninterrupted smooth line from roof to skirt. Metro-Cammell influence was evident in the design of the driver's cab windscreen, which was in two sections. The lower one-third was vertical and fixed while the upper two-thirds was angled into a deep recess and could be opened for ventilation. An electrically driven windscreen wiper was fitted to the upper section, fixed to the top of the bulkhead. The nearside screen was one flat fixed piece and had a windscreen wiper worked from the bottom of the screen.

The potentially plain appearance of the front was relieved by the layout of the equipment. The sidelights were set immediately below the screens at the outer extremities of the body, whilst the headlamps were slightly inset, flanking the registration plate immediately above the trim of the removable lower panel. Directly below the nearside headlamp and immediately above the skirt was a single foglamp. The most imaginative feature was the method used to conceal the radiator filler cap. This was situated behind the panelling immediately below the central windscreen dividing pillar and was hidden under a semi-circular hinged flap. This was incorporated into a 'bullseye' embossed with the fleetname 'LONDON TRANSPORT', which skilfully finished off the symmetry of the arrangement.

There were two entrance doors of the glider type employing Peters electro-magnetic gear, operated by compressed air supplied by a motor enclosed behind the front panelling alongside the entrance steps. Each leaf was fitted with two rubber glazed windows of unequal depth, the top section being the same depth as the windscreen, while the lower section was shorter and finished in line with the horizontal trim between the nearside panels, roughly in line with the top of the wheels. The lowest part of the doors was unglazed. There were five full-length saloon windows on each side, with another, shorter,

RF 1 at work from Putney Bridge garage passes the old Odeon cinema in Clarence Street, Kingston, in the spring of 1953. Alan B. Cross

one over the rear overhang. These were 'Simplastic' glazed in rubber and had rounded corners for ease of cleaning and maintenance. Four windows on each side had 'Widney Ace' wind-down opening windows which were described at the time as 'shallow half-drop' but which were actually of the quarter-drop type, designed to improve vision from the interior. Above these, in the coving of the roof and extending the full length of the passenger saloon, was a series of five large observation windows made of 'Triplex' toughened glass.

The basic angularity of the design was echoed in the shape of the mudguards which had a squared outline, rounded off at the corners, although the wheel housing was of conventional circular section. The lower side body panels had removable valances for access

to the engine, batteries and other components. This feature was specified by London Transport because the use of the more usual hinged flaps would have required wider spacing between parked vehicles in garages and therefore more garage accommodation. The fuel filler cap was situated in the middle panel of the nearside, while access to the oil filler was in the panel immediately behind the front offside wheel. 'Semaphore' trafficators were fitted immediately ahead of the first saloon windows on each side.

The curved rear end was interrupted in outline by a conventional indicator box, which stood proud of the roof over about half its width. The mark of Chiswick was finally stamped by the provision of a hinged emergency exit door in the centre, which

enforced the characteristic three window arrangement, so familiar on pre-war single-deckers from the same stable. The registration plate was situated between the door and the offside corner and was surmounted by the single brake and rear lamps, above which was a 'trafficator' in the form of an illuminated arrow, with a head at both sides. The intended direction of turn was indicated by the illumination of the appropriate arrow head together with the corresponding half of the shaft.

Internally, the basic design features closely followed those already established on the RT family of double-deckers. The totally enclosed entrance steps, which gave a step height of 1ft 2½ins on a laden vehicle, were panelled in stainless steel and finished with wooden strip treads. They were illuminated by two lamps, one inset into the first riser at its rearmost end and the other into the forward end of the second riser. The floors were finished with green linoleum. This extended up the side panelling to the seat rail above which olive green leathercloth was used as far as waist level. On the nearside, this arrangement was interrupted by the duct carrying the heating supply, which ran along two-thirds of the saloon from the front, in the curved section between the floor and the side panelling. The window finishers of pressed aluminium were covered with leathercloth, dark green on the lower third, up to the polished aluminium bracelet and what was described as 'putty green' (somewhat akin to Khaki in appearance) over the upper two-thirds.

These passengers look suspiciously like a group of London Transport office staff pressed into service for an official photograph. If so, the driver took a chance driving with his doors open, but this does help to illustrate the arrangement of the entrance steps and the position of the light at the rear end of the first riser. Lens of Sutton

Looking back from the top of the entrance steps, the deep squabs of the seats look inviting in the well lit interior of the RF1 body. On the left can be seen the single inward facing seat, with its armrest mounted on a polished aluminium guardrail. The second and fourth observation windows on the nearside have their concertina blinds drawn and fixed with press studs. The dark circle in the rear dome is the loudspeaker for the public address system. The forward looking view inside the Private Hire coach demonstrates the excellent visibility for passengers. LT Museum LTE/134/12/13

RF 2 returning to base over Elizabeth Bridge after completing the West End tour. D.A. Jones/LTPS

Partition edges were fitted with polished aluminium cappings. The ceiling was enamelled cream and rod controlled concertina blinds of leathercloth were fitted for use over the observation windows. Between the side and roof windows there was a moulding coloured cream but picked out in red.

The driver's compartment was separated from the saloon by a full height half-bulkhead, glazed between waist and cantrail level and echoed by a similar structure on the nearside behind the entrance steps. Access to the cab was through a waist-high hinged door. Apart from his usual controls, the driver was supplied with a set of door control buttons, identical to those in the main saloon for the use of the courier. The courier was also provided with a microphone, which was kept in a compartment immediately above the entrance door. A 'Trix' amplifier was situated under the rearmost offside seat and the loudspeaker was fitted into the dome at the rear of the saloon, behind a circular grille. Below this was a bell push, another being fitted to the front bulkhead on the door-well side. Alongside the loudspeaker was the access flap for the rear blind changing handle, secured by a 'budget' lock. Finally, to provide for emergencies when the vehicle was far from base, a set of tools was provided in a box under the rearmost nearside seat. To protect them from 'unnecessary loss' (theft?), they could be obtained only by first breaking a glass panel.

The thirty-five seats were arranged in pairs facing forward, except for one single seat which was placed immediately behind the driver's cab facing the nearside. This seat alone was given an armrest, surmounting a polished aluminium guardrail designed to prevent the passenger slipping off the end of the chair. The seat frames were of the standard London Transport aluminium tubular type, with polished 'MGT' top rails and a grab rail of the same material above them. 'Dunlopillo' was used for filling the cushions, which were covered in uncut moquette of a new geometric design which incorporated the main colours of the livery; Lincoln green, red and 'putty' green. The backs were also covered in putty green moquette and fitted with an ashtray. The headroom was a generous 6ft 6⅞ins and the total effect was of a light, airy and roomy interior.

Separate heaters were fitted for the driver and passengers. Both were supplied from a heat exchange unit utilising the engine cooling water, and a Clayton Dewandre electrically driven blower was used to circulate the warm air through the duct in the nearside of the passenger saloon. These units were contained under the floor at the front nearside. The driver's cab unit incorporated a windscreen demister, then something of a novelty on a PSV. The ventilating system was completed by a large extractor vent above the rearmost bay immediately ahead of the destination indicator box housing. Clean air for the engine cooling system was supplied through an air intake above the windscreen, which was connected with a Burgess intake-silencer under the roof of the driver's compartment. The air passed from there through a pipeline to the underfloor engine, where its circulation was enhanced by an engine driven fan.

Lighting was provided by twenty-three pearl twelve-watt lamps which projected from the cove panels, their fittings concealed but the lamps, in true Chiswick style, unadorned.

Externally the coaches were finished in a new livery which gave them a most striking appearance. The panels below the waist and the areas around the platform doors and destination indicator boxes were in traditional 'Lincoln' green but above this and extending over the whole roof, flake grey was used. The novelty of approach was extended into the lettering, all of which (apart from registration plates) was in red, which was also used for lining out. In line with the then current policy, bright parts were unpainted and this included an aluminium 'kicker' strip which ran around the bottom of the rear overhang. The new design did indeed seem to herald a bright new future for the single-deck fleet.

Douglas Scott had influenced the outside design and was particularly proud of certain features, notably the way in which the front destination box blended into the body, the continuous flow of relief colour around the windows, the squared mudguards and the bullseye hiding the filler cap. He also influenced much of the interior design, especially the coach-type fittings such as luggage racks on the Green Line version (chapter five) and the general décor.

The completed vehicle, which was given the classification 1RF1/2, was certainly no lightweight, turning the scales when unladen at 7 tons 12 cwt, two hundredweight heavier than the standard double-deck RT.

All twenty-five of the coaches were destined for the Central Bus department, which spread their allocation among eight garages, three each to Camberwell, Holloway (J), Merton, Middle Row (North Kensington), Riverside (Hammersmith), Streatham and Willesden and four to Upton Park.

RFWs being bodied in the Eastern Coach Works factory at Lowestoft in 1951, sharing the shop with just one double-decker, almost certainly a KSW.

RFW 1-15 Thirteen days after the delivery of RF 1 and only just in the nick of time to be available for the opening of the Festival of Britain, the first of the 'long-distance' coaches, RFW 1, arrived. Three more arrived on 30th April and three of the four (RFWs 1, 3 and 4) were licensed on the first day of the Festival, 4th May. One of them, together with one of the RFs, was inspected by the Executive at Victoria garage the day before and given its final seal of approval. The remainder came in ones and twos until the last pair (RFWs 13 and 14) were delivered on 29th May. Unlike the RFs, the registration numbers bore no resemblance at all to the fleet numbers, the batch chosen being LUC376-390, following the final Metro-Cammell bodied RTL (1000), which entered service at about the same time and immediately preceding the series allotted in February 1951 to Weymann RTs starting at 4042. They were classified 3RF3.

The chassis were of basically standard 9821E specification, though there were a number of details to LTE requirements. The resulting vehicles were almost identical to a batch of five built for the Tillings Transport (BTC) Ltd fleet, successor to the private hire department of Thomas Tilling Ltd, which was also a part of the nationalised British Transport Commission empire. Both batches had thirty-nine seat bodywork of a rather angular style and quite different from that evolved when ECW began production of its standard coach version of the semi-integral LS model as supplied to many Tilling group fleets. According to a report made by the Chief Mechanical Engineer to the Executive, the similarity was deliberate. The RFWs were designed to have as many features as possible in common with

RFW 1 (and the ubiquitous Morris Minor) in the familiar surroundings of Windsor on one of London Transport's conducted tours. On these vehicles, the emergency exit door was at the rear of the centre bay and can be identified by the additional grey pillar and the door opening handle just ahead of the rear wheel. Sports jacket, formal shirt and tie with raincoat folded over the arm, as sported by the man crossing in front of the coach, were standard wear for the average man on a Sunday outing in the 1950s.
Frank Mussett

the Tilling version so that vehicles could be lent by one operator to the other. The design was said to be suitable for touring on the continent, should the Tilling organisation need to borrow the LT vehicles for that purpose. Whether or not this was mere salesmanship on his part is not known but there are no recorded instances of RFWs being borrowed to run a continental tour. The design was certainly agreed with the Tilling Executive and the reason was undoubtedly to keep down the cost of manufacture.

Although somewhat austere by general coach standards, the RFW was more curved and luxurious in appearance than the RF. The front end was smoothly curved both laterally and vertically and the comparatively shallow dome was unimpaired by any destination indicator equipment. This feature was, in fact, absent from the vehicle altogether. Excellent exterior vision for the driver was achieved with a windscreen in four flat sections, two large ones covering most of the front and two smaller ones, angled at each corner, to give an overall

London Transport's coach tours are designed to show the visitor as much as possible of the best of London. Each tour is accompanied by a friendly and well-informed guide to point out the places of interest. The green coaches themselves are a new type, specially fitted with large glass roof panels, so that passengers can see even the top of Nelson's column without craning.

In the morning, the West End tour takes in the Changing of the Guard and Westminster Abbey. In the afternoon, there are tours to the City, including St. Paul's and the Tower of London, to Windsor Castle, to Hampton Court in the summer splendour of its gardens, and down the Thames by river-bus and by coach. The river tour also runs in the evening, and there could hardly be a pleasanter way of rounding off a day's sightseeing.

Finally, there are three new whole-day tours outside London. One goes to Windsor and Stoke Poges, where Gray wrote his Elegy, to Jordans, where William Penn is buried, and to Milton's Cottage in Chalfont St. Giles ; another to the splendid houses of Knole and Clandon Park ; and the third to Roman St. Albans and the Cathedral, to Luton Hoo with its treasures of art, and to Hatfield House, where the history of a great English family comes magnificently to life.

The West End and City tours each cost 7s. 6d., the Hampton Court and River tours 5s. ; fare for the Windsor tour is 12s. 6d., including tea at Windsor, and for each of the whole-day tours, 25s. including lunch and charges for admission to the places visited.

A free leaflet giving full details of these tours may be had and seats booked at the Private Hire Office, 55 Broadway, S.W.1 (over St. James's Park Station), any agent for London Coastal Coaches Ltd., or any branch of Dean and Dawson Ltd.

BY LONDON TRANSPORT

effect similar to a curved screen. The screen on the driver's side was, like the Metro-Cammell version, in two sections, the top two-thirds of which could be opened and fixed in any position. Each large screen was fitted with an electrically driven wiper, the offside one fixed at the top and the nearside at the bottom.

The sidelamps and headlamps flowed out of the curved corner panels in the form of half cones, immediately below the bottom of the screen, which gave an impression of speed. The foglamp was inset slightly and contained in a recessed circular aperture within the detachable panel which occupied the lowest one-third of the front panelling. As with the RF, the radiator filler cap was concealed behind a 'bullseye' composition, the top half of whose circle was hinged to open. The registration plate was situated in line vertically with this, immediately above the detachable panel, and comprised metalled lettering rather than the customary painted type.

There were six full drop opening passenger windows on each side, arranged in three bays separated by pillars, rounded at their corners and flush with the main side panels. Within the bays, the dividers between the two windows were slender polished aluminium and met the top and bottom rails at a right-angle. Along the top of each window was a 'louvre' to deflect rainwater. Above each of these was an observation window in the curved side of the roof panel. Although not immediately visible from the side, this sightseeing arrangement was complemented by two sliding panels in the centre of the roof. On the nearside, access to the saloon was by a hinged coach type entrance door, which opened towards the front of the vehicle. The glazed upper half of the door balanced the short fixed side window at the rearmost end of the saloon. On the offside, there was a hinged emergency exit door in the fourth bay, immediately ahead of the rear wheel. The contrast with the RF was continued into the treatment of the wings, which were in conventional circular section around the wheel arches. The fuel filler cap was on the nearside, in the middle of the second bay. Like the RFs, the RFWs had semaphore 'trafficators' fitted, in their case immediately below the window line in the extreme front corner on each side.

The rear view was the only feature which had a family resemblance to later models from the Lowestoft factory. In plan there was a continuous curve from nearside to offside and there was a comparably rounded line from roof to waistrail. The stamp of ECW was to be found in the arrangement of the rear windows, of which there were three, a large central one being flanked by two of about half its size. Immediately below the window mouldings was the registration plate, internally illuminated, behind glass. The rear 'trafficator' arrows were incorporated into this, one on each side of the registration number giving a much clearer and more practical arrangement than on the RF. Under that was a luggage compartment with two hinged doors, opened by means of a 'budget' key. A final touch of class was added by the provision of no fewer than four rear lamps, one on each lower corner panel and one on each side of the roof.

Advertisement from the Evening Standard, 15th June 1951.

The arrangement of RFW 6's saloon windows in three bays, split by a slender aluminium pillar, foreshadowed the panoramic windows of a later generation. The extensive use of polished aluminium trim and the four rear lamps were particular features which stamped the design as non-standard for London Transport.
LT Museum H/1623

RFW 15 doing what the RFWs were bought to do — contract hire work beyond the old statutory limits of the London Transport operating area.
Lens of Sutton

In every essential identical to the London Transport version, the Tilling Regal IVs were painted cream, with black mudguards and the fleetname in gold transfers. The bullseye cover for the radiator filler cap was replaced by the company's embossed fleetname. LYM732, the last of the five, is seen at Oxford.
R.H.G. Simpson

Left **Looking forward inside the RFW, the courier's control panel and the standard bell push can be seen on the front bulkhead.**
LT Museum 1849/R/B

Below **The RFWs had luggage racks suspended from the roof corners, which slightly interfered with the line of vision. Unlike normal London Transport practice, all interior lights were covered by glass lampshades, the individual switches for which were situated centrally on the inner side of the fitting. The loudspeaker grille is the large circular protrusion in the rear dome, above which is a standard bell push.**
LT Museum H/1628

Internally, the styling differed in one important respect from the RFs. There were thirty-nine individual seats to full luxury coach standard, arranged in seventeen pairs, with five across the rear, all facing forward. These had cushions, squabs and headrests filled with 'Dunlopillo' and covered in moquette of the same design as the RFs. The backs of the seats were covered with leather in a sun-burst design. Leather was also used as trim for the middle part of the headrests. One ashtray was fitted centrally to the back of each seat. There was a full length parcel rack on each side, hung from the ceiling alongside the roof windows but interrupted on the offside at the emergency exit door. There was a lamp above each row of seats, covered by a moulded shade and supplied with individual switches. Additional lighting was supplied by two lamps in the rear dome and by four others in the ceiling, all covered by the same design of moulded shade. In the rear dome was the circular grille containing the loudspeaker and above it a bell push. Another bell push was placed in the front dome, to the nearside of the courier's amplifier equipment.

The exterior finish was in the same 'Lincoln' green, grey and red livery as used on the Private Hire RFs but this was lightened further by a thin polished aluminium moulding strip which ran around the whole of the bottom of the skirt panelling. The unladen weight of the completed vehicle was 8 tons 8 cwt, five hundredweight heavier than the heaviest double-decker, the RTW.

These coaches were shared between both operating departments, nine to Central Buses

and six to Country for use on conducted tours and long-distance Private Hire jobs. Three Central area ones went to each of Chelverton Road (Putney), Dalston and Old Kent Road garages, while the Country department spread their six around to Northfleet, Reigate, Romford London Road (two), Watford (Leavesden Road) and Windsor.

Soon after delivery the RFs and RFWs had to have their public address equipment rewired because it was interfering with other electrical circuits on the coach.

The urgent need for these coaches and the RFs is interestingly illustrated by the way in which the operators went about staff training. The intention was that staff from eleven Central Bus garages and from most Country garages should be capable of driving both types, so that Private Hire work could be widely distributed. The imminence of the Festival of Britain was only one factor; there was also a British Industries Fair and a series of football cup-ties all of which conspired to leave insufficient time for the training programme, which was planned to be quite long because of the many novel features on the new vehicles. To get the vehicles into service as quickly as possible, training was restricted to only four men for each coach initially. The backlog was cleared once the main season was over.

There were those who were surprised and rather disturbed by the appearance of these wholly untypical vehicles in the London fleet. There were many coach operators in London who saw them as a threat to their livelihood at a time when excursions and tours business

was beginning to go into decline. London Transport's official response to this was to reassure their competitors that they had no aspirations to go into long-distance touring or to run trunk coach services. The decision to purchase vehicles to a full coach specification had been prompted by the extension of the Executive's permitted area of operation to a radius of 100 miles from London, for which the rest of the fleet was not considered suitable. In the event, they were mainly true to their word but, given the aggressive way in which the operating departments had already been pursuing competitive activities like bus excursions, the fears may well have had some substance.

The forty new Regals did not immediately replace any older vehicles as the existing fleet of AEC Renown coaches (LTC) and the sole surviving touring version of the TF were retained for use during the Festival of Britain. All twenty-four of the LTCs were delicensed in October 1951 and TF 9 in May 1952, seemingly for the last time, but six of the LTCs were again licensed for the 1952 season, when they operated between May and October from Chalk Farm (2), Merton, Old Kent Road (2) and Putney Bridge garages.

This RFW is alongside the River Thames and the courier is using the microphone to make an announcement. The connecting wire can be seen above the back of his head emerging from the light coloured equipment panel. The patterned leather on the seat backs was unique to this type in the LT fleet. LT Museum

6 THE GREEN LINE COACHES

The first thirty-foot Regal chassis for London (9821LT032) was despatched to Metro-Cammell on 16th February 1951 but it was to be nearly seven months before the completed vehicle appeared at Chiswick on 14th September. The delay was caused by an industrial problem with Metro-Cammell's shop staff over rate-fixing, compounded by one of the many bouts of material shortages which were so much a feature of the decade or so after the war. The Executive's plans had been framed on the assumption that the delivery of the coaches would follow immediately after the RF1 private hire vehicles, with the first going into service during June. First estimates were that the delay would be until August but, as the summer wore on, even this slipped by a further two months.

The consequences for the rest of the fleet were serious. The Central Bus operating department was under continuous pressure from drivers to remove the unpopular 9T9 and 11T11 buses as soon as possible and evidence that their patience was wearing thin was the demand of Uxbridge drivers in December 1950 that their 9T9s should be withdrawn in January 1951. They were persuaded to exercise patience until the new vehicles were due to arrive in June.

The Works Manager at Chiswick also had his problems. His work plan had been built around the release of the first thirty-seven 10T10s from Green Line service for overhaul, repainting and downgrading to buses, starting in June. He had ordered his materials and planned the rest of his throughput and output

from this starting point. This programme could not be altered except by leaving the Works with nothing to do, followed by a glut of work with which they could not cope. The Ts could have been turned out in green livery but this would have meant an expensive repaint to red within months and a surfeit of work in the paintshop. The Works wanted to continue with their plans and asked the Country department to accept the temporary operation of red 10T10s on the Green Line. This was completely unacceptable but it was agreed that the repainted vehicles could be used on bus work in the country area, releasing 10T10 buses in green livery for temporary use on coach services. In the event, ten vehicles were used in this way for periods varying between as little as five days to a full three weeks.

Above **This nearside view of RF 26 shows the basic angularity of the design, softened by gentle curves at both front and back.**
LT Museum LTE/141/8

Opposite **The inward curve of the sides above and below its centreline and the orderly arrangement of the equipment helped to soften the impact of the full frontal appearance of the Metro-Cammell body.**
LT Museum LTE/141/2

Right **This view of RF 26 shows how the side panels could be removed completely to allow access to the engine, mounted on the offside under the floor.**
LT Museum LTE141/12

After a difficult spring and summer, patience was finally rewarded with the licensing of RF 26 at Tunbridge Wells on 1st October. The Metro-Cammell body was directly derived from the Private Hire model, lengthened to take in the longer wheelbase and incorporating a longer rear overhang. The main effect on the external appearance was the addition of one more full size window on each side immediately behind the rear wheel and a glazed quarter panel at the extreme rear end of the saloon. The observation windows were omitted and replaced by plain metal cove panels. Directly above the windows and approximately within the wheelbase, metal clips were fitted to carry the traditional Green Line wooden route board. The design of this remained unchanged from those in use on the existing fleet, the route number and route details being in gold lettering on a 'Lincoln' green background. Provision was made for semaphore 'trafficators' of the type carried on the RF1s but the housing built into the bodywork was sealed under a metal plate and never used. The colour scheme introduced a new layout for Green Line, although a similar arrangement had been in use on buses for the previous six years. The use of 'Lincoln' green with a pale green relief was continued but the relief colour was reduced to a series of thin bands which followed the moulding around the passenger saloon side and rear windows, the windscreen and the driver's cab. Pale green was also used for the outline of the 'bullseye' cover to the radiator filler cap, on which the fleetname 'GREEN LINE' was embossed. This lettering, in common with the traditional side and rear fleetnames, legal lettering and fleet numbers, reverted to standard gold transfers, the use of red being confined to the Private Hire fleet. The total effect was dignified but dull. One modification which was introduced during the production run and subsequently made to all vehicles, was the introduction of a roof air intake ventilator into the third ceiling bay. The sliding grille vent was opened and closed by a laterally operated protruding knob.

The basic structure and interior finish of the new coaches was the same as the RF1s. The important visual differences were the absence of the observation windows and the addition, on each side of the saloon, immediately above the side windows, of parcel racks attached to which was a continuous polished aluminium grabrail. The cream coloured raised moulding above the windows was picked out in green, rather than the red used for buses. The main saloon lighting was from twelve-watt pearl lamps which were plugged directly into the

Above **The view forward in the passenger saloon of RF 26 makes interesting comparison with the Qs illustrated on page 10, the basic design features having changed little in the intervening fifteen years.** LT Museum LTE/141/11

Below **The closure of Windsor Bridge to traffic was long in the future when RF 26 made its first journeys to and from the Royal Borough in October 1951. The choice of Windsor Castle as a backdrop to this official view shows great pride in the new product and confidence in the future of the Green Line** LT Museum

Looking towards the back inside the Green Line version of the RF. The deep cushions are covered in a handsome moquette in tones of green, red and 'putty'. Douglas Scott's improved design of luggage rack flowing into the side panelling may be compared with the earlier type used on the Qs illustrated earlier.
LT Museum 17141

underside of the racks. Supplementary lighting for the gangway was given from a series of lamps in the central ceiling panels. Standard bell push fittings were installed in the rear dome and on the front bulkhead by the door. Additionally there were four elegantly designed oblong versions in stainless steel, on the underside of the offside parcel rack. The thirty-nine seats were of the special deep squab type used for coach applications by London Transport and were arranged in nineteen forward facing pairs, with one inward

facing single seat on the offside at the front. All but the rearmost row of seats was fitted with ash trays, as an added item of luxury for Green Line travellers. A neat solution to the problem of accommodating the faretable was found by placing it behind a lockable glass panel in the front panel above the windscreen. This was rather high for the average person to read with comfort but there were few other places for it to go and it was certainly an imaginative use of the limited space. Heating was provided for the passenger saloon and

driver's cab, as in the Private Hire model, but the equipment particularly associated with touring, the microphone, amplifier and loudspeaker, were, of course, omitted. The completed vehicle, classified 2RF2/1, had an unladen weight of 7 tons 17 cwt, seven hundredweight heavier than the standard RT double-decker.

The first one hundred Green Line RFs were registered LYF377-476, coming between two batches of Park Royal RTs the first finishing with RT 2651 in September 1951 and the other starting with RT 2830 in April 1952.

The order of priority for the deployment of the Green Line RFs had been worked out in the early part of 1951 and appeared to follow no particular geographical or garage based sequence. The choice of routes 704 and 711 to start the changeover seems to suggest that the most heavily used and high earning routes were given preference. The full plan, as amended by subsequent changes to the network, appears in appendix 6.

RF 26 ploughed a lonely furrow between Windsor and Tunbridge Wells for ten days, before it was joined by RF 27 and it was not until 1st November that the last four of Tunbridge Wells's allocation of eight was licensed for service. This slow progress continued to the end of the year, by when only eighty-five of the originally planned 215 had been received. Eventually the flow settled at about ten a week. Meanwhile, RF 33 was used for training at Windsor, who put its first Regal IV into service on 7th November. The allocation was completed on 14th November but 10T10s continued to appear on the 704 for some time, as the number of RFs allocated was sufficient only for the basic schedule; the pre-war vehicles were still used as engineering spares and for unscheduled duplication. Route 711 followed in sequence, the next batch of coaches going to the Country headquarters garage at Reigate, followed by High Wycombe and then, for routes 709 and 710, Amersham, Crawley and Godstone.

Almost exactly thirteen years separate High Wycombe's RF 54 from T 687 which it is following in Reigate, during which the curvaceous rear end of the 10T10 has given way to the more upright design favoured for underfloor engined vehicles.
F.G. Reynolds

RF 70 was delivered to Crawley in December 1951 but, in this picture, is operating on an Amersham running, having spent the night at the Buckinghamshire garage. This was a regular feature of operation on the long cross-London Green Line routes. F.G. Reynolds

In all these cases, the coaches released were 10T10s and this enabled the first stage of the replacement to proceed at last. The displaced Regals were submitted to Chiswick for a complete overhaul, during which they were stripped of all the features associated with Green Line standards of specification. These included the saloon heaters, still a facility which the Executive did not consider necessary for ordinary bus passengers, the ash trays attached to the seat backs and the linoleum floor coverings, which would not have been hard wearing enough for local bus operation. Equipment added included a Used Ticket box,

at the entrance and a clip for a route number stencil above the entrance door. The sliding door itself was retained but, in deference to the continuing requirements of the Metropolitan Police, was locked in the open position by means of a leather thong attached to the interior grab rail. Externally, they were finished in the standard single-deck livery of bus red with a single thin cream band applied to the beading around the waist and along the cantrail beading, which ran down in a rearward sweeping curve to join the lower one at the rear corners. The first of the downgraded buses, T 504 was delivered to Kingston garage

on 24th August 1951, where it replaced T 31. The extraordinary coincidence of this event cannot have been appreciated at the time but both of these buses were later preserved.

For the main programme of redeployment, the original order of priority was first to replace the 9T9s at Uxbridge (eight) and Hornchurch (six), then the seven 11T11s at Loughton. After this, eight would go to Kingston to replace a like number of TDs for release to various garages where odd 11T11s were held as spares against an official allocation of the Leylands. Finally, the remaining small allocations of 11T11s would

It is difficult to believe that these charming vehicles were so unpopular with staff. The 9T9s were the first type to have the built-in wing assembly on the nearside which was not to appear on production double-deckers until the RT. The bumper bar, which enjoyed a brief vogue in the 1930s, was unusual for a London vehicle. T 413 was among the first fifteen to enter service, starting work at Amersham in March 1936, fifteen years before this photograph was taken. Alan B. Cross

T 504 was the first of the 10T10 coaches to be downgraded and repainted red. It went to Kingston but is seen here, in Cromwell Road, Kingston, after it was re-allocated to Norbiton when that garage opened in 1952. Alan B. Cross

be replaced directly. This plan was not followed slavishly. Most of the vehicles displaced from Tunbridge Wells and Windsor were re-deployed, still as coaches, to garages all over the Country area from which other vehicles were selected for transfer to Central Buses. Most went to Hornchurch and Loughton, where they replaced the unpopular 9T9s and 11T11s respectively. Loughton's willingness to co-operate had been touch and go. As a token of London Transport's commitment to replacing the older Regals on route 254, a 10T10 had been sent to Loughton in January but the staff were apparently not as impressed by the 'new'

vehicle as had been hoped and put a number of obstacles in the way of operating it, which were not resolved until May. Meanwhile, five Country Bus 10T10s were transferred into the Central area on 1st March to replace 5Q5s for driver training in preparation for the Private Hire RFs. These remained in their green livery, as their turn in the overhaul programme had not yet arrived. The only immediate concession to their change of status was that the 'GREEN LINE' fleetnames were replaced by 'LONDON TRANSPORT', on the insistence of the Country Bus Operating Manager.

The plan for the TDs was knocked off course by the need for two extra buses on route 240A at Edgware, which was fulfilled by two of Kingston's Tigers, two others being sent to Muswell Hill to deal with another problem which had been brewing in that garage for some time. Kingston put the 10T10s onto route 201 but no other TDs were replaced at that time. Instead, the 11T11s at Edgware (four), Enfield (seven, including one still green), Leyton (one), Southall (two), Tottenham (one) and West Green (two) were replaced by 10T10s. Some of the 10T10s from route 711 replaced 9T9s at Addlestone and Leatherhead.

Almost at the end of its days and looking more than a little careworn, Hornchurch's T 428 shares a crowded South Street, Romford with Guys and RTLs in late September 1951. Alan B. Cross

The problem at Muswell Hill had its origins in the fact that, situated as it was in the northern heights, the terrain served by its single-deck buses was particularly hilly and arduous. To some extent, this was recognised in the allocation of TDs to routes 212 and 251 but, for reasons which remain veiled in the mists of history, the very busy and equally arduous route 210 had not been allowed a share of this type and was still soldiering on with some of the oldest buses in the fleet — single-deck LTs. The route was to be rewarded by being the first to receive the Central Bus version of the RF but this event was a long way off when the dispute first arose in March 1950. It was then that the drivers first objected to the continued use of petrol engined LTs but when they were offered diesel conversions instead, they did not like those either. Armageddon was avoided by an agreement to spread the use of the TDs over all three routes. (Route 244 does not, at that time, appear to have been a problem.) The disquiet bubbled up again in the summer of 1951 when the staff were reassured that the planned replacement of single-deckers at Enfield (on routes 205, 242 and 243) by double-deckers, would release enough TDs to meet the needs of Muswell Hill. Unfortunately, this particular source never did materialise as the double-decking of Enfield's routes had still not been carried out when the very last red RF went into service two years later.

An interim solution was found in the next round of coach replacements at Hertford and Guildford on route 715, one of the busiest coach routes, rejoicing in a twenty-minute headway over its entire fifty-mile length and needing no fewer than twenty-one RFs to fulfill its schedule. This is where the bulk of the Park Royal bodied 6Q6s were still running and it had been the intention (to the surprise of staff representatives, as recorded in chapter three) to withdraw the sub-class for scrap as soon as they were released from coach duties. Indeed, this was still the intention when Hertford received its first RFs in December 1951 and when Guildford completed its allocation in January 1952. It was not until March that, following renewed pressure from the Trade Union, the best twenty-four of the Qs finally went to Muswell Hill, where they replaced the whole of its allocation of single-deck LTs and started the final replacement of the class, out of the intended sequence and some six or seven months earlier than planned. The show of reluctance on the part of London Transport to do what to many must have seemed obvious, flowed from the fact that they were concerned about their ability to keep the Qs in serviceable condition for much longer, bearing in mind that they had deliberately been given minimal maintenance in preparation for their withdrawal.

The carefully laid plans were again disrupted in January 1952 when, instead of moving on to convert route 708, the next nineteen new coaches went to Grays garage, which had been almost at the end of the original programme. The professed reason for this change was an urgent desire on the part of the Country Bus operators to increase the capacity of route 723A which had been introduced in September 1951 to serve the newly developing Aveley estate. This change brought forward the release of a number of

TFs, which were not intended to be dealt with until the fifth phase of the replacement programme. Rather than re-allocate them to other coach duties, however, it was decided to bring forward parts of the fourth and fifth phases. All but two of the TFs went to St Albans, where they went into service on bus routes 355, replacing the remaining 6Q6s which had been in use as buses for some time, and on routes 365, 382 and 391, on which they replaced the oldest of the 4Q4s. The other two went to Epping.

Above T 485, on route 212 at 'The Victoria' Alexandra Park, still sports its front wheel disc trim and full Green Line livery during a temporary loan to Muswell Hill garage. G. Morant

Below Door locked open and faretable propped in the windscreen, Q 230, temporarily reprieved from scrapping to work on the somewhat arduous route 210, lays over in Wells Terrace, Finsbury Park in March 1952. At this time the terminal working at Finsbury Park was clockwise and the buses are standing on the south side of the road. Q 230 was first licensed in January 1937. Alan B. Cross

Two generations of AEC/Metro-Cammell collaboration at Aldgate bus station in April 1952. L1 class chassisless trolleybus 1368 pulls past Grays's RF 107, working the newly introduced 723A for which the replacement programme was amended at the beginning of 1952.
Alan B. Cross

Below TF 56 at St Albans in June 1952. It is still in the two shades of green of the coach livery, the only indication of its new status being the 'London Transport' fleetname.
Alan B. Cross

The planned sequence was resumed on 1st February when both East Grinstead and Two Waters garages licensed sufficient RFs to complete route 708, Hitchin completed its share of the 716 and Addlestone made a start on the same route. The rest of the 716 and Addlestone's share of the 717 was completed on 8th February, after which Hatfield received its allocation for route 717. Routes 701 and 702 at Staines changed over between 12th and 19th February, followed on 1st March by Northfleet's share of the same routes. Luton and Dorking got their first Regal IVs on 1st March, when the entire allocation for route 714 at Luton was renewed. The rest of Dorking's allocation on the 714 and then its share of the 712 and 713 was completed in stages up to 13th March. The changeover of routes 712 and 713 was completed on 25th March when St Albans licensed eight RFs. During this run, a new registration series started, at RF 126, the next one hundred deliveries being MLL513-612.

These changes enabled the original phase three of the plan to be completed. The released 10T10s were used to replace the remaining Country area 9T9s at Dunton Green, Hertford, Leatherhead, Luton, Northfleet and St Albans and the 11T11s at Watford (Leavesden Road). The last remaining 11T11s in the Central area, at Bromley, Dalston, Enfield and Muswell Hill were also ousted by 10T10s. Dorking's TFs were sent northwards to Hertford for bus service on routes 308, 308A, 329, 342, 372, 386, 386A, 389 and 390. At St Albans, the coach TFs were retained and joined the former Grays vehicles to give a complete allocation of the type for single-deck bus duties, ousting the 4Q4s. Luton's were also held back for use on routes 356, 364, 376 and 376A. In some cases, the TFs replaced Ts and these were redeployed as replacements for 4Q4s at Amersham, Crawley, East Grinstead, Hemel Hempstead, Northfleet, Reigate and Watford (High Street). Staines also supplied 10T10s to replace the last 11T11s running at High Wycombe.

The start of the final phase of renewal of the coach fleet was marked by the changeover of route 718, which started on 25th March 1952 when Epping's first five RFs were licensed, its other two arriving the following day. Windsor also ran route 718 and had its second bite at the class, five being received on 31st March and the balance of three on 3rd April. Chelsham was the next garage to become an RF operator, receiving eight between 3rd and 10th April for the 706 and 707. Tring also received its entire allocation of nine for these routes on 10th April. A batch of five went to Grays on 24th April for some improvements on the 723 and 723A, after which Epping's second batch, eight for route 720, were licensed on 2nd and 3rd May. Windsor got its third and final consignment, of seven, on 1st June, on which day route 705 at last joined its companion route 704 in being stocked with the new class, Dunton Green's batch of nine taking to the road simultaneously. The last series of registrations for the coaches started with RF 226 in April, the remaining 63 taking the batch MLL763-825.

The conversion of route 718 marked the start of the serious withdrawal of the 10T10 class itself. Epping retained some of its released TFs for use on route 399, the remainder being sent to Hitchin for its share

of routes 364 and 399. Others were used to replace 4Q4s at Crawley, Dunton Green, East Grinstead, Guildford and Reigate while some, still painted green, went to Central Buses to cover shortages there.

The last coach route to receive its new stock of Regal IVs was the 703. Swanley introduced theirs on 7th and 9th June, followed by Amersham's starting on 11th June. With the licensing of Amersham's RF 269 on 17th June, there remained twenty coaches to be delivered and allocated. Apart from RF 188, which was held at Chiswick until May 1953 when it

became the last to be licensed, these were the engineering and 'traffic' spares which had been withheld during the earlier part of the main delivery programme and were still being covered, in the main, by 10T10s. Twelve garages received their spares allocation between 12th August and October 1st and one also went to Romford, a garage which had no single-deck schedule to maintain. The last to be delivered was RF 287, which arrived at Chiswick on 14th October and was the vehicle selected to be the stand-by spare at Victoria, where it was licensed on 1st November 1952.

Above **On route 702 at a cloudy Sunningdale station five months after first entering service at Staines garage, RF 151 retains the gloss of newness.** J.H. Aston

Below **The 9T9s were finally ousted in March 1952, those at Hertford being replaced by TFs evicted from Dorking by new RFs.** D.A. Thompson

Wet springtime roads have conspired to mar the appearance of Chelsham's newly delivered RF 215, pausing mid-journey at Eccleston Bridge, Victoria on 8th April 1952. The bridge was two-way at this time and almost the exclusive preserve of the Green Line. Alan B. Cross

The last of the Windsor trio of routes to get Regal IVs was the 705, in June 1952, just in time for the summer season. Having set down its load in the town, RF 256 prepares to run down to Windsor garage to lay over. John Fozard

7 THE CENTRAL AREA BUSES

The first two chassis for the Central area batch were delivered to Elmdon on 9th May 1952. The first completed vehicle, RF 289, arrived at Chiswick on 1st September, accompanied by Green Line RFs 284 and 288 — and some weeks ahead of the last coaches to be delivered, for there was to be no interruption to the production flow of new vehicles. Nevertheless, this was a month later than had been expected as recently as December 1951 when the programme for the ensuing year was planned. The delay was again associated with a downturn in the national economy, which led the Government to impose restrictions on production for the home market, so that manufacturers could concentrate on exports. The original allocation for London, of 400 vehicles in the year, was reduced to 222. As things turned out, this total was bettered, just over three hundred being delivered in the twelve months.

The long awaited red RFs differed from the coaches only in those respects which marked out buses from coaches and Central area from Country area practice. Metropolitan Police requirements ruled out the use of platform doors, so the entrance arrangements followed the same pattern as the pre-war 5Q5 buses in having an unprotected opening leading directly to the steps up to the platform. This potentially dangerous arrangement was apparently acceptable to the Police in the interests of traffic movement, as they believed that the operation of platform doors would have prolonged stop times at Bus Stops to a serious degree in busy London traffic conditions. Above this entrance was the only

Above **The most basic design of the thirty-foot RFs was the Central area version, classified 2RF2. RF 292 is fitted with the old style of blind, though of a later provenance than that fitted to Q 232 behind it at Wells Terrace, where the Finsbury Park railway goods yard, to the right, is still in full swing.** J. Wyndham

Right **The entrance doorway of the RF2s was 2ft 5¼ins wide and open to the elements. This gave the driver excellent sight-lines to the nearside but presented a danger to last-minute boarders and alighters who were in danger of slipping under the front wheel. The route number plate was the same size as those fitted under the canopies of some RTs but in the RF family was unique to the Central version.** LT Museum H71273

other new external feature, a projecting block, angled slightly downwards, into which could be slid a route number plate. This was the same size and design as those used under the canopy on some roof-box RTs and was of black metal with the number applied in white transfers. There were, of course, no clips for side route boards. The additional roof air-intake ventilator in the third roof bay, which had been added during the production run of the coaches, was fitted to the red Regals from new.

Most of the major differences were to be found inside the vehicle. The floor covering was finished in hard-wearing wooden strips instead of the linoleum favoured in the coach version and the colour scheme followed the principles established in the RT family, with brown leathercloth below the waist, dark green covering the lower one-third of the window cappings and cream above. On later deliveries, the darker colour on the cappings was extended up to the level of the dividing rail for the opening windows, experience having shown that the constant rubbing of the ligther colour by seated passengers soon made it look grubby. A cream coloured moulding, picked out in red, ran around the saloon above the windows. There were, of course, no luggage racks and therefore no additional 'cleaner' lights were needed in the central ceiling panels. Seating followed normal bus practice, with sixteen pairs of forward facing seats in the rear part of the bus and a pair of inward facing longitudinal seats (five on the nearside, four on the offside) to provide extra circulating and standing space in the section immediately behind the entrance. Standard London Transport tubular aluminium chairs with cushions and squabs of a shallower profile than the coach version, were covered in the standard bus moquette of the period which contained a geometric pattern of horizontal lines of brown, green and black, broken by vertical red stripes. The cushions were trimmed in leather on the gangway side, to protect them from the extra wear and tear of local bus operation. Front and rear bell pushes were the same as for the coaches but, in common with contemporary practice on London Transport buses, a pull cord ran the length of the saloon on the offside, secured by polished aluminium rings. Finally, there was no heating system provided for passengers, as this was still not part of the specification for buses in either Central or Country area operation.

Externally, the buses were finished in the standard livery of bus red and cream, the relief colour following the same pattern as on the coaches. As was normal on red buses, the wings and underframe lifeguards were painted black. They were given the classification 2RF2, as representing the basic thirty-foot design. The red Regals started a fresh series of registration numbers, RFs 289-358 being registered MLL926-995.

A new style of destination and route blind display was introduced with these buses, similar in layout to the restricted display then still in use on some double-deckers and considerably less informative, if clearer, than the traditional type found on older single-deckers. The ultimate destination now ran the full width of the top or bottom one-third of the box, while the remaining two-thirds contained a large route number occupying the left-hand side of the display, and two lines of intermediate points.

Driver training for the unfamiliar buses had been carried out piecemeal, using the 5Q5s to give familiarisation with the set-back wheel arrangement and RTs for the main driving controls. Consequently, there was little delay in getting the buses into service once they had arrived. The first three, RFs 289, 291 and 293 were licensed at Muswell Hill garage on Wednesday 10th September and began running on the 210 the following day. Restocking of route 210 was completed on 9th October, releasing the half-dozen TDs to go onto route 244 and finally putting to an end the London service life of the 6Q6s.

The interior of the Central Bus version of the RF looking back from just behind the entrance. The bell rope, strung near the tops of the upright stanchions, proved rather inconvenient for all but the tallest passengers. On this version, the green covering on the window cappings runs up to the level of the dividing bar and the standard bus specification seats are covered in the design of moquette used on all post-war buses, notably the RT family with which it was particularly associated. LT Museum 843/9

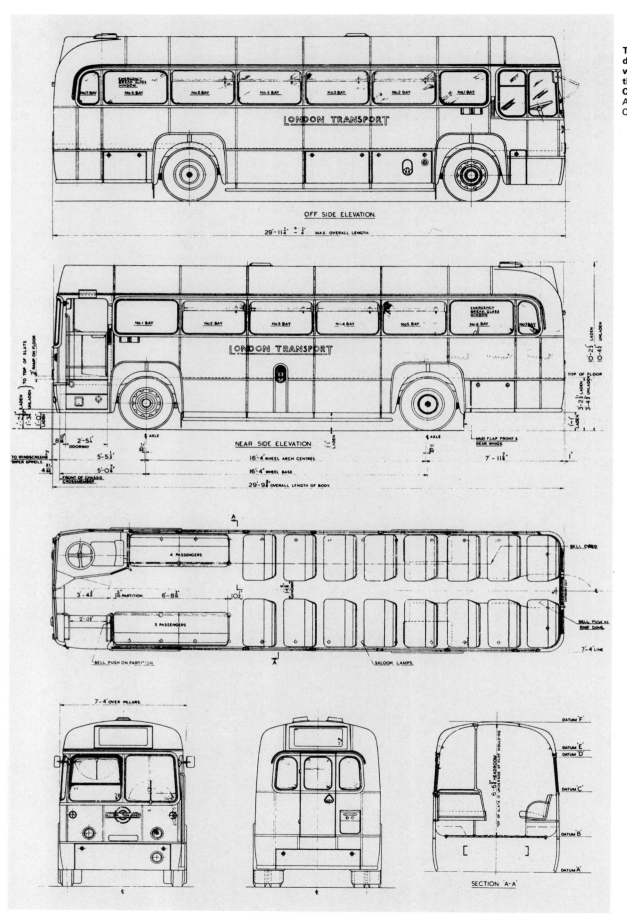

OFF SIDE ELEVATION.

29'-11¼" ± ¼" MAX. OVERALL LENGTH.

NEAR SIDE ELEVATION.

16'-4" WHEEL ARCH CENTRES.

16'-4" WHEEL BASE.

29'-9⅜" OVERALL LENGTH OF BODY.

SECTION 'A-A'

**These layout
diagrams of the RF2
were produced by
the Drawing Office at
Chiswick.**
Alan Townsin
Collection

The next to receive the new Regals was the 208A, another busy route on which Dalston garage ran single-deck LTs. There was then a brief pause while Muswell Hill received another injection of new buses, not this time for another route but to replace their entire original batch, all of which were taken away to form a training float for garages later in the programme. Only then did replacement of the oldest buses resume in earnest. Route 227, which was so busy that it boasted a four-minute peak frequency, was next in line, twenty-five RFs going into Bromley garage between 4th November and 12th December. Among Bromley's deliveries the registrations changed again, this time for a comparatively small batch of thirty, RFs 359-388 becoming MXX1-30. This short run was part of a series of manipulations by the licensing team at Chiswick who were trying to switch to registration numbers which matched the fleet numbers. In doing so they were constrained by the fact that many registration number blocks had already been allocated to manufacturers, so their room for manoeuvre was limited. The next batch was to be even shorter: RFs 389-411 being MXX277-299. It was the RLHs which 'benefited' in this case, the second batch of which (21-76) took the registrations MXX221-276.

Above **New in September 1931 at Sidcup and still going strong twenty years later, LT 1162 shares the Clapton Pond stand with Q 116, a 5Q5 4½ years its junior. After being displaced at Dalston, LT 1162 saw out its last days at Hounslow.**

Left **Setting off from Chislehurst War Memorial in late February 1953, Bromley's RF 350 displays the new style of destination blind, less informative but clearer than the old, introduced with the RF.** Alan B. Cross

Next for the new buses came Hounslow's 237, a rather quieter outer-suburban service, needing eight vehicles, which were put into service between 2nd and 9th December. Both the 227 and 237 had been operated by LT class AEC 'Renown' single-deckers but before any more of that type were removed, there was a complicated shuffle to take some 4Q4s out of Kingston. This was done by putting RFs onto Merton's route 200 (seven between 1st and 12th December) and Old Kent Road's 202 (seven between 13th and 24th December). Until then both had been operated by 5Q5s, most of which now went to Sidcup where they displaced post-war Weymann bodied Ts. These were sent to Southall whose complete stock of TDs was despatched to Kingston. Some of the rest of the Qs were needed to replace others of the same type which were now worn out and beyond economical repair.

The last two routes on which there were official allocations of LTs were the 213 and 234A, which were the next to receive RFs. Between 12th December 1952 and 20th January 1953, Sutton had twenty-three, which ousted its stock of Renowns. Croydon's five were licensed between 12th and 16th January; of these, two had been recovered from the training fleet and this was now becoming a common feature as the programme neared completion. Norbiton's rolling stock for the 213 comprised the much newer 14T12s but it nevertheless took nine RFs between 13th December 1952 and 1st January 1953 to enable the post-war Regals to displace 1T1s and the last of Kingston's 4Q4s on other routes. The last batch of registrations for the red RFs started at this time, MXX389-490 being allocated to RFs 412-513.

Twenty-four of the RFs delivered to Norbiton and Sutton had operational semaphore signals. They were a new design by Trico Folberth which was being tested to judge its suitability for PSVs. Nothing came of the experiment.

Of the original LGOC fleet, this left three Renowns at Dalston on the otherwise Q-operated route 208 and the last fourteen 1T1s at Kingston and Norbiton. Route 208 was not due for its RFs until after the 228 and 233 but a small advance allocation was made to Dalston to enable the LTs to be delicensed on 31st January. That proved to be the last day for the 1T1s as well, and therefore of the last

Top **Norbiton garage was itself quite new when this photograph was taken of newly delivered RF 375. In the background are delicensed STLs, stored in readiness for the needs of the Coronation the following June.** G.A. Rixon

Centre **The bulk of West Green's RFs entered service on 1st February 1953, just 4½ months after the first red ones began to grace Wells Terrace, Finsbury Park, where RF 458 is seen. Apparently there was a temporary shortage of the new style of blind, leading to the continued use of the crowded version transferred from a 5Q5.** G.A. Rixon

Right **Seven of Muswell Hill's new allocation of thirty-one RFs for route 212 can be seen in this gathering in the garage yard on 4th March, three days after the delivery had been completed.** Alan Townsin Collection

operational buses originally delivered to London Transport's predecessors. The problems of Walton Bridge had at last been resolved and the elderly Regals were replaced by 10T10s, displaced from Sidcup and Uxbridge. These moves came about as a result of Sidcup receiving its Regal IVs for route 228. Fourteen were delivered between 14th and 23rd January, releasing 14T12s to go to Southall and Uxbridge, who in turn sent 10T10s to Kingston.

The final onslaught started with the ousting of the 5Q5s from route 233 at West Green by twenty-two RFs between 1st and 3rd February, and from route 208 by thirteen at Dalston between 3rd and 9th February. The rest of February was occupied with one of the busiest single-deck routes, the 212 at Muswell Hill, which received thirty-one, the last of which was licensed on 1st March. The Weymann bodied 1TD1s removed from their original home on route 212 went to Loughton, where they replaced the 10T10s on route 254, whilst others went to Kingston. At Kingston some of them replaced Mann Egerton bodied TDs, which were sent to Edgware, Harrow Weald, Hornchurch, Leyton and Tottenham, in each case to replace 10T10s. The last route in the RF programme was the 241 at Sidcup, operated by the last of the 5Q5s, which took thirty Regal IVs between 1st and 25th March. The last two to be licensed for the first time were RFs 510 and 512, on 25th March 1953.

The completion of RF deliveries did not finish the replacement of pre-war single-deckers in the Central Area. There were still 10T10s working at Kingston and on route 205 from Enfield, while others were being used temporarily on airport services on behalf of BEA and some were stored for use during the Coronation. The Enfield allocation was awaiting the completion of work on the station bridge at Waltham Cross, which would remove the weight restriction and enable the three routes which crossed it to be converted to double-deck. This long awaited event had been dogged by many delays, the latest being caused by the diversion of Essex County Council's resources to deal with the serious flooding along the East Coast earlier in the year. The conversion finally took place on 6th May, using brand new RTs. The other buses then operating at Enfield were 2TD2s, which were sent to Kingston to clear out the last of the 10T10s on normal service work.

Top On 24th June 1952, Q 176 is just clearing a queue in Station Road, Sidcup, where the railway bridge a little further back dictated the use of single-deckers on routes 228 and 241. When new, in August 1936, Q 176 was green and allocated to Hemel Hempstead. It was repainted red in July 1948. Alan B. Cross

Centre Route 241 was the last to receive new red RFs, RF 493 being among the first to be licensed on 1st March 1953. F.G. Reynolds

Left The last route to have an official allocation of red 10T10s was the 205 at Enfield, awaiting the allocation of double-deckers. On their last Saturday, 2nd May 1953, Ts 552 and 563, both heavily laden, pass at The Queens Head, Cheshunt. Both were new in June 1938 and their first allocation was to Epping and Amersham respectively. Alan B. Cross

8 THE COUNTRY AREA BUSES

Five days before the last red RF went into service, on 20th March 1953, Aldenham took delivery of the first of the Country bus fleet, RFs 514 and 517. Chiswick had handed over responsibility for preparation and licensing of new vehicles at the end of February and Aldenham had already handled the last ten of the Central buses.

In almost every respect the design and appearance of this final batch was identical to the Central Bus version. The only difference of substance was the air operated folding platform doors which were of the same type as had been used on the coaches. The other minor difference was that no route number plate was carried above the doorway because the Country Bus department, whose buses made frequent changes of service, had adopted a policy of not using route number plates some years earlier. The first twenty-four (RFs 514-537) had modified window pans to take revised glazing by Beatonson, which included their 'Rapide' version of the high level drop window.

The livery was laid out in exactly the same form as on the Central buses but was, of course, in 'Lincoln' green and cream. Also, as was normal in the green fleet, the wings and underframe lifeguards were finished in the main body colour rather than black. The completed vehicle was classified 2RF2/2. A single registration series was allocated to the whole batch of 187 vehicles: NLE514-700, breaking up a batch on Park Royal bodied RTLs between 1426 and 1427, which entered service at about the same time. These careful manipulations by the licensing office to match registration and fleet numbers, were destined not to survive the modification programme of 1956 (see chapter 11).

With one exception at the end of the run, complete renewal, garage by garage, was adopted as the policy for replacement on basic scheduled services. The exception was of routes 435 and 462 at Leatherhead, which were delayed to the end of the programme because there was some uncertainty about being able to get approval for the larger vehicle on the 435.

It was the headquarters garage of Country Buses at Reigate which took the first seven-teen RFs, the first two, RFs 514 and 516, being licensed on 26th March with the entire allocation on routes 406C, 440, 440A and 447 completed on 8th April. This left only a few 10T10s for use as staff buses and for duplication. Reigate had taken priority in the programme because it was the last outpost of the once ubiquitous 4Q4, now the oldest single deckers still running. This flood of new vehicles triggered the sudden unceremonious departure of the last of this mould-breaking breed, surely the true ancestor of the RF itself. Some were to see some further operational use during the Coronation celebrations but all were delicensed finally on 1st July.

Above **The inspector proudly adopts a proprietorial air as he shepherds passengers onto glistening new RF 515. The extension of route 447 into Merstham 'LCC Estate' took place on 6th May 1953, and required the addition of two further Regal IVs to the original allocation. The equal size type of the destination display was a style used by the Country Bus department for circular or 'frying-pan' services, to stress the indirectness of the route followed.** F.G. Reynolds

The headquarters of the Northern Division at St Albans was next in line, taking no fewer than twenty-eight between 8th April and 6th May to replace its entire fleet of 'large' saloons on routes 304, 355, 365, 391 and 391A. Then came Hertford (twelve for routes 308, 308A, 329, 342, 372, 384, 384A, 386, 389, 390 and 399 between 7th and 28th May), Hitchin (seven on 1st and 4th June for routes 308, 364, 384 and 399), Luton (seven for the 356, 364, 376, 376A between 3rd and 10th June) and Windsor (thirteen for the 407, 407A, 458 and 459 between 10th June and 2nd July). This brought the programme to the traditional time for the start of summer duplication on the Green Line. There was therefore a brief pause in the replacement programme while nine of the new deliveries were sent to seven garages for coach work on 1st and 3rd July.

Up to now, all garages in the Country bus programme had already operated Regal IVs on Green Line but on 1st July, Garston which then had no Green Line responsibilities, became a new operator of the class. Between then and 9th July ten were delivered for routes 318 and 318A. Four of these were secondhand having been displaced at Hertford, Guildford, Reigate and Dorking by RFs 609, 611, 613 and 614, which had been fitted experimentally with stove enamelled window panelling.

This phase of the programme saw the clearance of all remaining TFs from regular service. Those not directly replaced by RFs were covered by other displaced vehicles. At Epping, these were 10T10s, while at Grays route 375 was given a permanent allocation of 15T13s, displaced by RFs at Garston. Garston's other Regal IIIs went to Crawley for routes 424, 426 and works services and to Tring for the 387. Some TFs were kept for special duties during the Coronation festivities but all had gone by 1st July. From this date until the end of the programme the vehicles displaced were to be exclusively the 10T10 sub-class.

Top **The 4Q4s had a friendly, almost cuddlesome, look compared with the more plainly workmanlike appearance of the RF. Their lifetime as buses did not quite make eighteen years as the last were withdrawn in March 1953. Reigate was the last bastion of the class, which had long been associated with the 447 and its predecessors. Q 73, in Reigate on a bleak looking March day in 1952, first went into service in October 1935 at Hatfield.** Alan B. Cross

Above **The old-world elegance of St Albans provides a nicely contrasting backdrop for RF 548, one of the twenty-eight of the class delivered to the local garage in April and May 1953.** G.A. Rixon

Right **Fittingly, Royal Windsor got its Regal IV buses during Coronation month, June 1953, RF 590 is on one of the peak hour short-working journeys from Windsor to Iver.** John Fozard

High Wycombe's 373, long the home of the 11T11 but now stocked by the fast diminishing 10T10, was next; it took five on 10th and 13th July. After these, deliveries switched to the south at Leatherhead (eight for routes 419 and 422 on 1st and 10th August) and Addlestone (six for the 427, 437, 456 between 12th and 26th August) before returning north, to Hemel Hempstead for route 322, which had eight on 26th August and 1st September. The Kentish Weald was the next to be graced by the Regal

IVs, with an allocation of four to Dunton Green for routes 404, 413, 413A and 421 on 1st September. Then came the Surrey Hills, on routes 425 and 432 from Guildford (eight between 1st and 3rd September) and six for the 412 and 425 from Dorking between 7th and 11th September. East Grinstead and Crawley bridged the geographical gap with allocations for routes 424, 434 and 473 (twelve and five respectively between 14th September and 1st October), before the last remaining

Northern Division garage awaiting attention, Epping, received a small allocation of four between 9th and 14th October for its share of routes 308, 308A, 384, 384A and 399. Routes 489 and 489A, run by Northfleet, were completed on 1st November with four vehicles, which left only routes 435 and 462, from Addlestone and Leatherhead. These received four each during November and December, the last vehicle in the main delivery run to be licensed being RF 699 on 8th December.

Above **The old order changeth. In 1953, the flags celebrate a new monarch, while Windsor's RF 582 represents the new Country bus order, alongside Chelsham's T 626 working a tour in its last summer in passenger service.** J.H. Aston

Left **RF 606 was one of the bus RFs allocated to Green Line duplication for the summer season of 1953 but is here working as a bus on Hertford's route 342 at New Barnet station.** G.A. Rixon

Above **Addlestone's RF635 in semi-rural north-west Surrey.** LT Museum 1259/3

Left **The territory to the east of Sevenoaks was shared by London Transport and Maidstone & District. This co-operation is symbolised in this view of Dunton Green's RF 652, sharing a stop with an M&D single-decker.**

Left **Route 434** defined the southern boundary of London Transport's operations for many years on its long cross-country run from Horsham to Dormansland. Crawley licensed RF 679 on 1st October 1953.
Surfleet Transport Photographs

Centre **Epping** was the last northern division garage to get bus RFs, in October 1953, but RF 569 was a Hertford vehicle which had presumably 'slept' overnight in the Essex garage, a fairly common feature of Country bus operations, RT 971, in the background, was one of Hertford's original 1948 batch which replaced the STs. By the time of this photograph it had already had its first overhaul and been given the new livery.
Lens of Sutton

Below **The last pre-war vehicles** to be replaced directly by RFs were the 10T10s at Addlestone and Leatherhead, where there had been some doubt about the suitability of the routes. Addlestone's T 525, still in the two-tone coach livery but with London Transport fleetname, at Leatherhead station in July 1952, is ignored by the waiting passengers, who presumably want the one that can be seen lurking around the corner.
Alan B. Cross

The three RFs which had not yet appeared in service at the end of 1953 were RFs 517, 647 and 700. They had all been taken into stock on time, alongside their contemporaries and, indeed, RF 517 was one of the first pair of the Country version to be delivered, but they had then been held, unlicensed, at works. They were being prepared for an experiment with single-manning, which at that time was confined, by Regulation, to vehicles seating no more than twenty-six, this limit having been increased only recently from the long-established twenty. The bus industry was beginning to struggle with the conflict of falling traffics and increasing costs and there had been some talk about adopting one-man operation on larger vehicles as an economy measure but there was by no means a wide-spread acceptance that it would work. The more adventurous operators were prepared to try the idea with flat fares or, in one case, with passengers being trusted to pay through an 'honesty box' but the thought of the driver collecting fares on a conventional scale on a vehicle which could carry in excess of forty passengers was generally viewed with some scepticism. It was therefore a bold decision on London Transport's part to try the system.

One of the pioneers in the field had been the Huddersfield Joint Omnibus Committee (jointly managed by the Corporation and British Railways), who had been running a couple of forty-three seater underfloor-engined Guy Arabs, delivered in 1951, on a one-man

operated service which had attracted a lot of publicity. The redoubtable Geoffrey Fernyhough, soon to become the Country Bus department's Operating Manager, accompanied by London Transport's Chief Draughtsman, Phil Lunghi, went to inspect the operation in August 1952 and was very enthusiastic about what he saw. This led, in December 1952, to a proposal being submitted to the Executive to carry out some experiments in the Country area, varying the scope of operation as much as possible, using routes of five to ten miles in length, with mainly end to end movement and little traffic in between. The expectations were quite modest, the maximum number of buses expected to be needed, should the experiment be successful, being only twenty. At that time, it was hoped that the recently negotiated payment of 10 shillings a week on the basic wage, for the operation of twenty-six seaters, would also hold good for the larger vehicles.

The first route chosen for the experiment was the Epsom local 419, operated by Leatherhead garage, starting on 3rd March 1954. RF 647 was licensed as a trainer (at Reigate) on 18th February, before going to Leatherhead where it was joined by RF 517, both being licensed for service on 1st March. RF 700 remained at Reigate until licensed on 3rd March.

The modifications to the vehicle were quite extensive by comparison with designs adopted later and, for that matter, compared with the

very simple arrangements on the contemporary twenty-six seater GS class. The half-height door to the driver's cab was replaced by a full length one, hinged from the centre bulkhead pillar at the front, on which was carried a glass screen, a shelf, coin trays and two 'Ultimate' ticket machines. At waist level, there was a handrail, below which the door was shaped inwards to provide adequate foot-room. When open, this door could lie flat against the front bulkhead, giving the driver and passengers the maximum of unimpeded space for entry to the cab and saloon. On the glass screen, there was a small lockable sliding panel through which the driver could talk to passengers, above which was a notice reading 'PLEASE STATE DESTINATION'. There were two coin trays, the forward one marked 'PAY HERE' and the rearward, which was positioned to receive change directly from a 'Brandt' change-giving machine, marked 'TICKET AND CHANGE'. The screen and trays could be lit by an overhead lamp, at the discretion of the driver. A 'Used Ticket' box was fitted below the change-giving machine.

Heralding a major shift in operating practice, RF 517 was London Transport's first 'large saloon' one-man bus. The only external differences were the altered driver's signalling window, in three sections instead of two, and the very discreet 'PAY AS YOU ENTER — Exact Fare Please' sign applied to the top of the nearside windscreen by transfers. Alan B. Cross

These two views show (right) the standard driver's cab, looking inward from the entrance steps and (below) the same view of the cab as modified for one-man operation. The main differences include: the introduction of a glazed screen, with metal trays for paying and for tickets and change; an external handle for opening the door; an outward 'bulge' in the cab door and side wall to allow a wider cab; the transfer of the Used Ticket box to a position behind the cab. Note that standing was not allowed.
LT Museum 6147/HP75959

The driver's cab was widened to line up with the door and the extra space was used to house the 'Brandt' change-giving machine and to enlarge the driver's locker above the cab. The fully enclosed compartment had to be provided with an emergency exit and this was done by combining into one unit the two glass panels on the offside. This incorporated a self-balanced vertically sliding signalling window for the driver and the entire unit could be opened and closed by handles inside and outside. Within the cab, an interior mirror was provided so that the driver could see the full length of the gangway.

Free access to the passenger saloon was also improved by the removal of the front pair of seats from the longitudinal bench on the nearside and replacing them with a luggage rack, reducing the capacity to thirty-nine. The bulkhead screen on the nearside was also made narrower. This arrangement also created more space for passengers to stand at and circulate around the pay window. Two posters were pasted, one at the bottom of the front nearside window, above the wheelarch, the other in the top of the nearside windscreen, reading 'PAY AS YOU ENTER — EXACT FARE PLEASE'. The modification was deemed to be sufficiently significant to justify an entirely new body classification and these vehicles were henceforth known as 2RF5s. The total cost of the work, for the three buses, was £2,027, just over £675 each vehicle.

After just over four months of apparently trouble-free operation at Leatherhead, the three experimental buses were switched to Hemel Hempstead. On 11th August, they started a new phase of the experiment on route 316, an interesting choice as it was one of the relatively few London Transport routes which were operated jointly with another operator, in this case Rover Bus Services. This also appears to have gone smoothly, to the extent that one of Hemel's own vehicles, RF 649, was delicensed on 1st October and became the fourth vehicle to be modified. It was relicensed as an OMO bus on 1st December, allowing RF 517 to return to Reigate, in readiness for it and RF 700 to go back to Leatherhead where route 419 once again became one-man operated from 18th May 1955, this time for good.

Facing Page Top Left **The cab door could be opened flat against the front bulkhead to maximise circulating space around it.** Alan B. Cross

Facing Page Top Right **A driver's-eye view of the passenger entrance. The two 'Ultimate' ticket machines can be seen mounted side-by-side immediately below the counter on which the cash and ticket trays are prominent. To the left of the counter is the 'Brandt' change-giving machine, linked by a chute to the change tray and, above that, a copy of the miniature faretable for reference by the driver. Just visible below the ticket machines is the leather Time Card container.** LT Museum 19258

Facing Page Lower **Looking forward from the middle of the saloon of the modified vehicle. The extra width of the cab and the inward sloping lower part are very distinctive. The rear-view mirror for the saloon can be seen above the middle of the nearside screen. The foreshortened longitudinal seat at the front has given way to a small luggage pen.** LT Museum 16603

9 THE AIRPORT COACHES

If the RFWs had taken many by surprise at the start of the delivery programme, the final member of the family was to outdo even that band of mavericks in its quirkiness and unorthodoxy. London Transport had entered into a contract with British European Airways from 16th July 1947 to run its airport coach services between central London, Croydon, Heathrow and Northolt. For this purpose, the airline owned a fleet of petrol-engined Commer Commando normal control coaches, fitted with eighteen-seat 1½-deck bodywork by Park Royal, the raised rear portion being designed to provide luggage accommodation under the passenger saloon. By the early 1950s, these vehicles were beginning to be too small to cope with the traffic and this inadequacy became particularly acute when the new higher-capacity Elizabethan aircraft began to enter service. BEA therefore sought London Transport's help to design a suitable replacement vehicle.

Under Chiswick's benign influence, the corporation was persuaded to move some way up the scale of quality and longevity by specifying the 9822E version of the AEC Regal IV chassis, as modified for the RFW, mounted with a special design of Park Royal body. The new bodies continued the principle of the 'deck-and-a-half' layout, with a rear 'observation' saloon but the treatment was exceptionally imaginative. Instead of the stepped roofline, traditional in such applications, the roof continued at the same level over the full length of the coach, the lower saloon at the front having an abnormally high and airy ceiling level. Sixteen of the thirty-seven seats were in this lower section, the remaining twenty-one being on the raised deck.

Above **MLL714, when new and before being fitted with destination blinds. The side access doors to the luggage compartment can be seen on each side of the rear wheel arch.** Automobile Engineer

Below **Two features which can be seen well on the vehicle on the left are the position of the hinged passenger door and the embossed 'BEA' shield, repeated on the front as a cover for the radiator filler cap. NLP637 on the far side has its passenger door open. The striking design of these vehicles, with its strong family resemblance to the RT double-decker, was only slightly marred by the 'eyebrow' effect of the heavily radiused upper windows at the front.** Frank Mussett

A year after the first BEA RF was delivered, the new terminal at Waterloo, on the site of the Festival of Britain exhibition, was opened. The confidence of the architecture is echoed in the new airport coaches, one of which is parked outside the terminal building. This rear view shows the large access doors on the offside and back, alongside which can be seen also the reflector plates, which became a requirement on all vehicles under new regulations introduced during delivery of the 4RF4s. F.G. Reynolds

Park Royal adopted a semi-integral form of construction, using extruded H-section light alloy pillars, directly secured to outriggers on the chassis. Stiffening for the side framing was given by interior truss panels of aluminium, supplemented to some extent by the exterior panels, to which they were attached by hollow rivets. Steel was used for crib rails, waist and cant rails and the roof sticks as well as the cantilever hoop sticks supporting the raised rear floor.

The baggage compartment, which was rubber padded to protect luggage from damage, had an exceptionally large capacity of 250 cubic feet claimed to accommodate one hundred full-size suitcases. The main access to the compartment was at the back, where there was a large top-hinged door, measuring 5ft 4ins by 3ft 6ins which could be held open by spring-loaded telescopic struts. Alongside this there was a smaller door on each side.

A hinged passenger door in the centre of the nearside led to the steps into the lower saloon; there were a further three steps to the upper deck. Immediately opposite, on the offside, was a hinged emergency exit door. Just inside the entrance door was a small enclosure for coats and hats. The interior trim and fittings were unmistakably from the Chiswick stable. The seats were to London Transport's standard polished aluminium tubular steel design and the extra deep cushions and squabs, filled with 'Dunlopillo' were covered in moquette of a similar design to that used on the RFs but with a predominantly grey colour scheme. Window finishers and lining panels were covered in burgundy and grey rexine, with polished aluminium cappings. Cork tiles were used on the floor and these were protected along gangways and on the steps by fluted rubber strips.

The windows were secured by 'Simplastic' glazing strips and five on each side, two lower, three upper, were fitted with 'Widney Ace' quarter-drop opening sections, operated by winding mechanism. Above the windows, there was a parcel rack for small items of luggage and clothing, a feature which was surprisingly not provided on the Commers. A Clayton Dewandre heating unit supplied warm air through ducts underneath the seats and there was a demister for the windscreen. Ventilation was completed by two extractor vents in the roof.

The influence of the RT was strikingly apparent in the external appearance, which was more curved in outline than the Metro-Cammell bodies on the RFs. A slightly dated 'thirties' look was given by the downward sweep of the side windows at the front and by the heavily arched shape of the front saloon windows, which were separated from the windscreen by two single aperture destination blinds, one on each side. Otherwise, the general appearance and layout of the side windows, the shape of the rear end and the detailed finish of the bodies followed closely RT practice. The layout of registration plates, side-and headlamps was the same as on the RFs and the radiator filler cap was concealed behind a hinged flap bearing, not a 'bullseye' but the familiar shield of the corporation's coat-of-arms. The angular shape of the mudguards used on the RFs was repeated.

An attractive adaptation of the Airways Corporation's livery was employed, dark grey being applied to the lower panels and a lighter grey to the upper, separated by a band of white at the waist rail. Further relief to the basic scheme was given by the polished aluminium mouldings which contained plastic inserts coloured burgundy and by the black painted

wings. The fleetname BRITISH EUROPEAN AIRWAYS was carried on the panels on both sides and embossed alongside this was the corporation's shield symbol.

Although not owned by London Transport, the completed vehicles were given the classification 4RF4. No fleet numbers were allocated and they were always identified in LT records by their registrations. An initial order for 40 was soon increased to 50 (MLL713-762).

The first completed vehicle (MLL713) was handed over at a formal ceremony on 21st April 1952 by Sir Wavell Wakefield, MP, chairman of Park Royal Vehicles Ltd, to Peter Masefield, the Chief Executive of British European Airways. Mr Masefield, who, many years later, was to find himself heading a much changed London Transport Executive, announced that he was expecting a seven year life from the coaches and, on that basis, he made the somewhat esoteric forecast that the cost per seat mile would be 1¼d, compared with 2½d for the latest turbine aircraft.

MLL713 was licensed at Victoria on 7th May 1952 and it then took just over a year for the remaining forty-nine to arrive. In the meantime, it had become clear that fifty would not be enough to meet the growing needs of the airline and a repeat order for fifteen was placed. These were registered NLP636-650 and were licensed between 5th August and 14th October 1953.

While the completion of delivery of the 4RF4s was awaited, there was a pressing need for some increased capacity on the airport services, partly caused by the move of the terminal to Waterloo in May 1953. BEA could not meet this from its own resources and therefore hired twelve redundant 10T10s during the summer of 1953 (Ts 474, 476, 511, 557, 575, 577, 588, 598, 637, 658, 676 and 702).

Like the Commers before them, the Regal IVs were housed in the basement at Victoria garage while the services they operated started from their main London terminal in a converted Festival of Britain pavilion on the South Bank at Waterloo. A purpose-built Air Terminal was installed at Cromwell Curve, alongside Cromwell Road a few years later and operations were transferred there in 1957. The operating base was then moved to Shepherds Bush garage, where there was a substantial amount of unused space, and all sixty-five coaches were transferred there on 6th October 1957. This arrangement lasted less than three years. With the abandonment of the trolleybus services operated by Hammersmith depot, the new motor bus services moved to Shepherds Bush and, to make room for them, the BEA fleet moved once more, into its final home at the disused depot, on 20th July 1960. The only exception to this series of block allocations was that one or two vehicles were stationed at Reigate between October 1957 and May 1965 to serve the needs of the newly developing Gatwick Airport.

Peter Masefield's forecast of the life expectancy of these vehicles proved to be extremely modest. Like so many models of the period, the BEA RFs were destined for a long life and continued to serve air travellers for about thirteen years receiving only one overhaul, at Chiswick Tram Depot, during 1957 and 1958. They were eventually replaced by a fleet of specially designed Routemasters in 1966 and 1967, the last five being delicensed on 1st April 1967. However one, MLL740, was relicensed on 10th April and remained in use until 14th May 1973, when it passed to BEA for disposal. It was put into the final orange and white of the Routemasters, to which it acted as a spare. Four (MLL725, 727, 729 and 735) were purchased by London Transport and spent another ten years modified to perform a new role as mobile uniform stores. They were withdrawn in October 1976 (727), November 1976 (725 and 729) and February 1977 (735).

Top **Interior view of a BEA 4RF4.**
Alan B. Cross

Centre **Manchester imitated London in adopting an identical layout for its airport coaches but used Leyland Royal Tiger chassis and Burlingham/Bond bodywork.**
Dennis Odd Collection

Left **The first and last, MLL713 and NLP650 parked at the County Hall end of the Waterloo terminal site, after MLL713's overhaul and repainting into the new livery.**
John Aldridge

The last of the second batch of fifteen 4RF4s, NLP650, passes its sister corporation's air terminal in Buckingham Palace Road, Victoria, some years later. By this time the corporation had altered its logo to a plain block italic *BEA* in white out of a red rectangle and its fleetname style to red capitals on a white background. The colour scheme was also simplified, with the dark grey extending up to the lower windows and along the luggage compartment panelling. The airport coaches all had operational semaphore trafficators, which can be seen as a black line at the bottom of the first lower pillar. Robert F. Mack

MLL740 was the last 4RF4 to remain in use with BEA and the only one to receive orange and white livery. It is seen at the West London Air Terminal in September 1970. Gerald Mead

Below **Former BEA airport coach MLL735 was one of four used by London Transport as mobile uniform issuing units between 1967 and 1976.** John Gascoine

10 THE FIRST FIVE YEARS

In its early days the RF was noteworthy for the smoothness and quietness of its running, in which many believed it surpassed its contemporaries. Achieving these features brought problems, however, and it was not long before its characteristics were changed and the RF became what it was always destined to be, the single-deck equivalent of the RT.

The leaf-life of the rear springs was already causing anxiety as early as the middle of 1952 and experiments were soon carried out on the soft suspension to overcome both this and difficulties with tightening U-bolts. From September 1952 onwards, various trials were mounted, including the use of standard AEC springs instead of those designed by LT, and experiments with modified stabilisers. The specification finally chosen used strengthened main leaves, which resulted in a harsher ride.

The Atlas Pilot Injection system used on the engines, undoubtedly resulted in uniquely quiet, smooth running but at the expense of unduly high fuel consumption and a worrying level of piston failures. In December 1952, authority was given for twenty-five RFs at Grays garage to be modified experimentally to standard injection by fitting replacement camshafts, delivery valves and holders. The experiment was widened in December 1953 to take in a Central Bus garage, Norbiton. This proved successful and the Pilot Injection system was removed from the whole fleet at first overhaul.

A modified fuel pipe layout was tried on twenty-four Green Line RFs at Dorking and Windsor in October 1952 but the AEC 9.6-litre engine was always more 'leaky' when laid on its side in the RF than when upright on the RT. Both types suffered flywheel problems and twenty-five RFs at Muswell Hill and a few at Windsor were included, from January 1953 onwards, in some large-scale tests then being carried out on RTs of improved glands.

Problems from water and grit, associated with the engine being under the floor, were encountered very early in the life of the class. This led to the adoption of waterproofed injector pumps and experiments, starting in March 1953, with belt shields for the compressor, fan and water pump drives, to assess their effectiveness in protecting the belts from stones, oil and weather.

Apart from the major changes associated with one-man operation and the longevity of the class, dealt with in later chapters, there were relatively few modifications to the RF bodies. One small change, made for safety reasons, was the addition of a handrail across the nearside front window. Another, already mentioned, was the amendment of the arrangement of the colours on the window cappings. This was further modified as the RFs went through their first overhaul, when the dark green colour was extended right around the window frames, eliminating the lighter colour completely.

More fundamentally, as built, the RF body could not be separated easily from its chassis and this was not consistent with the factory method of overhaul introduced at Aldenham in the mid-fifties. All of the class therefore had to be modified to allow the body to be detached from the chassis during visits to the works. As things turned out, none of the short-wheelbase version ever changed chassis or body but the remainder were changed regularly and most bonnet numbers were associated with three or four different bodies and chassis during their career. The only ones to retain their original units till the end were RFs 295-297, 307-309 (renumbered from 514-516, 526-528 in 1956).

The height of the overhead grabrails on the bus version created some problems for all but the tallest passengers and this led to an interesting experiment being carried out on twelve RF2s at Bromley (route 227) and seven RF2/3s at St Albans (routes 365/391) during 1953. Pendant-type hand-rail straps, as used on the Underground, were fitted to the rails in the forward section of the saloon alongside the longitudinal seats. The material was supplied from Acton Works and the straps were coloured brown. Whether or not they were liked by the passengers, the idea was not pursued.

Above **The RF in its heyday. Nine of the class share the bus park at London Airport (Heathrow) with a multitude of RTs.** John Aldridge

70

The arrival of the last of Addlestone's and Leatherhead's RFs in December 1953 left twenty-nine 10T10s still running as buses in the Country Area. They were replaced in two ways. At Hertford, routes 329, 386 and 386A were changed over to one-man operation on 21st April 1954, using newly delivered 'small saloons' of the GS class, seating twenty-six. The loss of four seats was acceptable on these lightly-trafficked routes. The same solution was used for routes 309 and 361 at Garston on 19th May, and on Windsor's routes 442 and 445 on 7th July. The other source of buses came from the double-deck fleet. On 19th May, part of route 318 at Garston garage changed over from single-deck to double-deck operation and on 7th July, Green Line routes 723 and 723A exchanged their RFs for a fleet of newly delivered RTs which had bodies inherited from the SRT class.

At Hertford and Windsor, 10T10s were replaced directly but at Garston it was post-war 15T13s that were released. These went to a new home at Amersham, where they went into service on the 394 group, replacing 10T10s. The Grays RFs were used to restore spares margins in the coach fleet. These had been covered by bus RFs since being depleted to supply additional rolling stock to route 725 when it was increased in frequency in April. The bus RFs which this released were used to cover the withdrawal of the last scheduled 10T10s at Dorking (route 412), Dunton Green (413), Hitchin (works services), Northfleet (489/489A) and Staines (441), all of which ran for the last time on 6th July.

Changes had also been taking place in the Central area which affected the deployment of the RF fleet. In the autumn of 1953, London Transport honoured a promise made to the staff at Loughton that they would be given priority if any RFs became available. This had now happened, as the running time reductions on routes 210 and 212 had released enough of the class to cover the needs of route 254 and eight RFs began running at Loughton on 7th October 1953. The TDs were not used immediately but lay idle for a full year while the future of the fleet was debated. They then went to Norbiton where they replaced its entire allocation of 14T12s, which became the first post-war buses to be withdrawn for disposal.

Top **Route 725 was again in the news in April 1954 when its frequency was increased, calling for then non-existent extra coaches. RF 246, parked here outside Windsor garage, was one of the original group gathered for the start of the service a year earlier.** Lens of Sutton

Centre **The lanes of north-west Kent, natural territory for the former Green Line coach Regals, were among the last areas to resound to the characteristic tones of the 8.8-litre AEC engine in the summer of 1954. Thirty-four seat T 648, a 10T10/1 new at Romford in September 1938, was one of the class which was exported for further service.** Alan B. Cross

Bottom **RF 294 was one of eight transferred into Loughton in October 1953, to replace TDs on the local route 254. Above the vehicle can be seen the top of a 'domed' Bus Stop flag.** W.J. Haynes

During the final run of deliveries of the RF, London Transport set about a fresh review of its single-deck requirements, covering the period up to 1957. The Executive's decision to order only 700 Regal IVs had left the Country department theroretically short of fifty-four buses. However, when considering the future of the seventy-strong 'small saloon' fleet in December 1951, the Executive had decided to order eighty-four new twenty-six seaters (the GS class), the balance of fourteen being intended to replace a similar number of large saloons. In theory, this left a shortfall of forty but a number of things had changed, or not happened, since 1951.

Whereas the forecast had expected augmentation and development of services to need twenty-five extra vehicles by 1954, only seventeen had been used, leaving an immediate surplus of eight. Not allowed for in the earlier forecast was that there would be service cuts, admittedly only modest at two vehicles, that there would be some loss of contract work (six vehicles) or that there would be some conversions to smaller vehicles. Unforeseen conversions to double-deck accounted for another twenty-five vehicles, while a further ten were contributed by a decision to abandon the concept of 'traffic' spares in the bus fleet as these had proved to be unnecessary. This reduction in the operational fleet also cut the number of engineering spares, reducing the total need by no fewer than sixty-two.

In the Central Area, also, there was already a surplus. This had come about for two reasons. Because the RFs had proved to be faster in service than the old buses they replaced on routes 210, 212 and 241, it had been possible to schedule shorter journey times saving seven buses. Another nine, in this case TDs, had come from routes 238 and 244 which had been converted to double-deck. Counter to this, four RFs had to be set aside for extra buses on routes 212 and 233 when the Alexandra Palace branch railway closed in 1954. After allowing for a reduction of one in engineering spares, there was a net surplus of thirteen but this comprised an actual shortage of eleven in the RF fleet, offset by a surplus of twenty-four Ts and TDs. This curious situation had arisen because the Regal IVs bought to act as spares to cover overhauls had been allocated for scheduled service when they were new, otherwise they would have had to be stored unused until the first red RF overhauls in 1956, which the Executive was not prepared to countenance. They were therefore covering duties identified in the original plans as being done by the Ts and TDs.

Looking further ahead, Central Buses foresaw a reduction of fifty-nine from yet more routes which had been earmarked for double-decking. Of these, thirty-nine were on routes then operated by RFs (200, part of 208A and 212) and the rest by TDs (221, 248 and part of 236). The timing of these changes could not be forecast with any accuracy, as they all depended on some action by highway authorities, either by increasing the headroom of overhead bridges or strengthening roadways over bridges. As an illustration of the frailty of forecasting, the conversion of route 236 to double-deckers has never taken place. Had all of these forecasts been realised, there would have been a surplus of seventy-two in the Central Area fleet.

Two members of the 84-strong 'small saloon' GS fleet, photographed at Hertford in the mid-fifties.
Lens of Sutton

The Green Line story was markedly different. There had been estimates in the early thinking about the size of the RF fleet that about eight extra coaches would be needed, but even this surprisingly modest allowance was omitted from the final orders. By 1954, the Green Line had reached an operating requirement of 281, compared with its fleet of 263 RFs and had already had to draw upon the new bus deliveries to meet the demands of the 1953 summer season. This had been in response to the growth of traffic directly related to the development of the New Towns and large estates in London's country ring which was expected to continue for some years. Between 1954 and 1957 the growth was expected to amount to a need for another sixty-six scheduled vehicles, bringing the total, after adding engineering spares, to 348 (eighty-five more coaches than currently owned). The eight surplus green bus RFs had already been co-opted as part of the spares fleet for the Green Line, leaving a final need for another seventy-seven coaches.

At the time of the review, many of the events which would lead to the surpluses had yet to happen and the operating departments were inclined to take the prudent view that the real and existing shortages in the RF fleet should be made good by ordering new vehicles and not by waiting for events to take their course. The Regal IV was by now an outdated design, having been superseded very rapidly by a new generation of lightweight single-deck models and it would not therefore have been appropriate to place a small repeat order for RFs. With this in mind, London Transport had been carrying out some trials with the new single-deckers. Three vehicles had been borrowed, a Bristol LS, a Leyland Tiger Cub and an AEC Monocoach and all three were run successively on Country Bus route 447, Green Line route 711 and Central Area route 208 between April 1953 and April 1954. Nothing came of these trials and the operators had to make do with the fleets they already had.

One of the problems which had been highlighted during the review, was the lack of

One of the possible candidates to fill the shortfall of single-deckers was the Tiger Cub, Leyland's contribution to the new generation of lightweights. This Saunders bodied demonstrator ran for a year with London Transport, first at Reigate then, towards the end of its stay in London, at Dalston who ran it on route 208.

vehicles to cover the overhaul of RFs. All the original estimates would have allowed an appropriate margin of buses for this purpose but, whereas the double-deck fleet was able to absorb the required inflation in its continuous delivery programme, the RFs were all delivered within two-and-a-half years, leaving a full year before the first of them would be due to go to works. Rather than keep brand new buses lying idle while older vehicles were still in service, the works spares were all allocated for service. The Green Line RFs were due to go for their first overhauls starting in late 1954, from which date a total of twenty vehicles would be needed at garages to cover the absentees. When the overhaul plans were being laid, it had been assumed that some 10T10s would be retained until the new light-weight vehicles were delivered. This event was confidently expected to occur no later than mid-1955, so it was envisaged that the 10T10s would continue in service until at least that time.

The Executive was not so easily convinced that there was a case for ordering new vehicles, as a careful reading of the figures showed that eventually there was likely to be a surplus within the existing fleet. Instead of authorising new coaches, they called instead for a major re-appraisal of the entire fleet requirement, both single- and double-deck. This was carried out in January 1955 and came to some quite different conclusions. One reason for this, not foreseen in earlier reviews, was that London Transport had now started to make some quite severe cuts in service in response to a decline in demand. The new assessment showed surpluses in both the Central and Country fleets, alongside a substantially reduced size of expected increase in the Green Line fleet. This can best be summarised:

Top **Private Hire RFs in their prime. Streatham's entire allotment of three, RFs 15 (leading), 4 and 13 line up in readiness to take a party somewhere unknown on 21st June 1952.** Alan B. Cross

Above **The handsome 1951 livery of the RF1s did not survive their first overhaul, when they were put into this startlingly drab allover green scheme. They retained their red lettering, which made the overall effect even more dreary. RF 9 was used in Green Line service during 1955 to cover the absence of RF2/1s during their overhaul programme. The additional handrail fitted transversely across the front nearside screen was covered in black plastic instead of the white of the upright bars, to reduce its visual impact on the driver.** Alan B. Cross

	CENTRAL		COUNTRY		GREEN LINE	TOTAL		
	RF	T/TD	RF	T	RF	RF	T/TD	TOTAL
1954/55 winter schedule	210	138	158	24	233	601	162	763
LESS:								
Service cuts	10	4	—	—	—	10	4	14
Conversions to D/D	23	4	6	—	—	29	4	33
ADD:								
Augmentation/development	–	—	5	—	19	24	—	24
Duplications	—	—	—	—	33	33	—	33
Traffic spares	—	—	—	—	12	12	—	12
Engineering spares	18	13	16	3	28	62	16	78
TOTAL	195	143	173	27	325	693	170	863
FLEET AVAILABLE	225	181	187	30	263	675	211	886
Surplus/*Shortfall*	30	38	14	3	*62*	*18*	41	23

Any idea of buying new coaches was now abandoned. Instead forty-four of the bus RFs were to be modified for use as Green Line coaches and fourteen of the Private Hire RFs recovered from the Central Bus fleet for the same purpose. The latter were not strictly speaking surplus to requirements as they were used on regular contract work but they were considered to be of too high a specification for such work. The intention was that they should be replaced by either Ts or TDs currently surplus in the Central Area, which would be fitted with platform doors and heaters to suit them for their new job. This proposal seems to have reached an advanced stage of preparation, almost to the point of ordering materials, before being finally abandoned. The reason for

not proceeding is not known but may have been because the contract work was lost.

Not surprisingly, the potential loss of thirty RFs from the Central Bus fleet also proved to be a stumbling block and arguments developed which were reminiscent of the frustrations of the late 1940s. The 'red' fleet already had a disproportionate share of the older, less popular vehicles and the operators were not prepared to make matters worse. This decision would leave a shortage of Green Line coaches, gradually increasing from four in 1955 to thirty-two in 1958. There were still twenty-five serviceable 10T10s in store for use in case of emergency and possibly to cover overhauls in the main fleet. Serious thought was given to making these fit for another four years service,

despite the fact that there were more modern surplus vehicles in the fleet. Indeed, the one thing which does not seem to have been worth considering was using the TDs to cover the shortages.

The final outcome of this prolonged saga was that ten (rather than fourteen) Private Hire, six (instead of thirty) Central Bus and nineteen (instead of fourteen) Country Bus RFs, were transferred to Green Line duties in 1956. The idea of using the elderly 10T10s to cover the overhaul programme during 1954 and 1955 was abandoned. Instead, up to eighteen of the Private Hire fleet operated, unmodified, on Green Line services. These changes were inextricably linked with other developments, dealt with in chapter eleven.

II THE LATE FIFTIES

The success of the single-manning experiment on Country routes 419 and 316 (chapter eight) confirmed the practicability of this method of operation on a significant number of routes. By the end of 1955, the Executive had authorised two further phases of conversion, requiring the modification of sixty-four buses in two batches, nineteen for operation in May 1956 and forty-five for May 1957. In the event, the first batch comprised only fifteen vehicles, those selected being RFs 682-696 inclusive, the balance of four apparently being made up by the experimental vehicles. The first two modified buses, RFs 684 and 687, were completed on 23rd February 1956 but the programme ran later than planned and the last (RF 686) did not appear until 11th July.

These fifteen were modified in substantially the same way as the trial batch but with a modified window between the driver's cab and the saloon to improve audibility. Stowage space was also provided for the cover of the change machine. An important new external feature, which was also fitted, later, to the original four, was a reversing lamp on the rear offside. The revised version was given the new body code RF5/1. Coincidentally, RFs 517, 647 and 649 were renumbered 697, 698 and 699 respectively, so that the entire fleet of OMO buses could be contained in the one series between 682 and 700. The numbers 647 and 649 were taken by RFs 698 and 699 in a straight exchange but RF 697 was involved in more complicated manoeuvres connected with the project for creating additional Green Line coaches.

The vehicles selected for conversion to Green Line coaches were RFs 16-25, 289-294, 514-516, 518-532 and 699. Externally, all thirty-

Above **During 1955 a new style of destination blind was introduced for the Green Line, to improve the readability of the route number. The old and new designs are seen side-by-side on two 'Relief' vehicles in the sidecourt of Victoria garage in September 1955. RF 684, on the right, was to be one of the 1956 batch of conversions to one-man form. Just in the picture on the right is one of the Scottish Omnibuses Regal IVs which worked the Edinburgh – London service.** Alan B. Cross

Right **The modifications for one-man operation from 1956 onwards had a much simpler cab arrangement than the prototypes of 1954. The glazed screen and the change-giving machine were both omitted and the driver's cab was not widened. Instead the cab door was modified to incorporate the ticket issuing machines on the driver's side and a simple cash tray on top. A standard Used Ticket box was fitted behind the cab door.** LT Museum 1107/D

Working as a bus at St Albans, RF 295 (formerly RF 514) has been modified for Green Line operation. The absence of side route boards reveals the special type of fitting used on these conversions, with its characteristic metal strip supporting the fixing clips. Alan B. Cross

Right RF 19 at Golders Green in August 1956 after modification for use as a Green Line coach. The use of light green for the relief colour, the 'Green Line' fleetname and the side route boards were the external features which changed. Just visible through the windows are the newly fitted lightweight luggage racks. G.H.F. Atkins

five were repainted in standard Green Line livery and supplied with fittings to carry the traditional side route boards. These were of a different type from those used on the purpose built coaches. Instead of the mounting clips being attached directly to the cove panels, they were fitted to a metal strip which ran lengthwise above the cant rail. When the boards were in place, there was no apparent difference.

Other modifications included the installation of central gangway lamps to all the converted vehicles, the fitting of saloon heaters and linoleum flooring to the former buses and the removal of the loudspeaker, microphones, First Aid and emergency equipment from the former Private Hire coaches. Entrance handrails were altered to the coach type and internal seat stanchions removed from the buses. The six Central Bus vehicles (RFs 289-294), also had to be fitted with platform doors.

Luggage racks were needed on all three types and it had been the intention to adopt a standard, solid, type as already used on the original coaches, in all cases. Equipping the buses was not done immediately but was carried out at their next overhaul. Although similar in concept to the original coach version, the racks were not the same as they were not contoured into the bodywork. In the case of the Private Hire coaches, there was a delay because of a temporary national shortage of steel tubing. During this pause, there was a change of heart and it was decided to fit these ten with lightweight racks which would not block the light from the cant glass panels. The former Private Hire vehicles were reclassified RF1/3 and the former buses, both Central and Country, all received the new body classification RF2/3.

RFs 1-15 remained on tours and Private Hire, RF 2 is in the second, cheerless, livery at Hatfield House. BTF

On the next overhaul of the former buses, starting later in 1957, the seating layout was modified to bring it into line with normal coach practice. The longitudinal seats on the nearside were removed and replaced by two standard transverse chairs, while those on the offside were replaced by an inward facing two-seat chair and one forward facing seat, to give accommodation for forty passengers. Although it was apparently intended to repitch the remaining seats, this was not done, the extra space being left in the area of the new transverse seating, which had greater than standard legroom. Bus seat cushions and squabs were retained.

There was also some renumbering and the complete changeover, including the OMO conversions can be summarised as follows:

RF16-25	Repainted in Green Line colours and reclassified 1RF1/3
RF289-294	Repainted and modified for Green Line operation, reclassified 1/2RF2/3
RF295-313	Renumbered 514-532, otherwise unchanged
RF514-516	Repainted and modified as Green Line, renumbered 295-297, reclassified 2RF2/3
RF517	OMO bus renumbered 697
RF518-532	Repainted and modified as Green Line, renumbered 299-313, reclassified 2RF2/3
RF647/649	OMO buses renumbered 698/699
RF682-696	Converted for one-man operation, reclassified 2RF5/1
RF697	Repainted and modified as Green Line, renumbered 298, reclassified 2RF2/3
RF698/699	Renumbered 647/649.

This elaborate reshuffle enabled Chiswick to maintain nice tidy blocks of basic types:

RF1-15	Private Hire coaches
RF16-313	Green Line Coaches
RF314-532	Central Buses
RF533-681	Country Buses, two-man operated
RF682-700	Country Buses, one-man operated.

The first bus to coach conversion to emerge was RF 294 on 7th March, followed two days later by the first two former green buses, RFs 310 and 312. The rest appeared between then and 25th April and most of them went into service more or less immediately. The Private Hire conversions followed between 16th and 25th May but six of them (RFs 16, 17, 18, 20, 21 and 24) returned for one last summer to their former duties with the Central Bus department.

The value of the enlarged fleet soon became apparent. Two new Green Line routes, needing eight coaches in all, started during the summer, the 719 (Hemel Hempstead — Victoria) on 11th July and the 715A (Hertford — London) on 8th August. The extension of route 718 from Epping to Harlow New Town, also in July, took another of the new vehicles while the rest were used as duplicates to help carry the continuously increasing traffic.

The changeovers to one-man took place on 11th July 1956 at Hertford, Epping and Hitchin (routes 308, 308A, 384, 384A and 399), Hemel Hempstead (317, 317A) and Amersham (394 group). On the same day, route 316, so recently involved in the experiment, lost its RFs in favour of GSs. At Amersham and Hemel Hempstead, the routes had been operated by 15T13s and this change absorbed some of the surplus RFs, while creating a surplus of nine Regal IIIs.

Events then became complicated by two issues which became intermingled. Arrangements had to be made to supply Central Buses with sufficient RFs to cover their next overhaul programme, which was due to start in the autumn; and a major row broke out with the Trade Union about the transfer of the six red RFs to Green Line work. The allocation of the entire post-war fleet had been carried out without major hitch because there had been full consultation with the Trade Union at every stage. They believed that, during these discussions, they had been given a firm undertaking by London Transport that the fleet of red RFs would be maintained at 225 and that any surpluses would be redeployed within the Central Bus area to replace Ts or TDs. They regarded the transfer of vehicles to the Country department as a serious and deliberate breach of faith. Needless to say, there was a comparable reluctance on the part of Country Buses to return its hard won vehicles but, after some tough bargaining, that was to be the final outcome. On 1st December 1956, RFs 533-538 were transferred from Country to Central stock and allocated to Sidcup garage. They remained green until they went for overhaul at the end of 1957, when they were repainted and had their platform doors removed. They re-entered service in this condition in February 1958. The true beneficiary of the transfer was Muswell Hill garage, which received six re-allocated red RFs, for use on route 251, replacing TDs.

In the meantime, a plan had been developed for deploying the fleet during the overhaul of the red RFs. This inevitably went through several metamorphoses, which included the possibility of transferring the surplus 15T13s into the Central Area. This was not acceptable to the operating department because of the loss of capacity on the smaller bus but the debate could have had an interesting sequel. Because of the superior specification of the Regal IIIs, compared with the TDs, it was actually agreed that thirteen of them should be overhauled and repainted red for use on Central Bus route 211 from Southall garage,

Above **RF 207 on route 718, newly extended to Harlow New Town, at Eccleston Bridge, Victoria.** Peter J. Relf

Below **The shape of things that didn't come. T 794 working in Central Bus service from Kingston garage might have foreshadowed the transfer of more 15T13s but the plan was abandoned.** B.A. Jenkins

Above Right **The first of the post-war Tigers to be withdrawn was TD12, in June 1956, indirectly replaced by redeployed RFs.** F.G. Reynolds

Right **RF 386 near the end of its overhaul at Aldenham in 1957. Above the heads of the two men can be seen the rear end of the chassis frame and part of the outrigger assembly.** LT Museum 1449/38

RF 188 was held at Chiswick after delivery to act as a test-bed for improving the efficiency of the system and in January 1953 road trials commenced using RFs 276 (RE), 278 (GF), 281 (DS) 282 (TG/SA), 283 (LS). The trials led to the ducted system being replaced by 'box' style heaters under the third nearside seat and the eighth offside seat. A 'float' of six vehicles was created, so that the work could be done quickly without reducing the availability of coaches. The vehicles chosen for this task were RFs 17, 26, 41, 125, 304 and 309, which were among those which had been allocated to Windsor for the peak summer period. The six visited each garage in turn during the next twelve months, starting at Epping on 23rd September 1956.

Another important modification which made its first appearance during 1956 was the addition of flashing trafficators. An experimental version, based on those fitted to the prototype Routemasters, was fitted to thirty-eight RFs (and also to eighty-seven RTs). The flashing units were contained in a metal housing attached to a box-like mounting just above the driver's mirrors on each side of the vehicle. They were wired so that they would flash in time with the double-headed arrows already fitted above the rear registration plate but which had never been used except on the Private Hire fleet and twenty-four Central Buses at Norbiton and Sutton in 1953. The experiment was successful and the whole fleet, including those fitted with the experimental model, was equipped with an improved version, incorporating a more flexible mounting, in 1959.

as replacements for 14T12s. This fascinating possibility came to nothing but three Regal IIIs had already been sent to Kingston in July 1956, still painted green, and these, later running from Norbiton on route 201 and joined from time to time by a fourth, continued in use until ousted by RFs in January 1959. Meanwhile, the needs of the 1956 overhaul programme were met by the Country department lending twelve surplus RFs to the Central department. These, still in their green livery, went to Sidcup, the first arriving in September, some three months before RFs 533-538. All eighteen ran with their platform doors permanently open, as required by the Metropolitan Police. The temporary loans were returned in December 1957, in time for the Country Bus overhaul programme.

While the buses were being overhauled, the coaches were subjected to an important modification to their heating systems, to take advantage of the improvements in design which had occurred in the previous six years. The original ducted system, by Clayton Dewandre, had soon proved inadequate and could not be made to reach a satisfactory standard even after the thermostats had been adjusted to open at a higher temperature.

Before conversion to OMO, RF 626 is seen on its way from Horsham to Edenbridge in August 1956, outside the White Hart, Crawley. Frank Hornby

The second phase of the plan for 'large saloon' one-man operation was introduced in the second half of 1957. The original intention to convert another forty-five vehicles was reduced to thirty-eight and the buses selected were RFs 562, 603, 607-629, 631-642 and 664. Experience with the trial batch led to a substantially simpler form of conversion being adopted for these and subsequent 'production' runs. The elaborate 'cinema pay desk' layout was abandoned and a half-height door retained on the driver's cab. The 'Ultimate' ticket machine was again fitted on the driver's side of the door but the ticket issuing and change-giving apparatus was replaced by two simple cash scoop trays on the top of the door. There was also a revised method of operation for the reversing light. The resulting body type was classified 2RF5/2. The seemingly random selection of fleet numbers came about because, by now, it had been accepted that all but the busiest town routes would become one-man operated in time and for this reason no attempt was made to renumber them either. Three further phases of modifications were eventually authorised and, by the beginning of 1959, only thirty-five green RFs remained suitable only for conductor operation.

RF 664 was the pilot for these conversions and came out of works on 1st December 1956. After a brief period of service at Epping, it returned to works for another two weeks between 23rd January and 6th February 1957. The main programme started with RF 562, interestingly recovered from Sidcup, which came out of Works on 4th October. The rest were all done by 30th October.

The service changes in October 1957 were in two phases. On the 15th routes 307, 307A and 337 at Hemel Hempstead, routes 342 and 390 at Hertford, route 364 at Hitchin and Luton and the 489 and 489A at Northfleet became one-man operated using the newly converted RFs. On the 30th they were joined by the 416 (which was extended from Leatherhead to Tadworth to cover the 435) and 422 at Leatherhead, routes 426, 434 and 473 at Crawley, the 432 at Guildford, and the 304, 365 and 382 at St Albans. RFs also replaced GS twenty-six seaters on routes 333 at Hertford (15th October) and 393 at Epping (30th October), beginning a trend which was to gather momentum in subsequent years. At Hemel Hempstead the buses displaced were 15T13s, absorbing some of the surplus RFs and rendering yet more of the older Regals redundant.

There was a delayed start at Leatherhead because of a strike by drivers who were unhappy with the terminal arrangements at Boxhill, which required buses to reverse. The staff believed that the absence of a conductor to guide the driver constituted a serious hazard and they based this belief on an experience earlier in the year, when an inspector was knocked down and seriously injured by a reversing bus. As a consequence of this, London Transport eventually adopted a policy of altering terminal workings when one-man buses were introduced, to avoid the need to reverse.

RF 618 was one of the second phase conversions to one-man form in 1957. The improved signing took the form of a plastic board on the front dash with orange coloured lettering and a larger board on the nearside, under the first window, with bright green lettering. Monday-Friday route 384B, which had only one journey in each direction, had been OMO since 1956. Ken Glazier

RF 648, a 1958 conversion to OMO, picks its way through New Town developments on route 393, which was given a Hertford allocation when it was extended to Welwyn Garden City in July 1958.
S. Hagerty

During 1958, seventy more RFs were modified. The three authorised phases of conversion effectively melted into one continuous programme running from January to November. It would presumably have finished a couple of months earlier but for the seven-week delay caused by the strike in May and June which brought all London Transport bus activity to a standstill. Six vehicles (RFs 542, 544, 545, 546, 550 and 551) which had gone into works for overhaul in the first half of January, came out between 29th January and 18th February as 'temporary OMO' buses and were used to form a float. The first vehicle to come out in the main programme of conversions was RF 663 on 28th April but only four more were to follow before work came to a halt during the strike. Deliveries resumed on 25th June and the programme was completed on 27th November, when RF 585 went to Amersham. During October, the original float vehicles were designated as permanent conversions. The vehicles converted during 1958 were: RFs 542, 544-546, 550, 551, 581-602, 604-606, 630, 643-663 and 665-681.

The first of the route conversions was made on 23rd July. At Epping and Hertford, the change coincided with a reorganisation of routes 342 (withdrawn between Hertford and Broxbourne), 372/372A (extended from Hertford to Epping, Coopersale Street), 393 (extended from Broxbourne to Welwyn Garden City) and 399 (withdrawn). The routes which had straight conversions were Addlestone's 427, 437, 456, 456B, 462 and 462A and Dunton Green's 404, 413 and 413A.

On 15th October 1958, there was another route restructuring associated with a conversion to OMO, this time at St Albans and designed to separate town services, which would remain conductor-operated, from country operations. The 'town service' section of route 355 between St Peter's Street and Firbank Road was withdrawn and the route extended instead to Harpenden via Batford, in which form it became one-man operated. Route 391 in turn, lost its Sandridge to Harpenden section and was diverted instead to Firbank Road, becoming in the process a purely local town service; it continued to operate with conductors. Other routes which changed over to OMO on this day were Garston's 319 group and route 331 at Hertford. On 29th October, Dorking, East Grinstead and Guildford made another contribution with routes 412, 425 and 428.

The changes to the 331 and 428 were of special significance as these were the first double-deck routes to be affected by the programme, in both cases releasing RTs for use elsewhere. Other newcomers to the RF fold were routes 386 and 481, two more examples where RFs replaced GSs.

The 1958 conversions coincided with a large programme of route changes and service reductions which followed the seven-week bus strike. In the Central Area, as part of those changes, the long promised double-decking of the two Sidcup routes (228 and 241) at last took place on 26th November. The reason for single-deck operation of these two busy routes was the low bridge at Sidcup station, which had now been completely rebuilt and the roadway widened and lowered to give adequate clearance for high vehicles. The 228 was not altered, except that its frequency was reduced, but the 241 was partly replaced by substantial changes to the 51 group.

All the changes, taken together, caused a cut in single-deck requirements of no fewer than fifty-eight. The surplus buses were used to replace the last of the 14T12s and a number of TDs. The displaced RFs went to Southall, for route 211, Uxbridge for route 222, replacing Ts in each case and to Leyton and Tottenham, where they replaced TDs on route 236. The Tigers, in turn, went to Uxbridge, where they took over the 224/224A/224B from 14T12s. This did not quite eliminate the vertical engined Regal from Central Bus service, as the three 15T13s were still running at Norbiton on the 201. This did not last long. Three more RFs which were spare were allocated to Norbiton for the 201 from 20th January 1959.

As part of the settlement of the 1958 strike, an undertaking had been given that operations would be reviewed to find ways of making economies. The service cuts have already been mentioned; associated with them was the closure of a number of garages. One of those which closed on 26th November 1958 was Old Kent Road, which had a small allocation of RFs for route 202. These went to New Cross, which became the first former tram depot to operate the class. Country Buses closed Hitchin garage after traffic on 28th April 1959, together with temporary premises at Fishers Green Road, Stevenage which had been operating coach RFs on the 716A since 1955. They were both replaced by new premises in Danestrete, Stevenage, which opened for business on 29th April 1959. Its starting fleet included eleven Green Line and three bus RFs, for routes 716, 716A, 392 and 392A. Hitchin's operation of route 364 was transferred, with two bus RFs, to Luton. This route was also extended to Flamstead (364) or Kensworth (364A), replacing double-deck routes 356 and 376 with one-man operated RFs.

The other principal source of economy was to be more one-man operation and this concept was now to be extended to the Central Area, which had last operated one-man buses (twenty-seat Leyland Cubs) in 1949. The routes chosen for the pilot conversion were Kingston's 216, 218 and 219, then operated by TDs and calculated to need thirty-seven RFs for the new style of operation. Following the dispersal of Sidcup's Regal IVs in November 1958, there was still a surplus of about eighteen and a further sixteen were released on 18th March 1959, when the remaining single-deckers on route 233, at West Green garage, were replaced by RTLs. The balance of three was at first to be scavenged from spares but ultimately came from route 208A whose fourteen RFs were replaced on 13th May 1959 by lowbridge double-deck RLHs on the 178.

Some additional one-manning was also proposed in the Country Area and it was now decided that the entire Country Bus fleet should be made suitable for use with or without a conductor. The purpose behind this decision was to give maximum flexibility in the use of the fleet and to reduce the number of spare vehicles which had to be maintained. Authority was given by the Executive early in 1959, therefore, for the conversion of thirty-seven red RFs and the remaining thirty-five green RFs.

The Country buses were the first to be modified, the programme being completed between 5th February and 11th March 1959 and embodying RFs 539-541, 543, 547-549, 552-561 and 563-580, all of which remained at the same garages. The red RFs chosen were in a continuous numerical sequence from 502 to 538 and the first to emerge from Works was RF 528 on 4th March. The last was completed on 8th May. The modifications followed the

pattern now set, except that, in the case of the Central Bus vehicles, platform doors had to be fitted. Ironically, in the case of RFs 533-538, they had to be re-fitted, as these were the vehicles recovered from the Country department in December 1956. This version was classified RF5/3. All vehicles numbered between 502 and 700 were now suitable for one-man operation. One minor improvement introduced at this time and ultimately extended to the whole fleet, was the introduction of orange-coloured plastic slip-boards reading 'Pay As You Enter', instead of paper bills.

Hitchin garage closed in April 1959 and most of its operations were transferred to the new Stevenage garage. Seen at Chertsey at the other extremity of route 716, RF 136 was destined for stardom six years later when it was selected as the prototype for the modernisation programme. Lens of Sutton

In the same programme of changes as the closure of Hitchin garage, two more double-deck routes succumbed to one-man operation. RF 576, a February 1959 conversion, works a journey from Luton to Flamstead on the newly extended 364, over the old route 356.

While the work had been going on, however, national negotiations had been taking place between management and Trades Unions about the rewards paid to staff for single-manning. The existing agreements gave OMO drivers fifteen percent more pay than 'crew' drivers but the Trade Union were seeking to increase this to thirty percent. The claim was resisted but, whereas in the Country Area there was an existing agreement which allowed the department to carry on with its plans, there was no such possibility for Central Road services staff, as the old agreement had been allowed to lapse after 1949. The planned conversion of the Kingston routes in May 1959 was therefore 'deferred'.

Nevertheless, preparations had been going ahead and the first (RF 512) was licensed at Norbiton on 20th April, followed by RF 515 on 22nd April and RF 516 on the 23rd. Three more (RFs 513, 517 and 524) were licensed on 1st May. Only one other of the batch was licensed at this time, RF 528 at Bromley from 8th April. On the day that they should have gone into service as one-man buses, they were delicensed instead and replaced by other unaltered ones made surplus from route 208A at Dalston. As there was no immediate prospect of securing an agreement with the Trade Union, after some time it was decided that the thirty-seven RFs should be deployed as two-man vehicles, not necessarily on the routes for which they had been intended but to the best overall economic advantage. If they had gone to Kingston as planned, three garages would have continued to operate mixed fleets of TDs and RFs, requiring costly duplication of spare parts. It was decided that the greatest financial gain would come from having one type in as many garages as possible and that the TDs at Norbiton and Uxbridge should be replaced by the spare Regals. A similar saving was made by allocating some of the remainder to North Street, for route 250, thereby removing the TD class from that Engineering Division altogether. This left sufficient for route 216 at Kingston to be included too.

Twenty-two of the red RF5/3s were re-licensed on 10th June 1959, at Norbiton (thirteen) and Uxbridge (nine), where the TDs ran on routes 206, 224, 224A, 224B and 264 for the last time on 9th June. The allocations to Kingston (eleven) and North Street (five) were not made until 1st July, as it took until then for the staff on routes 216 and 250 to be trained.

The Country department's plans went ahead unhindered and another phase of conversions, using eleven vehicles, was introduced on 13th May 1959. At Grays there was some restructuring of routes, which enabled some more double-deck workings to be taken over by the Regal IVs. A new route 399 was created, running from Bulphan to Rainham, covering sections of hitherto RT operated routes 323, 328 and 328A, as well as part of the 374, which was also converted. The local Rainham route, 375, was shortened to run only between the Ferry and the Clock Tower and also converted; but it ran in this form only until 30th June, when it was withdrawn altogether. At Reigate, routes 439A, 440 and 440A were converted and the 440A extended from Redhill to Wolding-ham to take over the country section of the 447.

Before the next stage of single-manning could be launched, it was necessary to carry out some redeployment in the fleet, to produce enough buses. A number of coaches, which had been doing duty as duplicates on Green Line services, were relegated to bus work on two-man operated routes, although they were not modified in any way for these duties. This in turn released sufficient bus RFs for use on the routes due for conversion on 10th June. The coach RFs were replaced on the Green Line by surplus RTs. The routes which benefited from this rearrangement were the 307B and 322, together with new routes 322A (Sundays only) and 322B (Saturdays only), run by Hemel Hempstead garage and Hertford's double-deck routes 350 and 350A, which were simultaneously extended from Hertford to Potters Bar, absorbing route 342.

RF 565 carries a full load around the Pond Cross Roads roundabout on its way into Watford on Hemel Hempstead's route 322, a June 1959 OMO conversion. S. Hagerty

Some coach RFs were replaced on duplication duties by RT class double-deckers during 1959 so that they could be released for use as two-man buses. RF 133, still in full Green Line trim, does duty as a bus from Windsor garage on route 458 in the deceptively leafy surroundings of Uxbridge bus station. Ken Glazier

In the short term, these arrangements coincided with the overhaul of the coach RFs and to meet the summer peak requirements, five of the red OMO RFs (509, 532, 534, 535 and 536) were lent to Reigate, for operation on the 447. This released some of the coaches which had been in use as buses, to go back to the Green Line for the time being.

In the autumn of 1959 there was a curious setback in the process of single-manning, when the Grays routes reverted to double-deck operation, using RTs. The buses displaced were sent to Reigate where they enabled the red RFs to be delicensed on 14th October. However, they were again relicensed on 29th October and remained there for another year.

12 THE SIXTIES

The RF family entered the 1960s with the oldest vehicles of the class about to celebrate their ninth birthday. In the normal course of events, steps would by now have been taken to find a replacement for the coaches, to keep a modern and high quality style on Green Line, excursion and Private Hire activities. Had earlier plans come to anything, seventy-seven (or, by a later estimate, forty-five) new vehicles would have been added to the fleet in the late 1950s. The next logical step would have been to buy new coaches and demote the RFs to bus work, replacing the early post-war fleet of Ts and TDs, totalling 211 vehicles. Unfortunately for the fleet planners, this option had been all but removed. At the start of 1960, only forty-four such vehicles were still scheduled for service and some of these were under imminent threat of indirect replacement by double-deckers.

Not that the needs of the Green Line were being neglected. One of the experimental Routemasters had been built as a coach (CRL 4), in the latest of a long line of attempts to develop a double-decker suitable for coach work. The future of the Green Line was seen as being closely related to the development of this vehicle and any idea of procuring new single-deckers for the service increases (which were still being forecast) had now been dropped in favour of using surplus RTs until the Routemaster coach went into production.

This change of policy became manifest in the summer of 1960 when the first of twenty-eight RTs came out of Aldenham in Green Line livery for use as peak duplicates. Looking beyond that, to the ultimate need to replace the rest of the class, a small experiment was carried out, using three AEC Reliance buses with Willowbrook 42-seat dual-door bodywork (RW 1-3), first on route 322 at Hemel Hempstead, starting on 26th September 1960, and later at Addlestone (routes 427, 437, 456 and 462) then at Reigate (440, 440A), at St Albans (route 355) and finally at Hertford, where they ran for the last time at the end of September 1963. The experiment was to have no immediate effect.

The RTs used on the Green Line had been fitted with saloon heaters, as was normal practice for coaches and, although not wholly reliable, they were popular. London Transport had already made the decision to fit all future new buses with saloon heaters and the Routemasters then entering service were the first standard buses to have them. Inspired by these successes, the Executive decided in 1960 that all Country buses should have heaters and a programme for installing them on the Country Area RFs was initiated during 1962. In the summer of 1963, when the programme was well advanced, the Board (as it had now become) decided that the same treatment should be given to the Central Area RT and

RF fleets, the only condition being that the vehicle should have a life expectancy of at least eight years. All RFs qualified and the red buses were modified starting in 1963. At about the same time, the differentials on all RFs were changed from $5\frac{1}{6}$-1, to $4\frac{4}{7}$-1, in an attempt to improve fuel consumption, and the two modifications together were recognised in the chassis classification being altered to 1/2RF.

During 1960, an attempt was made to brighten the appearance of the Green Line RFs with an experimental livery on the coaches allocated to Reigate and High Wycombe for route 711. No change was made to the basic layout of the livery, both the 'Lincoln' green of the main body panels and the paler relief colour being replaced by lighter shades. The wheel nut rings on the front wheels were painted black, and a ring of black was applied to the rear wheel discs. At a later date, the side route boards were also given a black background. Sixteen vehicles were given the new colours: RFs 33, 36, 41, 42, 51, 52, 55, 58, 69, 71, 72, 86, 126, 271, 309 and 313. The only other vehicle to receive this livery was the Routemaster CRL 4. The new scheme was never adopted but the lighter relief colour was chosen as standard, with Lincoln green still the main colour, early in 1962. The termination of the experiment led to an untypical series of compromise liveries on a number of coaches while stocks of various shades of paint

Facing Page
Reigate's RF 271 stands in the forecourt of its home garage in the experimental light green livery introduced for a short time from 1960. Gerald Mead

Left **Epping's RF 19 has been given a darker green relief colour in the aftermath of the livery experiments and looks decidedly dull as a result. Behind it at Aldgate 'Lay-by' is Grays' RT 4498, one of the hybrid vehicles with secondhand bodies recovered from the SRT class in 1954.** John Fozard

were exhausted. Some, for example, appeared with 'Lincoln' green main panels and a relief in the green which had been used for the main colour on the experimental bodies. When it reverted to a bus, RF 313 (and possibly RF 309) kept the light green but with cream relief.

In the meantime, the RF class gradually established a monopoly of large single-deck operations. A major shift in this direction occurred on 6th January 1960 when the short but frequent route 212, running between Finsbury Park and Muswell Hill Broadway, changed over to double-deck operation. It had been the weight restriction on the bridge at Muswell Hill station, over the now closed Alexander Palace branch railway line, that had latterly imposed the need for single-deckers but the bridge had now been strengthened, enabling the heavier vehicle to be used. The twenty-one RFs allocated to Muswell Hill for the 212, were sent immediately to Kingston, where they replaced TDs on routes 215 (Sundays), 218 and 219. Kingston's remaining single-deck operations on routes 215 and 215A had to stay with the smaller vehicle for the time being because of unsuitable roads on route 215A between Cobham and Downside. Authority was given in October 1961 for spare RFs to work on route 215 on specific runnings which did not have spells on the 215A. Approval for the use of RFs to Downside was finally obtained from the Traffic Commissioner in 1962. The buses to run on these two routes (from 9th May 1962) and then on the 240A (from 10th October 1962), were made available by yet more conversions to double-deck operation, following the rebuilding of the bridge at West Drayton station. The West Drayton to Hounslow section of Uxbridge's route 222 was absorbed into an extension of double-deck route 223 on 24th

Regal IVs came to Edgware in October 1962, when the 240A lost its TDs, London's last vertical front-engined single-deckers. RF 423 stands in the old forecourt at Edgware station, surrounded by the unfinished business of the Northern Line extension to Bushey Heath. W.R. Legg

March 1961; and then RTs took over responsibility for the 224A, 224B and 224C on 9th May 1962. Route 224 itself followed suit, somewhat surprisingly as it would appear to have been a prime candidate for OMO, on 8th May 1963. On the same day route 213 also lost its Regals, because double-deck operation had now been made possible by the rebuilding of Worcester Park station bridge. The scheduled allocation of red Regals dropped to only 175 as a result of these changes and was further diminished, to 168, when Southall's route 211 went over to double-deck RT operation on 1st July 1964. No immediate use was found for the displaced vehicles, other than to provide a float for the overhaul programme during 1964 and 1965, when a number worked for a time in the Country Area. Some which were delicensed at this time did not see service again with Central Buses for another four years.

All London Transport's 'large' single-deck operations were covered by the RF class from 10th October 1962, the last 15T13 having been withdrawn at Crawley the previous month. One final conversion to double-deck was carried out before the 'Reshaping' programme began the reverse process. After a long battle with the local authority and residents, route 200 changed over from RF to RT operation on 25th August 1965, removing Regals from Merton garage.

A Central Bus newcomer to the Regal IV and the first former trolleybus depot to operate the class was Fulwell, which took over responsibility for the five RFs needed for route 206 from its first day of operation as a motor bus garage, on 9th May 1962. Norbiton had exchanged it for Routemaster routes 282 and 283, successors to trolleybuses 602 and 603. Another interesting re-allocation was the 251 which was moved into Edgware.

During the rebuilding of West Drayton railway bridge, bus routes were split on each side of the work and the 222 provided the entire service along Cowley Road. RF 509, converted for OMO but still carrying a conductor, turns in West Drayton station forecourt at the end of a shuttle trip from Uxbridge in February 1961. Ken Glazier

Below A belated and perhaps untimely candidate for double-decking was route 200, then a short local route in Wimbledon, RF 321 on the South Park Road stand two weeks before the Regal IVs were displaced. Ken Glazier

The first major inroad into the dominance of the Regal IVs started on 29th August 1962, when the first of the production batch of Routemaster coaches went into service on route 715 from Hertford and Guildford, twenty RMCs replacing twenty-five RFs. This was followed on 24th October by routes 718 (Windsor and Epping), 720 and 720A (Epping), displacing another twenty-five Regals, on 21st November by route 719 (nine RFs — Garston) and finally, on 2nd January 1963, when sixteen RFs off routes 716 and 716A (Addlestone and Stevenage) were dislodged. Far from heralding a new phase of development for the Green Line, the introduction of the larger vehicles came at a time when passenger demand was beginning to decline and was accompanied by what was to prove the first in a long series of service cuts and modifications. The greater capacity of the vehicles was used, not to increase the passenger carrying potential but to enable some frequency reductions on routes 715 and 720, so that the sixty-eight double-deckers were able to cover the withdrawal of seventy-five single-deckers.

The principal casualties of this change were the ten former Private Hire coaches (RFs 16-25) which were withdrawn and soon sold. No thirty-footers were disposed of at this time but twenty-four coaches were eventually sold between January 1964 and January 1965. Also lost to Green Line work but not to London Transport was the entire batch of former Country Buses (RFs 298-313) which were now once again converted for bus operation. They did not revert to their original condition as they now had to be made suitable for one-man operation in common with the rest of the fleet.

They entered service as one-man buses between 5th September and 11th October 1962 but only the cab modifications were made at this time and the seating capacity remained at forty, in the 'coach' layout. It was not for another eleven months that a luggage compartment was installed on the nearside, as was usual on OMO buses. Between 4th and 29th August 1963 all sixteen had the front pair of nearside seats removed to make way for one. This reduced the seating capacity to thirty-eight, one less than the standard bus because the coach arrangement of mainly forward-facing seats was retained. The code given to this variation was 1/2RF5/4.

Before the arrival of the Routemaster coaches, the very strong presence of the RF in Country service is epitomised in this line-up in Epping garage on 12th August 1962. From the left are RFs 553, 690, 240 (a coach), 549, 610 and an unidentified coach. J. Gascoine

A smaller, neater looking, style of lettering was introduced on registration plates in the mid-1960s to enable the accommodation of the year suffix on new registrations. In this view at St Albans bus station, the new style transfers on RF 671, on the left, can be compared with the original type on RF 216, a former coach. E. Shirras

The 'new' buses were used to replace yet more GS twenty-six seaters from 24th October 1962 at Chelsham, where routes 464, 465 and 485 changed over to the larger bus, Amersham, where they took over routes 332, 348, 348A, 398 and 398A, and Epping where one replaced the last GS still running on the 381. As more Regals were released for one reason or another over the next few years, they replaced more of the Guys until all but two of the smaller class had gone after their substitution by RFs on route 309 in February 1969.

The rest of the ageing Green Line fleet was now left to keep going while major changes of policy were being worked out by the new London Transport Board. (This was the autonomous body newly created as successor to the London Transport Executive by the 1962 Transport Act which had abolished the British Transport Commission.) The failed attempt at introducing one-man operation to the Central Area in 1959 had not been the last word and the Executive had continued, so far unsuccessfully, to search for improvements in productivity, latterly by the use of larger double-deckers. On 20th November 1963 the Government stepped into the latest argument then going on between management and Trade Union and set up a Committee of Inquiry, under the chairmanship of Professor Henry Phelps-Brown, with wide-ranging terms of reference. The report which eventually appeared, in June 1964, provided a basis for the two sides to agree to far-reaching developments, including a substantial expansion of one-man operation.

RF 306, downgraded from coach to bus in 1962, at Hyde Heath in May 1963, working one of the last journeys to Hyde End, one of the many services withdrawn in the 1960s. Ken Glazier

Some Green Line RFs made surplus were formally downgraded to buses from 1965 onwards. RF 92, now a thirty-eight seat bus, in bus livery and with side route board clips removed, shares the bus station at Crawley with RT 4504. John Fozard

In preparation for the expected outcome of the report, the Central Bus department had put together what eventually became known as 'The Bus Reshaping Plan', which contained many revolutionary proposals involving new technical developments and the use of, as yet untried, new types of bus. The Country department also intended to try out some new ideas and included in the experimental vehicles ordered for 1965 was a batch of fourteen AEC Reliance coaches for the Green Line, intended to test the effect of higher specification vehicles for this form of work, with a view to determining what should replace the RFs. Like the proverbial rhinoceros, it takes a long time for an organisation the size of London Transport, in full cry, to stop and change direction and it was inevitable that some years would elapse while new techniques and new types of vehicle were tested. It was by now clear that the bulk of the RF class would have to serve for some years beyond their normal life expectancy, while these changes were developed.

Although an important side-effect of the Phelps-Brown report was to give a new lease of life to the bulk of the RF class, another of the reasons for the setting up of the Inquiry in the first place was to have a quite different impact on other parts of the fleet. Shortages of staff, in the Central Area particularly but also in parts of the Country Area, had been a problem since the early 1950s but had reached a serious stage in the early 1960s, with some garages suffering shortages of fifteen percent or more. With the coverage of the daily service schedules a constant battle, it became increasingly difficult either to justify or to operate the purely commercial private hire business. Gradually, from about 1962 onwards, the Private Hire department found itself having to turn more and more to independent coach

operators to supply its vehicle and staff needs. This came to a head in September 1963 when a dispute with staff about the operation of the service which replaced the Northern City Underground service while Victoria Line works were being carried out, led to the operation being taken over by Whitehall Motorways Ltd, using coaches, on contract to the Board. On 2nd April the following year, the Board formally announced that, due to the refusal of staff to work on tours and special services to sporting events (such as the Football Cup Final, the Derby and Wimbledon Tennis), contracts would be entered into with private operators. From then onwards, in the Central Area at any rate, all conducted coach tour, sightseeing tour and private hire work was carried out in this way.

The Country department continued to trade in these markets but came to rely for its vehicle needs on the standard bus and coach fleet for those in which the RFWs had been active. The result of this fateful decision was that the last full season for the Private Hire RFs and the RFW class was the summer of 1963, only RFWs 1, 6 and 14 being relicensed for the Country Bus department's 1964 season. The bulk of the fleet was delicensed for the last time on 1st September and 1st October 1963 but the very last 1RF1, RF 8, was still in use until 31st October at Wandsworth. The three remaining RFWs met a similar fate on 1st October 1964. All thirty were withdrawn and sold, the RFs finding a ready market among Independents at home, while ten of the RFWs went to Ceylon.

Transfer of private hire work to outside operators led to the withdrawal of the private hire RFs and RFWs and the abandonment of plans for a replacement coach for this work. RFW 15 in Buckingham Palace Road was one of ten which went to Ceylon. John Fozard

As the GSs were displaced from their traditional routes by the all-pervasive RF, new ventures were sought for them, like the 389 local in Harlow, almost foreshadowing the midibus boom to come two decades later, RF 644 and GS 65 in Harlow bus station. Lower case lettering had been introduced onto intermediate point blind displays in 1961. Alan B. Cross

There was one earlier casualty in the fleet which deserves mention as it was the first Regal IV to be withdrawn for scrap. In the early hours of 21st January 1963, RF 464 returned to Fulwell garage after carrying out a run as a staff bus. Shortly afterwards, it burst into flames, allegedly as a result of a carelessly discarded cigarette. Despite the firefighting efforts of the night engineering staff the bodywork was severely damaged. The vehicle was written off and the remains sold on 7th August that year.

The delay in replacing the Green Line RFs gave London Transport time to reflect on the future role of the coach services, in an increasingly congested road network and against a background of accelerating car ownership and improving railway services, as more suburban lines were electrified. The first example of a possible new approach appeared on 23rd August 1963, when the London to Windsor section of route 705 became 'Express', with fewer stops and a faster route using Chiswick flyover and the Colnbrook By-pass. The following year, on 4th November, a similar treatment was given to the 709, which ran express between Oxford Circus and Amersham, using Western Avenue between Shepherds Bush and Uxbridge and an attempt was made to capitalise on the M1 motorway with an entirely new route. Numbered 727, this ran between Tring and London via Hemel Hempstead, using standard RF coaches, still at this stage of development carrying a conductor. Coinciding with these changes, though, was a series of others which amounted to a significant curtailment of Green Line operation. Following the electrification of the Metropolitan Line north of Rickmansworth, coaches were withdrawn altogether from the Amersham to London section of the 703, while the London to Dorking service on routes 712/713 was reduced, generally to hourly, and the Luton service all but withdrawn; there were also substantial cuts on the double-deck routes in east London. The Wrotham service on route 703 was covered by an extension of the 717 from Victoria. Both Swanley and Hatfield lost their coach RFs, as the newly constituted 717 was operated by RMCs transferred from Epping, where they in turn had been replaced on routes 720 and 720A by RFs.

Sadly, the retrenchment proved to be more pervasive than the new ideas and route 727 ran for the last time on 30th October 1965, along with the express section of the 709 and Harlow New Town route 720A. A different tack was tried from the following day in an attempt to make the traditional services more attractive. To minimise the irregularities caused by traffic congestion routes 701, 702 and 714 were divided in London on Mondays to Fridays.

Top **The RT and RTW in the background and the Green Line RFs are still the types that dominate the central London scene in September 1965 but the cross-London operation of the 709 has only just over a month to run. Godstone's RF 77 is heading into Northumberland Avenue.** Ken Glazier

Right **Broad Sanctuary and Victoria Street was virgin territory for the Green Line and for the RF class when route 727 was introduced in 1964. Black and yellow side route boards are carried by RF 94, an innovation with this new route.** Ken Glazier

The rapid decline in the fortunes of the Green Line network had thrown up yet another surplus of coach RFs by the middle of 1965 but no disposals were authorised. Instead the Board decided to accelerate the pace of single-manning of bus services and gave authority for the downgrading of thirty-one RF2/1s to buses, the first of the breed to be so treated. The most important modifications were the addition of the necessary equipment to make them suitable for one-man operation and the removal of the front nearside seat, which was replaced by a parcel rack. Other 'coach' accoutrements were removed, such as the clips for the side route boards and the fleetname was altered from GREEN LINE to LONDON TRANSPORT. In this form the vehicles were reduced to thirty-seven seaters and were given the body classification RF5/5. The work was carried out between September and November 1965. One of the converted vehicles, RF 41, was returned to coach condition in August 1966.

Top **Route 703 disappeared in August 1963. A year earlier in the month of the vehicle's withdrawal, RF22, the Victoria-based emergency vehicle, substituted for a Swanley coach at Eccleston Bridge. The abbreviated destination blind display enabled all routes to be contained on the roller. 'GREEN LINE' was applied by transfers to the top one-third of the indicator glass, instead of being repeated on each display as was usually the case.** Ken Glazier

Centre **This rear view of RF 70 on the 727 shows the minor changes made over the years. The reflectors on the bottom panel were a requirement from 1954 and the additional arrow on the nearside was fitted when the new trafficators were installed at the end of the 1950s. The original left-pointing arrow head on the panel above the registration plate was painted out at the same time.** Michael Beamish

Undertaking new duties on East Grinstead local route 435 to Imberhorne Estate, RF 59 was one of thirty-one RF2/1s downgraded to buses and converted for one-man operation in the autumn of 1965. There were only superficial external changes: the route board clips were removed from the roof cove panels; the fleetname was altered; and 'PAY AS YOU ENTER' slip-boards were added on the front and nearside. E. Shirras

These experiences confirmed London Transport in its belief that an early decision on Green Line fleet replacement could be premature but they were also alert to the need to maintain an acceptable and recognisably up-to-date standard of comfort and appearance, if passengers were to remain loyal. They decided to investigate the potential for upgrading the existing fleet. RF 136 was chosen as the prototype, delicensed at St Albans on 19th July 1965 and taken into works. When it re-emerged in March the following year, it had undergone a remarkable transition. Externally, the main body colour of Lincoln green was retained and the most noticeable changes were the introduction of twin headlamps (very much a trend of the period), the single-piece curved windscreen on the driver's side and the application of a deep light green relief band immediately below the windows. This band was finished off both top and bottom with an aluminium strip running horizontally around the vehicle. The garage code and running number plate brackets were moved down to a position above the front wheel arch, so as not to intrude on the relief band.

At the front the bullseye device on the radiator filler cap flap had been removed as the light green band now ran across part of it. Instead, a new style of bullseye transfer was placed between the two groups of headlamps in the position formerly occupied by the registration plate. The modified design had the circle formed by two yellow lines and a solid yellow bar containing the GREEN LINE fleetname in green block capitals. The same style of bullseye was repeated at the back, on the bottom of the emergency exit door. The traditional style of fleetname also disappeared from the sides of the vehicle, being replaced by a version in large italic capital letters, yellow lined out in green, on the waistband under the front saloon windows. The extensive use of yellow was continued on the side route boards, whose background was of that colour, with the route details in black. The squared mudguards were replaced by a more conventional curved arrangement. A new position was found for the registration plate at both ends of the coach. The front plate was now placed at the very bottom of the lower panel while the rear one was removed from the offside and a new oblong recessed panel created for it immediately below the Emergency Exit. Finally, a new type of flashing trafficator was installed on each side at the front immediately below the waistband and a new style of fleet number, in very small yellow characters, was carried immediately above the front wheels.

Internally, the scheme followed the latest design standards set by Misha Black, most famous for his work on the Underground's Victoria Line. His philosophy favoured somewhat drab colours, the design justification being that grey was a surrogate for steel and depicted modern technical efficiency. Grey was used for the side panelling and the same colour was carried up over the whole of the window cappings continuing above this to cover the beading around the top of the windows. The ceiling was white. The moquette was of the same design as that introduced with the RCL double-deck coaches, a basically grey design with some red lining. The conventional saloon lighting was replaced by fluorescent tubes, covered by opalescent plastic shades. There

The prototype modernised coach, RF 136, poses for an official photograph to launch the project and is also shown on route 705 on its first day in service. The unpainted wheel nut rings and the restoration of bright parts to the rear wheel discs, did not survive into the production run. LT Museum F114440/Brian Speller

were four of these on each side of the saloon attached to the underside of the luggage rack and two more in the centre ceiling panel, replacing the 'cleaner' lights. The modified vehicle was reclassified 1/2RF2/5.

The completed vehicle entered service, to much acclaim, on 16th March 1966 alongside the newly delivered Reliance coaches on route 705 from Dunton Green garage, but it quickly moved to Tunbridge Wells on 21st March, where it started to run on the 704, the first home of the RF coaches. It proved to be a great success and it was not long before the Board decided to embark on a scheme for refurbishing the rest of the Green Line RF fleet. By mid-1966, the scheduled requirement for single-deck coaches had declined to a total of 169, of which twelve were supplied from the RC class. To meet this and the engineering spares required to support the scheduled fleet, the Board authorised the modernisation of another 174 RFs, giving a total of 175.

Opposite Top **The first one-man operated coaches ran from Romford and High Wycombe garages on Express route 724 between those towns from 10th July 1966. Modernised RF 234 is seen at Harlow. Yellow route boards with black lettering were, at this time, exclusive to 'Express' coach routes.** E. Shirras

Opposite Centre **The interior of a modernised coach looking forward. The contemporary obsession with rather drab grey colour schemes, pioneered by Misha Black in his Victoria Line designs, was carried through to the RF finishings. The side panelling was grey from floor to cove panels, the moquette mainly grey with some red lining and the ceiling white.** LT Museum 3440/19

Opposite Bottom **Looking towards the rear in a modernised thirty-five seater, the two luggage compartments can be seen on each side at the back, protected by lightweight bulkheads. The fluorescent lighting tubes can be seen above the windows and in the centre ceiling bays. The close-up view of RF 89 shows the luggage compartment on the nearside of thirty-five seater.** LT Museum 3440/11/J.M. Aldridge

The 'production' run of modernisations started with RF 26 in August 1966 and was completed with the licensing of RF 63 at Reigate on 12th July 1967. In most respects they were identical to RF 136 but one important styling change which was abandoned was the modification of the mudguards, which had not had a particularly beneficial effect on the appearance. A minor effect of this was to move the garage code and running number brackets further back, to a position behind the front wheel arch.

During the run of the project, two important new routes had started, both destined to be highly successful and both, even more significantly, one-man operated. The first of these was the long-awaited (although much changed in concept) northern orbital route, numbered 724, which started on 10th July 1966 and was the first OMO Green Line route. Standard coach RFs were allocated to High Wycombe and Romford, re-introducing scheduled single-deck operation to the east London garage for the first time since the war. These were replaced by modernised vehicles in April 1967. The second new route was a yet bolder western orbital, the 727, which started on 13th May 1967, also one-man operated but, because it served both Heathrow and Gatwick airports, required additional space for passengers' luggage. The modernised coaches dedicated to this service, which were allocated to St Albans and Reigate garages, therefore had the rearmost row of seats removed and replaced with luggage racks, reducing the capacity to thirty-five. The upshot was that three different classifications of modernised coach appeared: the OMO thirty-nine seater — RF2/4; the conductor operated thirty-nine seater — RF2/5; and the OMO thirty-five seater — RF2/6.

The thirty-four remaining RF2/1s which were not included in the modernisation programme were downgraded to buses between May 1966 and July 1967. Like their predecessors, they were classified RF5/5. Of the original 263 Green Line RFs, 175 were still in use on coach services, having been modified, sixty-four were now buses and twenty-four had been sold.

A well-loaded RF 99 passes a group of VC10s in London Airport on the highly successful 727. Another example of the many attempts to develop new business for the Green Line was the summer weekend extension of route 706 to Chartwell, which started in July 1966. Modernised RF 44 (opposite) shares the virtually deserted coach park with one uncertain looking woman and a Maidstone & District Harrington bodied AEC Reliance coach. John Aldridge

The immediate effect of the Phelps-Brown report was to remove the shackles preventing the introduction of one-man operation in the Central Area and no time was wasted in making use of this new freedom, although not exactly as planned in 1959. On 18th November 1964, four routes were converted, the 201 from Norbiton, the 206 from Fulwell, the 216 from Kingston and the 250 from North Street (Romford). Two more followed on 27th January 1965, routes 237 (Hounslow) and 251 (Edgware). The small (one bus) Sunday

operation on route 203 was added to Hounslow's operation from 4th July 1965. The different approach compared with the 1959 plan was designed to spread the human effects of the change around as many garages as possible, minimising the amount of redundancy among conductors in any one place and giving as many garages as possible the opportunity for higher earnings for some drivers.

To meet the increased and increasing demand for OMO buses, a further modification

programme of sixty-eight buses was authorised for completion during the first half of 1965. The bulk of the conversions coincided with overhaul and came out of works between 7th January and 10th June. Four of the vehicles which went to Luton in June 1965 were adapted to take Setright ticket machines only and were classified RF5/6. Ten others which went to Crawley and East Grinstead, also in June 1965, were designed to accept both Setright and Ultimate ticket machines and took the classification RF5/7. The RF5/6 classi-

The complex tracery of tram tracks in the garage yard had survived over thirty years, albeit filled with tar, since Fulwell's last tram, an unusual foreground to RFs 531 and 359. Lined up against the building are three RTWs, 200, 30 and 172, by now relegated to training duties. John Aldridge

fication disappeared in July 1966 when the vehicles were modified to take both types of machine and were reclassified RF5/7.

The steady advance of single-manning of Country Bus services had also continued, exclusively by use of the RF class. Double-deck routes 327 (4th November 1964), 429/439 (3rd October 1965) were converted, as was London's longest established 'lowbridge' double-deck route, the 336, together with companion route 359, whose RLHs were the first to be withdrawn. From 20th March 1966, the Watford to Hemel section of 318 had its RTs displaced by OMO RFs and the 313 and the Dunstable — St Albans portion of the 343 (renumbered 342) followed on 15th May. Even more sweeping displacements came in December 1966, when OMO RFs appeared, from New Year's Eve, on routes 323, 374, 431, 445 (replacing a GS), 460, 471 (replacing GSs) and 854 (renumbered 493). The last remaining single-deck routes still carrying conductors, the 391, 391A and 447 were also converted, the earlier belief that such town services were unsuitable now having been proved unduly cautious. This left only a handful of RFs still running on works and other special services which still had conductors because their duties included some double-deck work.

The vehicles for these changes came from the pool of spare vehicles thrown up by the continuing decline in service levels but the changes in the autumn of 1965 coincided with the start of a further overhaul cycle and some of the newly modified red RFs were used temporarily at Amersham, Reigate and St Albans.

Newly modified and overhauled, red RF 368 was placed on temporary loan to the Country department for the conversion of route 336 to one-man operation in October 1965. It is seen at the Watford Junction terminus in Woodford Road to which the route had transferred when its traditional terminus, Leavesden Road garage, closed. Alan B. Cross

The Central department continued to make use of its new agreement in advance of the main Reshaping Plan, by single-manning as many routes as possible using RFs. The first example of a red double-deck route to succumb, was included in the third stage of conversions on 3rd October 1965, when the Loughton — Epping section of route 20 became RF OMO, under the number 20B, signalling the abandonment of the rigid segregation of single-deck route numbers in the series above 200, which had prevailed since October 1934. Loughton also converted its established single-deck route 254 from the same date. In the same programme, the comparatively new and poorly patronised Ilford — Barking section of route 129, was also amputated and turned into a one-man operated route, numbered 291, using RFs. Further straightforward conversions took place in the Kingston area on 23rd January 1966, involving routes 215, 215A and 264 and, from 7th August, Enfield (double-deck route 121) and Croydon (route 234A). Also on 7th August, Harrow Weald started running a new route 136, demonstrating the advantage of one-man operation in allowing the introduction of services to otherwise commercially unpromising areas like Harrow Hill. For these conversions a further pro-gramme of vehicle modifications had been in progress, resulting in alterations to forty-two more RFs between 18th May and 30th September 1966.

Barking garage became a Regal IV operator in October 1965 when route 291 was created out of part of the 129. RF 506 is seen at the Barking end of the route. Capital Transport

The lowest numbered route on which RFs were officially scheduled was the 20B, though unscheduled appearances were made on sister route 20. The 20B, on which RF 518 is seen, was the first Central area double-deck route to be converted to single-deck one-man operation. Capital Transport

One of Harrow Weald's first allocation of RFs, in service at Harrow-on-the-Hill station during the first week of new route 136 in August 1966. College Road was then two-way. Capital Transport

Eight of the fleet of sixty-five 4RF4s take their layover at Gloucester Road Air Terminal. They were superseded by Routemasters in 1966-1967. W.H. Godwin

While these convulsive developments were affecting the standard RFs, the one remaining non-standard variety, the 4RF4, was still quietly going about its business on the airport services of British European Airways. Peter Masefield's assumption of a seven-year life had been doubled in practice and the coaches were still giving good and reliable service in the mid-sixties, the only casualty having been MLL742 which was withdrawn in July 1963 after being involved in an accident. However, the airline was anxious to improve its 'image', especially now that its fellow airline, BOAC, was using stylish new Atlanteans, which made the RFs look rather dated. London Transport persuaded BEA to adopt a variant of the Routemaster (ironically, a basic body design only two years younger than that of the RFs) and the first of these went into service in October 1966. All but one of the remaining sixty-three Regals was withdrawn in the following six months, spending their last days at the new BEA operating base at Chiswick Tram Depot, the last five being delicensed on 1st April 1967. The exception was MLL740 which was retained as a spare in support of the Routemaster fleet until May 1973. Many of the others then saw further service as specialist vehicles of one sort or another, such as mobile showrooms, caravans, and dining rooms for film crews. Four (MLL725, 727, 729 and 735) were retained by London Transport for use as a mobile uniform issuing stores, in which form they endured for another ten years, the last being withdrawn in February 1977. This (MLL735) and one other (MLL740) survived for preservation.

Just before the departure of the 4RF4s, BEA had embarked on another new venture, with the help once more of the RF class. On 1st August 1965, RFs 290-297 were licensed at Hammersmith to operate on the new 'Executive Express' service, which took passengers carrying only hand baggage, direct from the aircraft, on the apron at Heathrow, to West London Air Terminal. The vehicles remained in their green livery but a large white panel was added immediately below the saloon windows carrying the name 'executive express' in red lower case lettering (lower case was the design rage at the time) alongside the

contemporary symbol of the airline which carried the title 'BEA' in white italic capitals on a red rectangle. Side route boards were later fitted proclaiming the same message, in the same style. The Regals were used only as an interim measure until the airline could take delivery of eight new purpose built Willow-brook bodied 2U3RA model AEC Reliance coaches. These were all licensed on 20th July 1966 and the Regals were returned to London Transport service between 20th July and 25th September. Curiously, RF 91 was drafted in to help out the new Reliances from the end of September until early January 1967.

Above **RFs 295 and 293, dressed for the new Executive Express service of BEA, in the former trolleybus depot at Hammersmith in October 1965.** Alan B. Cross

RF 296 'airside' at Heathrow, waits to pick up a load from a British European Airways Vickers Vanguard airliner. BEA

Now that all its mainstream single-deck operations were one-man operated, developments in the Country Area concentrated on single-manning those double-deck routes which were considered suitable. At first this still meant using the RF, but the new generation vehicles of the MB family began to arrive in October 1967 and it was an RF route, the 447, which received the first of these to enter service in April 1968. Sadly, this was not the only source of Regals for use as double-deck replacements, because demand was melting away so fast that the Country Bus department found it necessary to make stringent economies each year during the late sixties and service levels were constantly being cut. These also hit the Green Line, which suffered a schedule cut of no fewer than twenty runnings during 1968 alone. In consequence, less than two years after their modernisation, twenty-four Green Line RFs were demoted to buses. Modification work included the removal of the front nearside seat, reducing them to thirty-seven seaters, and the side route board clips. The light green relief band was replaced by a band of yellow, the relief colour then being adopted on the new generation rear-engined buses. The fleetname was carried in Johnston type capitals in green, while the front and back bullseyes were also of a new style, the circle being in solid yellow, the bar in black and the legend LONDON TRANSPORT in yellow. The modified vehicles were given the body classification RF5/8. Another consequence of the continuing decline of fortune was the return of RFs to route 719 from 30th December 1967. The RMCs were used on route 708 so that its frequency could be reduced.

Meanwhile, the remaining coach RFs still not fitted for OMO were converted in readiness for an important change of direction for the coach services. The success of OMO on the 724 and 727 had convinced the Country department that the future wellbeing of the main network lay with single-manning and the entire single-deck operation was changed over in two stages, on 23rd November 1968 (routes 701, 702, 710, 711, 714, 719 and 720) and on 15th February 1969 (routes 706, 708, 712, 713, 725). These and the 724 and 727 were now the sum total of single-deck coach operation. Route 708 had now lost its RMCs, after just over a year's operation, while routes 707 and 715A had been withdrawn in the February cuts and routes 704, 705 and 709 had been converted to RCL operation in earlier changes.

The mixture of service cuts and replacement of some RFs by the new Swifts had created by now a surplus of Regals in the Country Bus fleet and it was decided to transfer thirteen of them to Central Buses, who had more scope for their use. The transferred vehicles were RFs 545, 563, 570, 580, 590, 598, 602, 603, 608, 617, 627, 632 and 685 and went, still painted green, to Muswell Hill on 1st January 1969. They were repainted red between 30th May and 21st July 1969.

Right **A contrast in RF styles, RF 157, on the left, was modernised in September 1966 then downgraded to bus in March 1968, but was still used for a time on coach work from St Albans garage. Alongside it at Golders Green, in the spring of 1968, Tottenham's RF 447 was almost in the same condition as when it first entered service at Dalston in February 1953.** Michael Beamish

Less than two years after being modernised for the relaunched Green Line 'image', RF 215 was one of twenty-four surplus coaches transferred to bus work in 1968. The relief colour was altered from light green to canary yellow and the Green Line roundels replaced by standard London Transport versions. In the background is a Godstone RML on route 410 indulging in the time-honoured custom, dating from East Surrey days, of making a connection at Westerham. E. Shirras

Modernised RF 38 in the last days of conductor operation of the Green Line, on route 717 at Sidcup on 26th October 1968. Route 717 was replaced by an extended 719 on 23rd November. Michael Beamish

Left **Looking more than ready for the repaint it was to get in June 1969, RF 617 was one of thirteen Country Bus Regals transferred to the Central area in January of that year. It is here setting off up North End Road, past the old Golders Green Hippodrome, on the Sundays only through working over route 236 to Leytonstone.**
Capital Transport

Centre **RF 56, a former coach, on St Albans local route 391 from which the class was ousted in February 1969 by 'Autofare' MBS class AEC Swifts.**
Michael Beamish

Below **Still carrying the 'DS' code of its former garage allocation at Dorking, RF 161 participated in London Transport's last conversion to one-man operation of a Country bus service, the 371 group of routes at Grays, in October 1969. This vehicle started its career with LT across the river at Northfleet seventeen-and-a-half years earlier and was modernised in December 1966.**
E. Shirras

During its last year as part of London Transport, Country Buses indulged a major onslaught on the lighter trafficked double-deck routes, converting to one-man operation no fewer than thirty-two routes during the course of the year. It also all but completed the removal of the GS class, with the conversion of route 309 to Regal IVs from 15th February 1969. By now, it was principally the MB family which provided the rolling stock for OMO conversions but the RF still had much to contribute and found itself being used to replace its double-deck contemporaries on many routes. It too was being replaced, however and the first examples of this came on 15th February when the RFs on St Albans's routes 391 and 391A were displaced by 'Autofare' MBS thirty-six footers, while those on Garston's 318 were pushed out by the 'conventional' OMO MB class. RFs appeared on many routes for the first time, albeit on Sundays only, as more services turned to single-manning on the quietest day of the week, using buses and drivers made available by the depressingly long list of routes from which Sunday services had been withdrawn. Routes 312, 338, 338A, 339, 358, 405, 406A and 476 were Sunday only conversions, while routes 402 from Dunton Green and Dartford's 486 were full conversions on 15th February. At the same time, the Crawley to Horsham section of double-deck route 405 was covered by an extension of OMO routes 434 and 473. On 14th June, the 468 got OMO RFs in place of RTs. The last conversion of all under LT auspices was the somewhat surprising use of RFs to replace RTs on the formerly extremely busy and frequent 371 group of routes in Grays, from 5th October 1969.

The fifteen-or-so-year old RF was also destined to play an important part in the development of the Central department's Reshaping Plan, whose start was severely delayed by labour relations conflict and did not get going until 7th September 1968. The class featured in the very first stage, providing the rolling stock for the conversion of route 90C (renumbered 290 and needing four buses) and for a new one-bus local Potters Bar route 284. Existing RF routes 218 and 219, which had been in the original 1959 list, were now also, at last, converted to OMO. Potters Bar and Twickenham garages were both new operators of the Regals. Within a matter of weeks, on 26th October, the first Central Bus route and garage to lose RFs was the 202 at New Cross, which was absorbed into new flat-fare routes P1 and P2, using MBS class standee single-deckers. Regals were again used to replace double-deckers on 22nd March 1969, when the outer ends of routes 80 and 80A were hived off and diverted to Morden as one-man operated services, using twelve RFs and reintroducing the class to Sutton garage after a lapse of over seven years. Another RF joined the fleet at Croydon, when new route 233 was introduced to serve Roundshaw estate on 31st May, but this lasted only until 21st November as the 233 became London's first double-deck OMO route, using an Atlantean (XA), the following day. Another route to lose RFs in favour of the new generation vehicles, this time the 'conventional' MB variant, was the 20B at Loughton which was withdrawn and replaced by an extension of route 20 on 14th June. Hounslow's small RF allocation was given a modest boost on 23rd August, when a new route 211, requiring three buses, took over the Hounslow to Hampton operation from the 111 when an experiment with 'split-entrance' operation of MBS buses started on that route. In passing it is interesting to note that the Sunday service on route 285 was converted to OMO using RFs from Fulwell and Norbiton, from 20th July 1969. This was the only example of a former trolleybus route being operated by the class.

The end of the sixties saw the RF still as the mainstay of both red and green single-deck fleets as London Transport stood poised for its first fundamental organisational shake-up since the LPTB was formed in 1933. Under the terms of the Transport (London) Act of 1969, the Central Bus operations were to be placed under the policy control of the (then Conservative) Greater London Council, day-to-day control being in the hands of a newly-constituted London Transport Executive, while the Country Bus department was to cease to be part of the undertaking altogether.

Above **The first Central Bus route to lose RFs was the 202, operated by New Cross garage, a curious back street route serving mainly factory areas, like the western terminus at Canal Bridge, RF 330 was the number borne by the example of the class which was displayed at the Commercial Motor Show in 1952 but by 1968, when this photograph was taken, the Aldenham factory overhaul process will have left little of the original.** Ken Glazier

Centre **Regal IVs returned to Sutton garage in March 1969 to introduce 'conventional' one-man operation to substantially modified routes 80/80A. The garage is in the background, as RF 454 turns from Bushey Road into Collingwood Road on a section formerly served by route 156.** Alan B. Cross

Right **The Sunday conversion of route 285 to one-man operation from July 1969 brought RFs to a former trolleybus route for the first and only time. RF 423 is seen at Hanworth.** Colin Stannard

13 THE LONDON COUNTRY YEARS

The Transport (London) Act of 1969, detached the Country Bus and Coach department from London Transport and incorporated it as a new subsidiary of the National Bus Company, the wholly owned government company responsible for the nationalised bus sector in England and Wales, outside London. The new company was given the ambiguous name 'London Country Bus Services Ltd' and its headquarters was established at the former Country department head offices in Bell Street, Reigate. On 1st January 1970, ownership of the entire 'green' fleet was transferred to LCBS which therefore inherited 413 RFs, only thirty-seven short of the number originally taken into stock by the Country Bus and Coach department between 1951 and 1954. Of these, 150 were 'modernised' Green Line coaches; interestingly, this left 263 buses, exactly the same number as had originally been coaches, aptly illustrating the change of relative fortunes of the two sub-types. Twenty-five of the buses were former coaches which had been modernised in 1966/67. A complete list of the transferred vehicles is shown in appendix five. There were also five red RFs which had been borrowed from Central Buses on 4th October 1969, to cover shortages in the Country fleet, which remained in London Transport ownership. RF 393 stayed until 24th November 1970 but RFs 325, 341, 374 and 388 were not returned until 5th March 1971.

Only one LCBS garage, Godstone, had no RFs allocated and the company's starting schedule called for a total of 241 buses and 132 Green Line coaches. This left twenty-seven buses and eighteen coaches, seven of which were unlicensed for various reasons (such as accident repairs) and the remainder allocated as spares, either as normal engineering support to the scheduled RF fleet, or to cover shortages in the more modern fleet of Swifts and Reliances. St Albans, with twenty-four buses and thirteen coaches, had the largest total allocation and the largest number of coaches, while Hatfield's three buses, held only as support vehicles to the otherwise wholly MB family and double-deck allocation, was the smallest. Hertford had the largest quantity of the bus version, its holding of thirty being sufficient to cover its entire single-deck operation.

The only immediate indication that anything had changed was the new 'legal owner' panel displaying the name and address of the fledgling business. As time wore on, the fleet was gradually repainted into the new livery, which was based on the 'Lincoln' green and canary yellow scheme which London Transport had already adopted on new single-deckers since 1968. The fleet name LONDON COUNTRY was applied in canary yellow block capitals in place of the LT name and a new company symbol replaced the traditional bulls-

eye. The new design, which attracted a number of ribald nicknames, betrayed some influence from the bullseye, although the company stoutly denied any connection. A solid circle was surrounded by a larger circle surmounted by a series of horizontal parallel lines, gradually diminishing in width and joined at their outer edges by sloping lines, all in canary yellow.

Above **One of the first targets the new London Country company set itself was 100% one-man operation. RF 572 works a crew journey on a works service to the large Slough Trading Estate in 1970.** E. Shirras

Facing Page Upper **Looking spick and span nearly three years after its last repaint in 1968, London Transport RF 388 spent just over two years on loan to the Country area and London Country, the last few months up to March 1971 at Crawley, working routes like the 426.** E. Shirras

Facing Page Lower **London Country's first corporate style was a close family likeness of its London Transport parent. The fleetname on the side in Johnston type; the other lettering, the destination blinds and the livery all look at home on RF 114 as it enters Butterwick from Hammersmith Road. The company symbol below the radiator filler cap housing generally appeared where the LT roundel had been carried previously.** J. Gascoine

The AEC Reliances which helped replace the RFs proved to be less reliable and durable. Route 727 was allotted RPs in August 1971 and RP 2 is seen at Watford in June 1973 after repaint into NBC corporate livery. Tom Maddocks

Opposite **Regal IVs increasingly appeared on some seemingly unlikely routes on Sundays. Hertford's trunk route 310 was converted in this way in 1971. RF 626 at Waltham Cross could still be mistaken for a London Transport bus.** Colin Stannard

From October 1972, the London Country fleet gradually began to appear with a main body colour of light 'national' green and white reliefs. Fleetnames, fleet numbers and wheel centres were finished in grey. During the remaining lifespan of the RF class, an untidy variety of liveries was to be borne, ranging from the old London Transport standard to the final NBC corporate style, depending on the life expectation of individual vehicles and the dates when they were due for overhaul or repaint. Another mark of the new owner's different approach to the appearance of vehicles was the gradual removal of wheel nut ring covers and rear wheel decorative discs.

On the day the company started business there were already 138 new Swifts on order, many of which had been intended by London Transport as replacements for the RF class, but the company almost immediately ordered ninety Leyland Atlanteans and a like number

of AEC Reliance coaches and announced that it was giving priority to the elimination of conductors as quickly as possible, in line with NBC policy. The new vehicles were accordingly earmarked to supersede RTs on bus work and the Routemasters on coach work. One of the company's earliest decisions, therefore, was that the RF would not be withdrawn for some time. A programme of overhauls was organised, using the facilities of London Transport's works, where 120 coaches got the full Aldenham treatment between February 1970 and September 1971.

Nevertheless, replacement of the class began in the autumn of 1970, when RFs on route 711 were replaced, from 18th October, by the much troubled RC class which had been idle for some time, all but two of them having been delicensed at the time of the company's formation. No Regals were withdrawn, however, the bulk of those released going to

Garston, Hemel Hempstead and Northfleet as additional spares. Reigate retained one and one went to St Albans, both being required for route 727 whose allocation was increased on the same day.

Further Green Line retrenchment came on 20th February 1971, when route 710 was withdrawn between Uxbridge and London. The four RFs which this released were used to replace the borrowed London Transport vehicles, which were returned to their owner the following month. In the same programme of service changes, new route 405A at Crawley used a mixture of RF and MB vehicles. Other new recruits to the class, on Sundays only, were Hemel Hempstead's 320 and 320A, St Albans's 330 and Harlow's 397, 397A, 805, 805A and 805B. There were also some weekend withdrawals, a feature which was now becoming so commonplace that detailed reference would become tedious.

Between February 1970 and October 1972 route 710 ran only between Uxbridge and Amersham, RF 165, sporting the short-lived LCBS company symbol, leaves Uxbridge in March 1971. Alan B. Cross

Some rescheduling in Grays on 3rd July 1971 brought RFs to routes 370 and 370A for the first time, although only for occasional journeys on Mondays to Fridays. Double-deck route 300 also went over to RF OMO on Sundays. A major programme the following month had a considerable impact on the Regal fleet. From 8th August, routes 329, 351 and 381 were withdrawn and substantial reductions were made on routes 322, 355, 364, 365, 413 and Green Line 712, mainly as a result of reduced County Council financial support. There were also some further newcomers to RF operation, routes 306 (shared wth MBs), 310, 310A and 396 all being converted to one-man operation on Sundays. Later in the same month, on 27th August, Green Line route 711 once again became RF operated, the Reliances being returned to their former home on route 727. Not that this was to last long, as these in turn were replaced by the new Reliances (RP class) that December. At about the same time Dunton Green garage received an allocation of AEC Swift (SM class) buses which displaced a number of bus Regals. Between September and November, another twelve coach RFs were downgraded to bus specification and the combined effect of all these changes was to release fifteen Regal IVs for sale.

One effect of the wider spread of operation by RFs was that the destination blinds became substantially longer and began to exceed the capacity of the rollers. To overcome this problem, a more abbreviated display was introduced so that the top and bottom sections of the display glass had to be masked with black paint. The first garage to need this treatment was Amersham, whose vehicles were altered in March 1971.

Amersham was the first garage where it was necessary to reduce the size of the destination display to allow more routes to be included on a given length of blind. RF 305, seen here at Chesham Broadway, originally a bus, then a coach, reverted again to bus to replace Amersham's GSs on routes like the 348. Dunton Green was among the garages which followed. RF 653 passes RF 686 in Knockholt Pound. E. Shirras

One of fifteen Swifts acquired from South Wales Transport in 1971, SMW 11 was one of twelve Marshall bodied vehicles allocated to St Albans garage to assist RFs with one-man conversions.

London Country's vehicle policy in this period can best be described as 'grab what you can, as quickly as you can' as the company tried to reduce the average age of its fleet and eliminate rear entrance double-deckers, whatever their age. In addition to the new buses on order, the company was able to take a large number of vehicles, owned or ordered by other NBC companies and not now required by them. Among these was a group of Willowbrook bodied AEC Swifts transferred from South Wales Transport, which arrived between June and October 1971. These were classified SMW and used, not to replace RFs but, alongside RFs, to convert St Albans routes 338, 338A, 343 and 358 to one-man operation from 8th January 1972. From the same date, in Kent, the 431A, 431B, 451, 480A, 489 and 489A routes were withdrawn, as was the Brasted to Sevenoaks section of 413. Double-deck routes 454 and 454A were simultaneously converted to one-man operation, using some of the displaced RFs at Dunton Green. Nine more Regals were withdrawn, five in October (when the first of the SMWs had been licensed at St Albans) and four in January. Less than a month later, on 5th February, there were more withdrawals, routes 337, 352, 359, 364A and 394 disappearing in whole or in part. Luton's double-deck (RT) route 360 took over some of the released resources and became a new user of Regal IVs. More Sunday-only recruits at this time were Windsor's 446, 446A and 458 (the latter actually reverting from MBS, which had been allocated in July 1971). Six more RFs joined the increasing list of withdrawn vehicles. The vehicles selected for withdrawal were the buses due for overhaul, leaving the recently overhauled former coaches to continue in service.

Another batch of twenty-one Alexander bodied Swifts (the SMA class), originally intended for South Wales Transport, were put into service on Green Line route 725, from Northfleet, Dartford and Windsor garages on 4th March 1972, replacing RFs. The displaced coaches were transferred to bus work, twenty being modified during March. Seventeen buses were released for disposal (although two of these were later reinstated).

The second half of 1972 saw no letting up in the relentless cutting back of services as the company struggled to balance its books. From 14th October, part or all of routes 333, 373, 388, 445 and 710 were withdrawn, while further losses to the RF family of routes came with the conversion of the 460 to MBS from Staines garage and the replacement of RFs by Atlanteans (AN class) on the 805 group at Harlow on Sundays. There were some modest off-setting advances: a new experimental route 372 was introduced on 18th September between High Wycombe and Amersham, which used RFs (but only until 24th November, after which MBSs took over); and some of the double-deck journeys on the 384 were converted to RF OMO.

Thirteen more coaches were demoted and modified for bus work between April and October, releasing thirteen buses for withdrawal in October (nine) and November.

Above **In February 1972, Luton town service 360 lost its RT double-deckers in favour of one-man operated RFs released by major service cuts following the withdrawal of County subsidies.** Peter Graves

Left **A remarkable error which appeared on some blinds in 1972 was the reversal of the fleetname to read 'LINE GREEN', as displayed on bus RF 667 at Hitchin on a soggy August day.** John Gascoine

Between February 1969 and January 1973, Crawley's route 434 was operated by a mixture of RF and MBS class vehicles. In the last days of London Transport's stewardship, RF 672 and MBS 379 share Crawley Bus Station with two Southdown single-deckers on their New Town service 79 to Gossops Green.

The company's next order for Green Line vehicles was part of its first clutch of Leyland Nationals. The original intention had been that sixty-eight of the seventy ordered would be used on Green Line work, starting the replacement of the Regals in earnest, but there was a change of approach. The company really wanted a single-door version of the National for use on the Green Line, where speed of boarding and alighting had a lower priority than a comfortable seating arrangement, and had been lobbying Leyland to produce one. Leyland was reluctant to break with the principles of rigid standardisation and 'mass-production' on which the success of the model was supposed to be based but London Country finally succeeded in breaking the manufacturer's determination in time for this first order to be modified. Forty-seven were built to the new specification and assigned to the Green Line, while the remaining thirty-three dual-door vehicles were diverted to bus work.

The first Regals to be toppled by Nationals (LN class) were at Dunton Green, where the four RFs on route 493 were replaced on 1st January 1973. The next batch went to Hatfield, where they replaced SMs and MBSs. The SMs went to Addlestone to replace RFs on routes 427, 437, 456 and 462, while the MBSs went to Crawley for the 426 and to replace the remaining RFs still working the 405, 405B, 434 and 473. Further deliveries of LNs to Hatfield later in the year went onto trunk routes 303 and 303A, until then operated by MBs. The displaced MBs went to Dorking to replace RFs on routes 412, 425 and 439 between June and September and to Guildford, for route 425, during September. Some of the Regals went, in turn, to Amersham where they replaced vehicles in the 289-297 series for disposal.

Canary yellow replaced the cream relief colour on unmodernised Regals too and was used for fleet name and number, as on RF 42 at Dorking bus station. J. Gascoine

The Green Line version of the National (LNC) went first to route 721 at Romford, where, on 3rd March 1973, vehicles of this type displaced Reliances onto routes 720 (Harlow) and 724 (Romford and Staines), from which the coach RFs were withdrawn. The thirty-five seat RFs which had been running on the 724 since May 1972 were sent to Staines and Northfleet for use on routes 701 and 702. Later deliveries of the LNC went onto routes 706 at Tring (during April and May) and 711 (from 26th May at Reigate; 1st June at High Wycombe), where they replaced Regals directly. Despite the age of the RFs, they were in good condition and still gave a quiet and comfortable ride, so the sudden appearance of the much noisier and harder seated (though softer sprung) Nationals must have come as something of a shock to passengers.

Although the first half of 1973 had been relatively quiet in terms of service changes, this was put right on 7th July with another round of alterations which included the withdrawal of RF operated routes 337, 364, 494 and 702. Over the nine months from January to September, sixty-four RFs had been withdrawn and seventeen coaches downgraded to bus specification.

Route 721 received the first Leyland National coaches in March 1973 but, in August 1974, had borrowed RF 125 from Grays to work this journey from Aldgate, presumably to cover vehicle shortages. By this time, RF 125 had been repainted into NBC corporate green, a much lighter colour than the traditional 'Lincoln' green but retained the original style of fleetname. In this version of the livery, the wheel centres were painted grey. G.F. Walker/J. Gascoine

Vehicle orders for 1973 included forty-five short wheelbase Nationals (SNC) for the Green Line and twenty-three Bristol LHS single-deckers (the BL class) for bus work. Most of the BLs entered service on 20th October 1973, at Dunton Green (routes 404 and 421) and St Albans (routes 304, 313 Sundays, 355 and 382). The rest went to Amersham where they replaced RFs on the 348 and 359 on 15th December and the 349 and 394 on 5th January 1974. The 349 was the new number given to the 348A and 348B because the three-track number blind displays fitted to the BLs could not cope with suffix letters. St Albans had another intake of BLs starting on 4th May, this time for routes 338, 358 and 361. This coincided with the allocation of new short-wheelbase bus Nationals (SNBs) to route 313.

The SNCs entered service between December 1973 and April 1974, progressively replacing coach RFs. The first went onto route 708 from East Grinstead and Hemel Hempstead on 15th December 1973, then came Garston's route 719 (26th January 1974), Dorking and Luton's 714 (9th March), routes 712 and 713 at Dorking and St Albans garages (6th April) and, finally, route 701 at Northfleet and Staines (7th September).

This part of the fleet renewal programme led to the withdrawal of twenty-eight RFs between October 1973 and May 1974 but such was the parlous state of the rest of the fleet that no fewer than fourteen of them were reinstated in January and February. Ten more coaches were downgraded to bus specification during December. Only four more were to be so treated during the remaining lifetime of the class.

During the summer of 1974 and before any more fleet renewal took place, there were some fairly severe service cuts in the Addlestone, Amersham, Grays and Leatherhead areas which allowed the withdrawal of six more RFs in July and August.

Above **Unlike the RFs which it replaced, BL 8 is in every respect an NBC corporate bus, transforming this St Albans scene to one that could be seen almost anywhere in the country.** Alan B. Cross

Left **RF 75, downgraded from coach to bus in December 1973, heads north out of East Grinstead on a short-working run to Victoria on 11th September 1974, still helping out on route 708, normally operated by short Leyland Nationals (SNC).** J. Gascoine

Below **The Regals were constantly being used to cover for deficiencies in the rest of the fleet, which was in a pretty poor state in the mid-1970s. RF 169, back on home ground working as a Green Line coach at Butterwick, Hammersmith in June 1974 has the reduced indicator display introduced in 1971 to accommodate the larger number of routes operated by the class at many garages.** J. Gascoine

Two applications of the standard NBC livery to RFs are seen in the mid-1970s on RFs 65 and 550, the former being relieved by grey painted wheels and the retention of unpainted metal beading where the relief colour was once carried. G.F. Walker/Capital Transport

Dorking's Regals were replaced in November 1974. Pioneer Green Line RF 26 survived to receive full NBC corporate livery, as seen here at Golders Green when the Dorking management allowed it one day to relive former glories by doing a turn on route 713. RF 26 was withdrawn in December 1975.
Michael Beamish

Thirty more Bristols were ordered for delivery in 1974 but this time they were 7ft 6ins wide and intended as replacements for RFs working on routes where road widths were inadequate, for full size vehicles. The specification, which required a length of 26ft 5¾ins, was therefore very reminiscent of some of the early thoughts on the RF class. On 28th September the first deliveries went to Northfleet, where they operated on routes 450, 489 and 490 and displaced the last Regals from that location. Dorking and Guildford garages were next, from 9th November, their allotment going to routes 412 and 432 respectively, with some appearances on the 414, 415, 425 and 449. Guildford's last scheduled RF was replaced by an MB from 9th December. The remaining BNs went to Chelsham, for routes 464, 465 and 485, from 21st December, Hertford for routes 308, 350, 351, 386, 388, with journeys on most of Hertford's other routes (22nd February 1975) and, finally, Leatherhead for routes 416 and 419, with journeys on the 462, 468 and 481. The process was somewhat delayed and long drawn out by the need for drivers to be trained on and acquire licences to drive manual gearbox vehicles. The 468 was itself converted to BN in two stages in March and November 1975.

Apart from the direct replacement of Regals by new buses and coaches, there was also a programme of redeployment going on in the rest of the fleet. London Country had finally succeeded in convincing Leyland that a coach version of the National was needed and had placed an order for thirty-two of the so-called 'suburban coach' version for delivery during 1974. As these new Leyland Nationals came in, they were used to replace the earlier examples on the Green Line, these in turn going elsewhere to take over from Reliances, SMs and MB family vehicles on the busier bus routes. The vehicles released by this game of musical chairs ultimately replaced RFs.

Route 387 at Tring received redeployed LNCs, replacing its sole remaining RF and MBS vehicles from 23rd March; then on 3rd August 1974, the RC class Reliances which had been running on the 723 from Grays were replaced by SNC class Leyland Nationals. The Reliances were sent to Hertford and downgraded to bus work, in which guise from 10th August they replaced RFs on routes 327, 331 and 337 and the Hertford share of routes 390, 392 and 393. They were also used instead of RFs, from 12th August, on routes 350, 351, and 384. From 19th October 1974, displaced MB or MBS buses were allocated to route 426A at Crawley, 425 and 439 at Guildford and Dorking and 440 at Reigate, while routes 462 and 462A at Addlestone and Leatherhead (and 468 on Saturdays), were taken over by the short version of the AEC Swift (SM class). Other Regals were replaced directly by SNB class Leyland Nationals, those at Dunton Green for route 402 and at East Grinstead for routes 428, 434, 435 and 473 being displaced on 15th March 1975. Later in the year, on 30th August, further route changes in the Dartford and Reigate areas led to the withdrawal of the last RFs still running on routes 440, 447 and 486. On the same day Dunton Green ceased Saturday operation of the class, the remaining workings on the 431 and 471 being converted to BL and, at Harlow, route 380 lost RFs in favour of farebox Atlanteans.

On 3rd October 1975 Green Line route 701 was withdrawn and the SNC class Leyland Nationals which had been running it were transferred to Chelsham for route 706, replacing the last RFs scheduled for all-day coach operation, and Staines, where they dislodged the RPs from the 724. Chelsham's Regals were distributed around the fleet as additional spares. Further inroads into the remaining scheduled operations of the class were made on 29th November; the RF runnings on Amersham's route 305 switched to BL; all but one of those on route 336 were replaced by SMs; Leatherhead's 418, 468 and 481 lost their last RFs in favour of SMs; and High Wycombe lost its last Regal, from route 442 which got an MB instead.

All of these losses were minutely compensated during the summer by two interesting 'reversions'. During June, RF 166 was allocated to permanent two-person operation on routes 452, 457 and 458 at Windsor in support of the ailing double-deck fleet. Then, on 4th July, a new route 365 was introduced between Luton and Kimpton (on Fridays and Saturdays only), replacing one formerly operated by Jey-Son Coaches and using an RF. Again, for purposes of crew rostering, some journeys carried a conductor.

In the fifteen months covered by this phase of the vehicle renewal programme, from September 1974 to December 1975, one hundred and fifty-five Regals were withdrawn, a total of 300 of the original 413 having by now gone.

Another 1975 withdrawal, this time in January, was RF 610 which, in this view at Slough station, demonstrates the neglect apparent in much of the fleet in the mid-1970s. The 458 was one of the last routes to have an official allocation of Regals. Alan B. Cross

RF 68 at Kimpton on a crew operated Saturday journey on route 365 between Luton and Codicote taken over from an independent operator by London Country in July 1975. Bob Turner

Regal renaissance at Leatherhead, RF 54 and two others were drafted in during 1977 to cover the temporary absence of BNs. Normally used on the 416 and 419, they sometimes strayed elsewhere, as in this case on route 418 at Leatherhead garage where RT 2836 is about to terminate.
Lens of Sutton

Left **Modernised RF 145 at Bennetts Gate, Hemel Hempstead, in May 1975, downgraded to bus work, has a three-line intermediate point display on its destination blind for route 320A.** Ian Pringle

Below **Looking very sorry for itself indeed and wearing its twenty-six years wearily, RF 200 leaves Garston garage on 6th May 1977 to work a journey to Hemel Hempstead on Green Line route 719, one of the last operated by this bus. The chalked route number was a symptom of the generally run-down state of the company in the mid-1970s.**
Roland Hummerston

RF 125 at Windsor bus station in December 1977, flanked by an SNC and RP on the right and an SM on the left, the modern fleet it was held in reserve to support. R.M. Gillespie

The next order for new vehicles, for delivery during 1976, concentrated on the 10.3 metre version of the Leyland National and comprised a further thirty coaches and, the first to be ordered as buses, twenty-five SNBs. The same combination of direct and indirect replacements was continued during the delivery of these vehicles, which, when complete, all but removed the RF class from the fleet.

The first of the bus Nationals went to Luton garage between 22nd and 29th January 1976, where they replaced the Regals on routes 365 and 366, as well as route 360 on Sundays, although it was not until October that Luton lost its last RF. Over the same period and continuing until 7th February, the first coaches of the 1976 batch were going to High Wycombe and Reigate for route 711. Reigate retained its displaced LNs as buses, replacing MBSs which were sent to Crawley. There they replaced SMs which went to High Wycombe, whose MBs were supposed to go to Hemel Hempstead to allow the withdrawal of RFs from route 322. But this did not happen and instead, they were dispersed around the fleet as urgently needed spares. The remaining SNC deliveries during February went to Romford, again for the 724 and this time releasing RP class Reliances for deployment as late-running coaches at Dunton Green and Windsor, which had been the last scheduled allocation of RFs to Green Line work.

February's bus Nationals went to Harlow, where they operated on routes 390, 392, 393; Hertford for routes 308, 333, 350, 351 and 384; and Grays, for routes 323, 357, 371, 371A and 371B (plus the odd runnings on 328, 367 and 368). They dislodged the last of Harlow's Regals, as they did at Grays, except for one solitary vehicle retained for the 374 until a major route reorganisation could take place on 3rd April. The Grays changeover was otherwise completed on 6th March. Starting on that date and over the next few weeks, most of the RFs still working at Dunton Green, principally on routes 431 and 471 but also for odd journeys on most of its other routes, were replaced by short wheelbase Swifts, released from 'Superbus' service at Stevenage and repainted. The clearance of Regals from Dunton Green was completed on 22nd May, when some SMs displaced from Crawley by a schedules revision, were transferred to the Kent garage for use on route 413.

The next garage to say farewell to the Regal was Amersham, where the remaining workings on 332 (school days) and 336 switched to SM between 3rd and 20th March, while the RFs still at work on the 349, 353 (Saturdays), 359 and 394 gave way to BLs. The Swifts made available by the arrival of SNBs at Chelsham (from Garston which had got new SNCs for the 719), allowed also the completion of route 486 at Dartford with the class.

The chequered history of the Green Line continued its downward spiral with a substantial reduction of route 716, including the withdrawal of the Chertsey service altogether, in May 1976. This released a quantity of RP class Reliances which were demoted to bus work at Stevenage, after less than five years in use as coaches, to replace RFs on routes 303, 383 and 384 and Hertford, where the last Regals were removed, primarily from route 384 but also from 327, 331, 337, 350 and 351, on which a few scheduled runnings had still existed.

There was also a big programme of service changes in Hemel Hempstead on 15th May, followed by yet more changes on 19th June, which led to RFs disappearing from routes 307 (apart from odd journeys), 317, the 319 group, the 322, 334 and 344. Hemel finally lost its Regals at the beginning of October as a direct result of Green Line route 703 being withdrawn and the 721 severely reduced. These changes released LNB Nationals for use on routes 300 and 303 at Hatfield who in turn sent SNBs to Hemel Hempstead. Garston also lost most of its remaining RFs by the same means but was unable to replace those on route 309 which was not physically suitable for the larger bus and therefore had to await the availability of smaller new vehicles. Other displaced SNBs were used to complete the conversion of Staines garage (route 460, 466 and 469).

By the end of 1976 the only routes to have an official allocation of RFs were the 309 from Garston garage and the 446A (Sundays only), 452 (Sundays) and 458 from Windsor. None survived for long. The Windsor routes received an allocation of SMs on 7th January and route 309 was given BNs when it was reallocated from Garston to Amersham on 29th January as part of a series of service changes in Hertfordshire and Buckinghamshire. This hardy class was not yet finished, though. On the very day that Garston lost its scheduled allocation, Windsor started a temporary service, numbered 335, on behalf of Chiltern District Council between Gerrards Cross and Little Chalfont, using RFs, to cover one of the services lost in the schedule changes. This ran for the last time on 26th February. Then, when the experimental 'Dial-a-Ride' minibus in Harlow was replaced by a new route operated by BN class buses in April 1977, the vehicles were obtained from Leatherhead garage, where they were replaced by RFs 54, 79 and 218 until further Bristols could be delivered in August and October 1977. They normally ran on the 416 and 419 but sometimes appeared on other routes when there were vehicle shortages in other classes. There were also another fifteen Regals sprinkled all over the fleet, providing essential spares support to the more modern fleet of less reliable buses.

This support role sustained the small number of RFs for a couple more years but the bulk of them were withdrawn between May and October 1977, four more going between January and May 1978. The last of this group to be withdrawn was the only survivor of the original bus version, RF 684, which saw out its last days, still in traditional 'Lincoln' green, at Chelsham, where it was delicensed on 20th May 1978.

The only two to survive this clearout were RFs 202 and 221 which had been recertified in June 1977, after which they saw service at Northfleet and Chelsham respectively. RF 221 was a coach which had not been modernised and appeared in the final form of National Bus Company corporate livery, while RF 202 was a modernised coach and received the GREEN LINE fleetname within the corporate livery. In October 1978, RF 221 developed a defect which was not worth remedying and the bus was abruptly withdrawn.

RF 202 continued to serve on routes 489 and 490, with the occasional outing on Green Line routes 725 and 726 until it too was withdrawn just as abruptly after experiencing a gearbox failure in July 1979. Although it had outlasted its siblings in the London Transport fleet by four months, therefore, the London Country RF disappeared from formal service operation without ceremony. Fortunately, the rites due to such a thoroughbred had been carried out by London Transport in March, as will be recorded in the next chapter.

RF 202 itself was resurrected and continued as a preserved service bus with LCBS and later Kentish Bus. It was overhauled and repainted in original Green Line livery in May 1980 as part of the Green Line Jubilee celebrations. It was withdrawn in about June 1989 but nevertheless received a new registration (XKE164A) in November 1989. RF 202's registration, MLL589 was transferred to a Leyland Tiger.

Above **The side panels were authorised for advertising but on vehicles with the fleetname in the traditional position, this was often covered up, as in the case of RF 214 at Slough bus station in January 1976.** Alan B. Cross

Below **The longest surviving example of the traditional 'Lincoln' green colour scheme was on RF 684 which spent its last days at Chelsham and was not withdrawn until 20th May 1978. In this photograph, taken ten days before it was withdrawn, it is in Salmons Lane West, Whyteleafe on route 453.** Roland Hummerston

Facing Page Upper **RF 221 started and finished life at Chelsham garage, twenty-seven years elapsing between the two events. In its final form, as here at Oxted station on 28th September 1978, it had the later version of the NBC 'corporate identity', with the fleetname in white lettering on the roof panels and the red and blue 'double-N' symbol. It was abruptly withdrawn within a month of this photograph being taken.** Paul Hulyer

Facing Page Lower **The ultimate survivor. RF 202 was still a Green Line coach and one of only two Regals still in service when photographed at Market Square, Bromley on 29th July 1978. It was withdrawn in July 1979 but returned as a preserved vehicle and, at the time of writing, is still owned by Kentish Bus, one of London Country's successor companies.** Roland Hummerston

14 THE LAST YEARS WITH LONDON TRANSPORT

Having handed over 413 of the class to the newly-formed London Country company, London Transport started the new phase of its history with a total of 233, of which seventy-eight were still in their original condition and suitable only for use with conductors. Thirty of these were converted for one-man operation, starting with RF 324 which went to Aldenham Works in June 1970 as the pilot conversion, the remainder being done between November 1970 and the end of January 1971. These conversions could be distinguished from earlier examples by having a modified cab door and one-piece glazing on the glider doors. They were given the classification RF5/9. Some of these buses were made available by their displacement from route 208, which changed its identity on 18th April 1970, when it became flat-fare route S2 and received an allocation of MBS class thirty-six footers. The remaining forty-six were the first major block of the class to be formally withdrawn, those at Bromley being replaced on route 227 by SMS class AEC Swifts on 2nd January 1971 and those at Dalston and Leyton, on route 236, similarly ousted on 18th April 1971.

Meanwhile the role of the class in the 'Reshaping' programme continued. On 24th January 1970 the route which had been the original home of the red RF, the 210, was converted to one-man operation, still using RFs. There was then a lull in conversions until the first of the modified vehicles was available. The change to route 210 had coincided with a large number of alterations connected with the opening of the Victoria Line and some reductions on OMO route 143. To maintain the level of one-man operation at Highgate, part of the revised 210 was allocated to that garage, introducing the RF class to another site for the first time. On 18th April, Riverside followed this trend by taking over the operation of RF-operated route 290 from Twickenham garage which closed that day. Two route numbers which appeared on the class for the first time were the 151, which was reintroduced as a foreshortened off-peak only operation using one RF from Sutton on 10th October 1970 and the 71, which was converted to one-man operation on Sundays only, using RFs released from cuts on route 218, from 2nd January 1971. The indifferently

supported 151 lasted only until 16th April 1971. The 71 proved to be more enduring and had a different claim to fame, in that the use of the longer single-decker enforced a Sundays only re-routeing.

The newly-modified Regals made an appearance on 10th January 1971, when the routes serving the Uxbridge to West Drayton corridor lost their RT double-deckers in favour of RFs, reintroducing the class to Uxbridge garage and introducing one-man operation to routes 204, 223, 224 and 224A. From the same date, the recently introduced 211 was absorbed into an extended route 111 and the RFs supplied to it by Hounslow garage were replaced by SMSs. Another route to lose RFs, this time being displaced by the MBS class, was Harrow Weald's 136, from 24th July 1971.

Above **The RF was the longest vehicle which could be accommodated at Riverside garage, which got an allocation of the class in April 1970 when Twickenham closed. RF 412 is leaving Wakefield Road bus stand, Richmond, in December 1972, advertising bus driver jobs at £37.50 a week.**
J. Gascoine

RF 525 at Carshalton Beeches on the reduced 151 operation introduced for an unsuccessful six-month trial between October 1970 and April 1971. J.G.S. Smith

A Sundays only RF conversion was that of the 71 from October 1970. RF 369 is seen in Kingston the following year. Colin Stannard

The series of vehicles from RF 359 were given what today would be cherished registrations. RF 359 is seen at Hounslow on that garage's 211 route, withdrawn in January 1971. Colin Stannard

Hounslow's RF allocation was boosted again from 18th September 1971, when route 202 was single-manned. From the same day, Palmers Green joined the list of garages operating the veteran class with the conversion of route 212 (Palmers Green — Dollis Hill) from RT to RF, again one-man operated. The vehicles for both of these changes came from Highgate and Muswell Hill, where route 210 had lost its Regals, after almost exactly nineteen years continuous operation by the class, in favour of the increasingly dominant SMS class.

The Regals continued to operate reliably despite their age, while the buses of the new generation were giving serious trouble. The changes and delays to the main 'Reshaping' programme preoccupied the Executive during most of 1972 and 1973 but a decision on replacing the RFs could not be delayed much longer. Most of the OMO RFs had been given a fourth overhaul during 1971 but a number became due during 1973 and, rather than undertake another overhaul programme at such a late stage, it was decided that they should be withdrawn. To release the required number, Barking received DMS double-deckers for route 291 on 10th March 1973 and Uxbridge received a batch of SMS class buses for route 204 on 30th June. This bought time for arrangements to be made for the systematic withdrawal of the remainder of the class in 1975/76.

RF 443 undergoing overhaul at Aldenham in 1972, one of the last to be given this treatment, and shortly after in service on route 202, from Hounslow garage, rounding the corner at The Quadrant, Richmond.
John Gascoine

202 Twickenham Whitton
Hall Rd Bridge Rd
HOUNSLOW BUS STATION

LONDON TRANSPORT

PAY AS YOU ENTER
PLEASE

MXX 420

The Executive sought authority in the autumn of 1973 for a major bus purchasing programme, which was eventually sanctioned by the Greater London Council. The orders, announced in March 1974, included ninety-five Bristol LHS chassis with thirty-nine seat bodywork by Eastern Coach Works of Lowestoft, most of which were intended as replacements for RFs on routes where the larger modern vehicles were not suitable. Another important part of the programme was a plan to modify 115 of the standee version of the AEC Swift (SMS) to fully seated layout (classified SMD), in which form some were intended to replace RFs on routes where larger vehicles were acceptable. A few routes were also identified as being worth converting to double-deck operation and the orders for new Fleetlines made allowance for this. The routes identified for SMD were 215, 218, 219, 251 and 264.

The planned use of the SMDs was substantially modified as the programme proceeded because routes 215, 251 and 264 were found, after all, not to be physically suitable for the larger (SMD-class) vehicles. Routes 212, 254 and 258 were found to be in need of larger capacity vehicles and were in turn removed from the BL programme. Finally, in the case of routes 218 and 219, it was the inadequate size of the inspection pits in Kingston garage which prevented their operation by the 33ft SMD class.

Towards the end of RF operation with London Transport, the layout of the front destination blinds on single-deckers changed. Edgware was one of only three garages (the others being Norbiton and Uxbridge) to receive RF blinds which had nearside route numbers. RF 352 is seen at Mill Hill in April 1976. Capital Transport

Regals, like RF 401, served the newly opened Brent Cross Shopping Centre for only a matter of weeks, before being replaced on route 212 by SMS class AEC Swifts in March 1976. Capital Transport

There were the seemingly inevitable delivery delays and the withdrawal of the class did not start in earnest until 22nd March 1976, when Palmers Green's allocation of RFs on route 212 was replaced by SMSs, released from route 239 which received Fleetline double-deckers. Loughton's route 254 followed with a similar exchange on 10th April 1976. The first Bristols went to North Street on 24th April, replacing Regals on the 250 (and RTs on the 247). Riverside's small allocation on route 290 was changed over on 9th May, then came routes 80 and 80A at Sutton (27th June), 264 and 206 at Fulwell (19th July and 22nd August respectively), the 216 (and 71 on Sundays) at Kingston (26th September) and route 215 at Norbiton on 24th October. The 121 at Enfield was one of the routes which was reckoned to justify double-decking and its Regals were replaced by DMS vehicles with twice the carrying capacity, on 25th October 1976. More Bristols arrived at Kingston and Norbiton on 8th November to cover the operation of route 201 and completing, for the time being, RF replacement at those garages. RF operation at Uxbridge garage came to an end for the second and final time on 12th December 1976, with the introduction of double-deck DMS class one-man buses onto routes 223 and 224B and standee Swifts onto the 224. The remaining conversions to BL took place in the new year. On 23rd January 1977, Croydon lost its Regals from route 234A and Edgware from route 251. Hounslow's allocation on routes 202 and 237 was displaced by Bristols on 17th April 1977.

At about this time the last of the class should have been withdrawn but the restrictions imposed by the inspection pits at Kingston still prevented the operation of anything larger than the RF from that garage. The consequences gave a curious echo of the situation in the early 1950s when the replacement of the vintage 1T1s had to be delayed because of the weight limit on Walton Bridge. Route 218 was again one of the culprits, this time joined by the 219. The number of buses needed for this joint operation exceeded the number of BLs still available and no new vehicles were on order. To keep the service going while a solution was found, it was decided to recondition twenty-five of the class, to a standard sufficient to obtain three-year Certificates of Fitness. Most of the buses so treated appeared in the contemporary livery (first introduced in the summer of 1973) in which the traditional LONDON TRANSPORT fleetname had been replaced by a white roundel, devoid of lettering, which was carried in some cases on the panel immediately below the second saloon window, and on others below the third window. The fleet number was also applied in white letters and numbers. Some, however, retained the traditional gold transfer underlined fleetname or the later version in straight Johnston capitals. The work was done at Hanwell and Stonebridge garages. On 12th March 1978 code RF5/10 was officially introduced to denote that an Almex ticket machine could be fitted.

Upper Left **Passingford Bridge saw its last RFs in April 1976 when North Street received Bristols to replace RF 428 and its siblings.** Capital Transport

Left **RF 517 at Sunbury Village on 13th April 1977, four days before route 237 received its allotment of Bristols.** J. Blake

This vestigial but not insubstantial operation continued for just under two years, the Regals continuing to give a high standard of reliability and quality of ride, while the future of yet another generation of its successors, the SM family, was under review. The vehicle chosen for the premature replacement of many

of the Swifts was the Leyland National and it was to be this class which eventually replaced the Regals at Kingston. The solution to the problem of the inspection pits was elegant in its simplicity: the two routes were reallocated to Norbiton garage, which had pits of the correct dimensions.

Top **Twenty-five Regals were recertified in 1977/1978 to keep the 218 and 219 going, RF 522 was given the treatment at Hanwell**. J. Blake

Above **RF 520, originally RF 301, was over twenty-five years old but still looking very healthy when photographed working on route 219 in the late seventies.** Capital Transport

Left **An early morning journey to Shepperton in the last days of RF operation, worked by RF 492 at Hersham**
R.M. Gillespie

Below Left **The last journey to the BAC works at Weybridge by a Regal IV was worked by RF 507, which was also the last service bus, with the same driver, arriving at Kingston in the early hours of 31st March.**
R.M. Gillespie

The last full day of service operation was 30th March 1979 and the buses which ran on that day were RFs 314, 369, 381, 428, 437, 441, 471, 481, 492, 495, 502, 504, 505, 507, 516, 520 and 522. The last scheduled journey was worked by RF 507, which had been restored to its original 1953 livery and decorated for the occasion with balloons and streamers. Correctly anticipating the tremendous interest generated by the event, London Transport operated two duplicates to carry the overspill of people celebrating the departure, RFs 314 and 492 being the chosen pair for this honour. The importance of the event was marked by a large crowd of champions waiting to cheer the arrival of RF 507 at Kingston, in the early morning of Saturday 31st March.

London Transport did not leave it at that. Three Regals had been kept out of service on the Friday to be prepared for a commemorative run the following day. On the morning of Saturday 31st March, the Mayor and Mayoress of the Royal Borough of Kingston-upon-Thames, Councillor John and Mrs Mollie Greenwood, took part in a small ceremony, honoured guests at which were the three drivers chosen to take the buses on their last public trip, John Boylett, James Stockham and Ernest Atkinson. The Mayor was presented with one of the unique bullseyes from the front of an RF, mounted so that it could go on permanent display in Kingston Museum. He sent RFs 510, 511 and 512 on their way from Kingston bus station at 10.30, to run via route 219 to Weybridge BAC Works. They then returned to Weybridge station where they ran via the old, now disused, stand before continuing to Hersham to pick up the route of the 218 to Staines. They made their final run back over route 218 to Kingston. Those who travelled on this historic trip received a special commemorative ticket. Sadly, RF 512 had problems with overheating and with its gearbox during the journey but the old warhorse managed to complete the course and took the honour of being the last RF into Kingston garage.

Although London Country Bus Services continued to run RF 202 for a few more months, the withdrawal of Kingston's allocation effectively marked the end of the class in regular service, after almost twenty-seven years of excellent performance, having outlasted many of its successors. It was the last single-deck class to be designed specifically to London Transport's exacting requirements and the stringent specifications of Chiswick and Southall clearly stood the test of time.

COMMEMORATIVE RUN OF LONDON TRANSPORT'S LAST RF BUSES SATURDAY 31 MARCH, 1979

The run starts at 10 30 from Kingston Bus Station and covers routes 218 and 219 visiting Weybridge, Hersham, Staines, before returning to Kingston.

Top **Preparing for the commemorative run, RFs 510, 511 and 512 are lined up in Kingston bus station, while Leyland National LS 181, represents the new order on route 218.**

Above **On the commemorative run, RF 511 turns in Weybridge station approach, by now abandoned as an operational turn.** R.M. Gillespie

Left **The souvenir ticket for the commemorative run had coloured silhouettes of a Green Line RF and, at the bottom, a Central Bus example. The lettering was green, while the roundel was red, the whole being on a cream background.** R.M. Gillespie

15 THE SURVIVORS

Unlike its double-deck contemporaries in the RT family, the RF was not subjected to large scale premature withdrawals and the London influence which permeated so many independent double-deck fleets in the fifties and sixties did not extend to the single-deckers. Instead, for the most part, the RFs saw out their full life in London Transport or London Country service and were then withdrawn for scrap. Nevertheless there were some interesting exceptions to this general rule and, as a postscript to the RF story, it is worth spending a little time surveying what became of the survivors.

The principal exceptions to the longevity rule were those vehicles withdrawn between 1962 and 1964, as a result of the Executive's decision to withdraw from 'own account' contract work and of the arrival of the Routemaster coaches. The first to go were Private Hire RFs, the largest single group being snapped up by Premier Travel of Cambridge in the autumn of 1963. This operator added to its Regal IV fleet the following year when it acquired four redundant Green Line thirty-footers, bringing its total fleet to twelve. They operated on most of the company's local services and were almost as common a sight in Drummer Street bus station as the London ones were on their home ground.

Above **Redundant RFs found many different uses with all manner of new owners. RF 367 fell into the hands of a private owner who gave it some undignified decoration.** John Gascoine

Left **Former Private Hire RF 9 in the colours of Premier Travel at the Drummer Street terminus, Cambridge in April 1966.** Ken Glazier

The first disposal in 1962, however, went elsewhere. Four of them were bought by Super Coaches of Upminster, who were establishing themselves as an operator of local services in the Hornchurch and Romford areas, on routes either abandoned by London Transport or on which the larger undertaking did not wish to operate. An associated company, Redbridge and District, took two of the RF2s in 1964. Other single examples went to Midas Motors of Brentwood, Simmons of Letchworth (who took another in 1964), Pete's of Hockley and, most far flung of all, to Garelochhead Motor Services in Scotland and to Keneally of Waterford in Ireland. Garelochhead took another two in 1963 which, together with the RT family vehicles which they bought, gave their fleet the look of a branch of London Transport for a time.

Another operator, rather nearer home, who took on the appearance of a department of London Transport was Osborne of Tollesbury in Essex, whose red and cream livery gave even greater emphasis to the apparent association. They took two RF1s and four RF2/1s during 1963 and 1964. In their elegant and well maintained livery, they graced the lanes of south-east Essex alongside similarly acquired RTs for many years. The other 1963 disposals of the RF1s went to Hampson of Oswestry.

The largest batch of Green Line RFs sold in this period was purchased by British European Airways, who used ten of them for various duties in Heathrow Airport. Two others went to operators in Hemel Hempstead, Chiltern Counties and Ronsway.

Above Right **Super Coaches of Upminster bought some RFs to run on local services in east London, some of which, like this one, later ran under the trading name of Redbridge and District. The destination blind appears to be an imitation of the layout then in use on Green Line. MLL598, previously RF 211, is seen at Barkingside in August 1965.** Ken Glazier

Right **RF 5 in the handsome cream and two-tone red livery of Osborne's had lost the front roof glazing panel by the time it was photographed in July 1968.** Gerald Mead

Below **Two of the large BEA purchase, RFs 266 and 273 in use as 'Airside Coaches', for which role they have been fitted with radios, whose aerials can be seen projecting from the offside of the roof. Contemporary coach styling is represented by a Duple Super Vega bodied Bedford VAL, also on airport duties.** John Aldridge

Only one RFW survived within the British Isles as a PSV, RFW 1, which went to Elm Park Coaches of Hornchurch. Four others were sold for other uses but the bulk of the class found an unlikely new home in Ceylon, ten of them having been included in the agreement between London Transport and the Ceylon Transport Board which was intended to rejuvenate bus operation on the island. They retained their status as coaches and were allocated to the Special Tours Department of CTB, operating from Moratuwa garage, south of the capital Colombo. They were given a version of the red and grey colour scheme which the new Board had adopted for its bus fleet and went into service with little modification for their new operating conditions. The main changes were the insertion of a grille in the removable panel on the front of the vehicle, to improve the flow of cooling air around the radiator, and the addition of a matching offside lamp to balance the existing foglight. The seats were also given a fresh covering of blue cloth. Most of them survived until at least the late 1970s, latterly in a new livery of cream, blue and red.

No further sales took place until the main programme of replacement got into its stride in the seventies. By then the vehicles were so venerable that there was only a fairly limited market for them. Nevertheless, some operators found them useful, often to pioneer new services where the choice of a low-cost, almost life-expired bus helped to reduce the financial risk.

Two such operators in west London were Continental Pioneer, who bought nine, four from London Transport and five from LCBS, at various dates; and Hall of Hounslow, who took no fewer than twenty-eight from LCBS, mainly in 1971. Hall was a company which enjoyed spectacular growth in this period, much of it based on the development of contract work at Heathrow Airport, where they ran many of the courtesy services. Other significant purchases were by Blue Saloon of Guildford, a name with historic resonance as an important local operator before the formation of London Transport and one which was about to rise to greater prominence again.

The operators themselves found the usual range of further uses for some of their discarded relics, including staff transport, trainers, mobile recruitment offices and, modified, as towing lorries. The unique design of the RF4 airport coaches lent itself especially well to the special function which London Transport allocated to four of them between 1967 and 1976. They were used as mobile uniform stores and could be seen all over London visiting garages to supply staff with their replacement kits.

Finally, the RF was much loved by enthusiasts and has been a favourite model for preservation. No fewer than ninety-eight RFs and two RFWs are preserved and can still be seen regularly at rallies every year. Whether or not it is sensible for so much preservation effort to be lavished on one type of vehicle and one, what is more, that proved to be a short-lived, if important, 'blip' in the development of the single-decker, is debatable but the fact that so many are devoted to the task is a wonderful tribute to the quality and style, perhaps even the end of the line, exemplified by this classic vehicle.

Facing Page **Two survivors of the RFW class which stayed in the United Kingdom were RFWs 1 and 6, both of which saw service with St Thomas's Hospital. Apart from the pale green livery, the only modifications made to the vehicles since they were new are the reflector discs at the back and the flashing trafficator in place of the semaphore type.** John Aldridge

Left **Halls of Hounslow bought twenty-eight redundant RFs in 1971 for their flourishing business in and around Heathrow Airport.** John Gascoine

Facing Page **RF 43 had been a modernised Green Line coach before it was sold to Continental Pioneer who ran it on former London Transport route 235 in Richmond, one of the services handed over to private operators during the overtime ban in 1966. It has acquired an AEC badge of the type seen on Reliances but is otherwise little changed.** Capital Transport

Left **RF 254 last ran for LCBS at Chelsham, only a short hop over the downs from Orpington, where Tillingbourne Valley used it and others to set up a local operation under the name North Downs Transport in succession to Orpington and District.** John Gascoine

Facing Page **In 1938 Blue Saloon sold out its stage services in Guildford, via Aldershot & District to London Transport. Forty years later, RF 683, bought from London Transport, works on a local service in Guildford helping Blue Saloon start the renaissance which was to blossom under deregulation.** John Gascoine

Left **The Essex operations of Blue Triangle have included the use of RF 401, seen at the Two Brewers, Ongar, on an Essex County Council supported Sunday service.** Keith Wood

RF 78 stands in the forecourt of Godstone garage on a spring day in 1960. A.J. Wild

APPENDIX 1
SUMMARY DETAILS OF RF FAMILY

FLEET NUMBERS	REGISTRATION NUMBERS	BODY NUMBERS	TYPE CLASSIFICATION	FLEET NUMBERS	REGISTRATION NUMBERS	BODY NUMBERS	TYPE CLASSIFICATION
RF 1-25	LUC201-225	7379-7403	1RF1/2	RF 389-411	MXX277-299	7907-7929	2RF2
RF 26-125	LYF377-476	7419-7518	2RF2/1	RF 412-513	MXX389-490	7930-8031	2RF2
RF 126-225	MLL513-612	7519-7618	2RF2/1	RF 514-700	NLE514-700	8691-8877	2RF2/2
RF 226-288	MLL763-825	7619-7681	2RF2/1	RFW 1-15	LUC376-390	7404-7418	3RF3
RF 289-358	MLL926-995	7807-7876	2RF2	Not allocated	MLL713-762	Not allocated	4RF4
RF 359-388	MXX1-30	7877-7906	2RF2	Not allocated	NLP636-650	Not allocated	4RF4

CHASSIS NUMBERS

RF1-66	9821LT001-025, 032-051, 058, 053-056, 063, 062, 059, 064-067, 057, 070, 072-076, 079, 078
RF67-90	080-082, 085-088, 092, 060, 083, 093, 052, 094-097, 099, 084, 098, 100, 077, 102, 103, 068
RF91-108	089, 108, 110, 112, 116, 115, 117, 119, 121, 122, 125, 126, 128, 129, 109, 131, 132, 111
RF109-131	133, 134, 071, 135, 136, 061, 091, 105, 130, 138, 139, 141, 143, 142, 141, 145-151, 153
RF132-150	090, 118, 124, 107, 113, 140, 117, 152, 154, 114, 110, 156, 157-159, 137, 155, 160, 104
RF151-180	161, 162, 123, 163, 164, 101, 165, 166, 1008-1010, 106, 1011-1023, 1025, 1024, 1026-1028
RF181-241	1037, 1030, 1029, 1031-1036, 1038-1070, 1072-1076, 1071, 1077-1084, 1086-1088, 1085, 1090
RF242-257	1101, 1092, 1093, 1097, 1094-1096, 1099, 1098, 1106, 1102, 1107, 1111, 1091, 1104, 1105
RF258-272	1089, 1108, 1100, 1113, 1115, 1114, 1103, 1110, 1112, 1116, 1119, 1117, 1118, 1121, 666
RF273-289	689, 671, 1109, 1129, 1120, 1122, 1126, 1133, 1135, 069, 649, 672, 656, 662, 659, 660, 1124
RF290-304	650, 673, 1127, 653, 1128, 676, 683, 668, 678, 652, 658, 647, 651, 686, 670
RF305-322	691, 664, 684, 689, 666, 681, 667, 674, 1134, 692, 708, 663, 698, 680, 1132, 679, 657, 694
RF323-340	661, 687, 682, 675, 697, 706, 1123, 696, 700, 701, 703, 690, 704, 711, 705, 693, 699, 707
RF341-359	712, 717, 715, 702, 710, 714, 648, 654, 695, 713, 718-720, 716, 725, 729, 1130, 726, 721
RF360-377	723, 724, 730, 733, 734, 727, 1131, 728, 731, 732, 736, 739, 737, 738, 740, 688, 696, 735
RF378-407	742, 748-751, 746, 747, 1125, 655, 743, 744, 752, 755, 753, 754, 741, 756-763, 765-769, 777
RF408-440	783, 792, 793, 770-775, 778, 781, 782, 786, 776, 785, 787-790, 794-802, 805, 804, 803, 808, 818
RF441-458	821, 809, 810, 813, 816, 823, 824, 835, 836, 841, 844, 832, 845, 677, 685, 709, 722, 745
RF459-478	764, 779, 791, 806, 807, 811, 812, 814, 815, 817, 819, 820, 822, 825-828, 830, 831, 839
RF479-503	833, 837, 838, 840, 842, 843, 846-848, 850, 851, 856, 862, 853-855, 859-864, 866, 867, 870
RF504-521	874, 875, 879, 880, 882, 884, 885, 892, 915, 917, 780, 784, 829, 834, 849, 857, 858, 865
RF522-542	869, 872, 873, 868, 871, 876-878, 881, 886, 891, 899, 888, 894, 898, 897, 901, 900, 887, 890
RF543-624	893, 895, 889, 896, 902-908, 910, 911, 913, 909, 912, 914, 916, 918, 919-979, 982, 980
RF625-650	983-989, 991-993, 990, 994, 995, 971, 996-998, 1002, 999, 1007, 1001, 1000, 1003-1006
RF651-700	1320-1326, 1329, 1328, 1330, 1331, 1327, 1332-1336, 1338-1340, 1337, 1342, 1341, 1343-1369
RFW1-15	9821E318-332
MLL713-726	9822E1175, 1176, 1178, 1177, 1190, 1187, 1184, 1183, 1186, 1188, 1182, 1179, 1207, 1185
MLL727-741	1180, 1195, 1205, 1208, 1197, 1181, 1194, 1212, 1202, 1211, 1201, 1210, 1189, 1196, 1198
MLL742-756	1214, 1204, 1213, 1486, 1192, 1488, 1509, 1206, 1191, 1209, 1491, 1203, 1492, 1193, 1200
MLL757-762	1489, 1199, 1490, 1493, 1487, 1485
NLP636-650	1498, 1496, 1500, 1499, 1494, 1502, 1504, 1501, 1508, 1495, 1507, 1503, 1497, 1506, 1505

New to Norbiton garage in December 1952, RF 383 is seen the following summer.
G.A. Rixon

APPENDIX 2
MONTHLY SUMMARY OF VEHICLES INTO SERVICE AND INITIAL ALLOCATIONS

APRIL 1951	*RF 2 (Q)*
MAY 1951	*RF 1, 6, 10, 16 (R); RF 3 (U); RF 4, 13, 18 (AK); RF 5, 14, 15 (AL); RF 7, 8, 12 (Q); RF 9 (J); 11, 19, 20 (X); RFW 1 (D); RFW 2, 7 (P); RFW 3 (RG); RFW 4 (AF); RFW 5 (WT); RFW 6 (RG); RFW 10 (NF); RFW 12 (WR).*
JUNE 1951	*RF 17, 22, 24 (U); RF 21, 23 (J); RF 25 (AL); RFW 8, 9 (D); RFW 11, 15 (AF); RFW 13 (P); RFW 14 (RE).*
OCTOBER 1951	RF 26-29, 31 (TW).
NOVEMBER 1951	RF 30, 32, 34, 35 (TW); RF 33, 36-40, 42, 43 (WR); RF 44, 45, 48 (RG).
DECEMBER 1951	RF 41, 46, 47, 49, 50 (RG); RF 51-54, 56, 57, 59, 60 (HE); RF 55, 58, 61-63, 67-69 (MA); RF 64-66, 70, 71 (CY); RF 73, 77-79, 82 (GD); RF 74-76, 83-86, 89 (HG).
JANUARY 1952	RF 72, 80, 81, 87 (HG); RF 88, 90-99 (GF); RF 100-115, 118-120 (GY).
FEBRUARY 1952	RF 116, 117, 121-124, 127, 128 (EG); RF 125, 126, 129-133 (HH); RF 134-137, 139 (HN); RF 138, 140-146 (WY); RF 147-150, 152 (HF); RF 151, 153-158 (ST).
MARCH 1952	RF 159-165 (NF); RF 166-173 (LS); RF 174-184, 186, 187, 189-191 (DS); RF 185, 192-198 (SA); RF 199-203, 205, 206 (EP); RF 204, 207-210 (WR).
APRIL 1952	RF 211, 212, 214 (WR); RF 213, 215-221, 224 (CM); RF 223 (TG); RF 222, 226-230 (GY).
MAY 1952	RF 225, 231-235, 237, 238 (TG); RF 236, 239-244, 246 (EP), BEA: MLL 713 (GM).
JUNE 1952	RF 245, 247-252, 254 (DG); RF 253, 256, 257, 260-263 (WR); RF 255, 258, 264, 265 (SJ); RF 259, 266-269 (MA), BEA: MLL 714 (GM).
AUGUST 1952	RF 270, 277, 280 (HG); RF 271, 272 (WR); RF 273, 275 (EP); RF 274 (TW); RF 283 (LS), BEA: MLL 715 (GM).
SEPTEMBER 1952	RF 276 (RE); RF 278 (GF); RF 279 (GY); RF 281, 284 (DS); RF 282 (TG); RF 285 (NF); RF 286 (ST); RF 289-297 (MH).
OCTOBER 1952	RF 288 (WY); RF 298-302, 315-322 (MH); RF 303-314, 330 (D), BEA: MLL716 (GM).
NOVEMBER 1952	RF 287 (GM); RF 323, 325-329, 332 (MH); RF 324 (D); RF 331, 333-351 (TB), BEA: MLL 717-719 (GM).
DECEMBER 1952	RF 352, 353, 358-360, 369, 377 (TB); RF 354-356, 368, 370, 371, 373 (AL); RF 357, 361-367, 376 (AV); RF 372, 374 (A); RF 375, 379, 383 (NB); RF 378, 380, 382, 384, 385, 387 (P), BEA: MLL 710-729 (GM).
JANUARY 1953	RF 381, 386, 388, 393-407, 415 (A); RF 389-392 (NB); RF 408, 410, 412 (TC); RF 409, 411, 416-422, 439, 455 (SP); RF 413, 414 (D), BEA: MLL730-738 (GM).
FEBRUARY 1953	RF 423-435, 438, 454, 456-461 (WG); RF 436, 443, 449-453, 462, 466, 467, 469-473, 475-478, 480-482, 484 (MH); RF 437, 440-442, 444-448, 465, 468, 474 (D); 463 (TB), BEA: MLL739-743 (GM).
MARCH 1953	RF 464, 479, 488-498, 500-513 (SP); RF 483, 485-487 (MH); 499 (A); RF 514-516, 521 (RG), BEA: MLL744-755 (GM).
APRIL 1953	*RF 518-520, 522-531 (RG); 532-537, 539, 541 (SA), BEA: MLL756-759 (GM).*
MAY 1953	*RF 188, 552, 557 (RG); RF 538, 540, 542-551, 553-556, 558-561 (SA); RF 562-574, 577 (HG), BEA: MLL760-762 (GM).*
JUNE 1953	*RF 575, 586-589, 591 (LS); RF 576, 578, 580, 581, 583-585 (HN); RF 582, 590, 592-596, 598, 601, 605 (WR).*
JULY 1953	*RF 597, 602, 614 (DS); RF 599 (CY); RF 600, 611 (GF); RF 603, 612 (EP); RF 604, 610, 616 (WR); RF 606, 609 (HG); RF 607 (HN); RF 608 (SA); RF 613 (RG); RF 615, 617-621, 624 (GR); RF 622, 623, 626-628 (HE).*
AUGUST 1953	*RF 625, 629-635, 639 (LH); RF 636-638, 640, 641 (WY); RF 643 (HH), BEA: NLP636-639 (GM).*
SEPTEMBER 1953	*RF 642, 644-646, 648-650 (HH); RF 651-654 (DG); RF 655-661, 663 (GF); RF 662, 664-668 (DS); RF 669-671, 673 (EG), BEA: NLP640-643 (GM).*
OCTOBER 1953	*RF 672, 674-676, 683 (EG); RF 677-682 (CY); RF 684-686, 688 (EP), BEA: NLP644-650 (GM).*
NOVEMBER 1953	*RF 687, 689-691 (NF); RF 693 (LH).*
DECEMBER 1953	*RF 692, 694, 695 (LH); RF 696-699 (WY).*
MARCH 1954	*RF 517*, 647* (LH); RF 700* (RG).*

NOTE: Vehicles shown in italics were delivered in green livery.
*Modified for one-man operation before entering service.

APPENDIX 3
SUMMARY OF BODY AND CHASSIS CLASSIFICATIONS

Chiswick had a long tradition dating back to the days of the LGOC of allocating a type code to each chassis and body variation. The criteria for deciding when a variation needed a new code were apparently quite elastic but in the 1950s, when the RF was being delivered and developed, it was customary to give new codes to most significant changes which were made. The following list summarises those allotted to the RF family.

CHASSIS CODE	DESCRIPTION
1RF	27ft 6ins long. Private Hire chassis.
1/1RF	Private Hire coaches converted for Green Line operation.
2RF	Standard 30ft long chassis, Green Line, Central Bus and Country Bus.
1/2RF	2RF chassis with modified differentials and fitted for saloon heaters.
2/2RF	2RF chassis fitted with forty gallon fuel tanks.
3RF	RFW chassis — 30ft long; 8ft wide.
4RF	BEA coach chassis — 30ft long; 8ft wide, AEC model 9822E.

BODY CODE	
RF1	Not used (possibly reserved for 27ft 6in Central Bus version).
RF1/1	Not used (possibly reserved for 27ft 6ins Green Line version).
RF1/2	27ft 6ins long Private Hire coaches, thirty-five seats.
RF1/3	Former RF1/2 vehicles modified for Green Line operation, fitted with luggage racks and side route boards.
RF2	30ft long Central Area buses, no platform doors, forty-one seats.
RF2/1	30ft long Green Line coaches, platform doors, thirty-nine seats.
RF2/2	30ft long Country Area buses, platform doors, forty-one seats.
RF2/3	Former buses converted for Green Line operation, platform doors, forty seats.
RF2/4	Former RF2/1 coaches, modernised and modified for one-man operation; thirty-nine seats.
RF2/5	Former RF2/1 coaches modernised in two-man operation form; thirty-nine seats.
RF2/6	Former RF2/1 coaches, modernised with additional luggage space (for route 727) and modified for one-man operation; thirty-five seats.
RF3	RFW coaches.
RF4	BEA airport coaches.
RF5	Experimental Country Area buses fitted for OMO; thirty-nine seats.
RF5/1	Second version of Country Area OMO bus with modified cab door; thirty-nine seats.
RF5/2	Simplified version of Country Area OMO bus, with modified cab equipment; thirty-nine seats.
RF5/3	Central Area buses modified for one-man operation, thirty-nine seats.
RF5/4	Former RF2/3 vehicles, downgraded to buses and modified for one-man operation; thirty-eight seats.
RF5/5	Former RF2/1 Green Line coaches, downgraded to buses and modified for one-man operation; thirty-seven seats.
RF5/6	Country OMO buses equipped for Setright ticket machines only.
RF5/7	Country OMO buses equipped for Setright and Ultimate ticket machines.
RF5/8	Modernised coaches downgraded to buses; thirty-seven seats.
RF5/9	Central buses modified for one-man operation (1970 batch); modified glider doors; thirty-nine seats.
RF5/10	Central Buses equipped for Almex ticket machines.

APPENDIX 4
DATES OF MODIFICATIONS AND RENUMBERINGS

RENUMBERING

The exchange of numbers took place simultaneously on both vehicles on the dates shown.

295/514	23/3/56	302/521	12/4/56	309/528	29/3/56
296/515	22/3/56	303/522	19/3/56	310/529	9/3/56
297/516	4/4/56	304/523	16/3/56	311/530	5/4/56
298/517/697	28/3/56	305/524	16/4/56	312/531	9/3/56
299/518	22/3/56	306/525	28/3/56	313/532	23/4/56
300/519	11/4/56	307/526	18/4/56	647/698	26/1/56
301/520	11/4/56	308/527	28/3/56	649/699	26/1/56

BUS AND PRIVATE HIRE COACH TO GREEN LINE COACH CONVERSIONS

(a) RF1/2 to RF1/3

FLEET NO.	DATE MODIFIED	DATE INTO SERVICE	FLEET NO.	DATE MODIFIED	DATE INTO SERVICE
RF16	16/5/56	1/7/56 (AF*); 1/10/56 (DS)	RF21	23/5/56	1/7/56 (J*); 1/10/56 (NF)
RF17	16/5/56	1/7/56 (Q*); 1/10/56 (SJ)	RF22	25/5/56	15/6/56 (EP)†
RF18	17/5/56	1/7/56 (NX*); 1/10/56 (NF)	RF23	25/5/56	1/8/56 (NF)
RF19	23/5/56	11/6/56 (HN)	RF24	17/5/56	1/7/56 (P*); 15/8/56 (ST)†
RF20	17/5/56	1/7/56 (AK*); 1/10/56 (NF)	RF25	23/5/56	4/7/56 (HF)

*Temporarily retained on Private Hire duties.
†RFs 22 and 24 returned to Central Buses after overhaul in 1958.

(b) RF2 (red bus) to RF2/3

RF289	21/3/56	25/3/56 (GM)	RF292	19/3/56	25/3/56 (R)
RF290	15/3/56	18/4/56 (TG)	RF293	15/3/56	5/7/56 (MA)
RF291	16/3/56	25/3/56 (HG)	RF294	7/3/56	4/4/56 (RG)

(c) RF2/2 (green bus) to RF2/3 (new numbers — see above for renumbering dates)

RF295	23/3/56	23/3/56 (RG)	RF305	16/4/56	16/4/56 (RG)
RF296	22/3/56	22/3/56 (RG)	RF306	28/3/56	1/5/56 (LH)
RF297	4/4/56	9/4/56 (WR)	RF307	18/4/56	18/4/56 (RG)
RF298	28/3/56	6/6/56 (RG)	RF308	28/3/56	28/3/56 (GD)
RF299	22/3/56	1/5/56 (EP) as a bus until 11/7/56, then coach.	RF309	29/3/56	4/4/56 (SA)
RF300	11/4/56	5/7/56 (SJ)	RF310	9/3/56	25/3/56 (RG)
RF301	11/4/56	1/8/56 (NF)	RF311	5/4/56	5/4/56 (WY)
RF302	12/4/56	12/4/56 (RG)	RF312	9/3/56	25/3/56 (RG)
RF303	19/3/56	19/3/56 (DS)	RF313	23/4/56	8/8/56 (NF)
RF304	16/3/56	19/3/56 (HG)			

COUNTRY BUSES MODIFIED FOR ONE-MAN OPERATION

(a) RF2/2 to RF5/1

FEBRUARY 1956:	RFs 684, 687.
MARCH 1956:	RFs 683, 685.
APRIL 1956:	RFs 682, 689, 694.
MAY 1956:	RFs 690, 691, 695.
JUNE 1956:	RFs 688, 692, 693, 696.
JULY 1956:	RF 686.

(b) RF2/2 to RF5/2

DECEMBER 1956:	RF 664.
OCTOBER 1957:	RFs 562, 603, 607-629, 631-642.
JANUARY 1958:	RFs 542*, 544*.
FEBRUARY 1958:	RFs 545*, 546*, 550*, 551*.
APRIL 1958:	RF 663.
MAY 1958:	RFs 653, 665, 667, 671.
JUNE 1958:	RFs 654-657, 662, 670, 673-676, 678.
JULY 1958:	RFs 658-661, 666, 668, 669, 672, 677, 679-681.
AUGUST 1958:	RFs 581, 582, 587, 590, 599, 605, 630, 643, 647, 649-651.
SEPTEMBER 1958:	RFs 584, 586, 588, 589, 591, 592, 593, 594-598, 600-602, 604, 606, 644-646, 648, 652.
NOVEMBER 1958:	RFs 583, 585.
FEBRUARY 1959:	RFs 539-541, 543, 547-549, 552-561, 563-565, 567, 570, 572, 573, 576.
MARCH 1959:	RFs 566, 568, 569, 571, 574, 575, 577-580.

*Officially these were 'temporary' conversions; official conversion was made in October 1958.

CENTRAL BUSES MODIFIED FOR ONE-MAN OPERATION

(a) RF2 to RF5/3

MARCH 1959:	RFs 502-505, 507, 514, 528.
APRIL 1959:	RFs 506, 508-513, 515-524, 530, 531, 533-535.
MAY 1959:	RFs 525-527, 529, 532, 536-538.
JANUARY 1965:	RFs 343, 353, 356, 360, 369, 392, 399, 408, 420, 423, 431, 437, 454, 459, 468.
FEBRUARY 1965:	RFs 415, 422, 424-426, 436, 463, 470, 472, 476, 479, 492.
MARCH 1965:	RFs 318, 323, 326, 329, 333, 334, 336, 338, 340, 363, 366, 367, 375, 417, 427, 428, 440-442, 458, 461, 481, 485, 495, 498, 499, 503.
APRIL 1965:	RF 449.
MAY 1965:	RFs 352, 358, 359, 368, 381, 384, 387, 412.
JUNE 1965:	RFs 414, 419, 432, 455, 460, 483.
MAY 1966:	RFs 448, 452, 453, 462.
JUNE 1966:	RFs 320, 411, 421, 429, 439, 443-445, 450, 465, 480, 486, 488-491.
JULY 1966:	RFs 314, 382, 473, 497.
AUGUST 1966:	RFs 315-317, 321, 327, 328, 331, 342.
SEPTEMBER 1966:	RFs 322, 354, 362, 438, 456, 457, 471, 478, 482, 487.

(b) RF2 to RF5/9

NOVEMBER 1970:	RFs 324, 330, 349, 385, 396, 398, 404, 406, 407, 409, 418.
DECEMBER 1970:	RFs 346, 350, 355, 365, 370, 383, 401, 402.
JANUARY 1971:	RFs 345, 351, 364, 371, 379, 380, 389-391*, 400, 403.

* RF390 used equipment withdrawn from RF590, a 5/2.

GREEN LINE COACH MODERNISATION PROGRAMME

(a) RF2/1 to RF2/5

MARCH 1966:	RF 136.
AUGUST 1966:	RF 26.
SEPTEMBER 1966:	RFs 40, 56, 74, 85, 157, 159, 183, 184, 192, 196.
OCTOBER 1966:	RFs 44, 45, 48, 57, 61, 62, 65, 67, 83, 103, 104, 108, 177, 191, 201, 202, 235.
NOVEMBER 1966:	RFs 30, 46, 49, 60, 64, 75, 93, 107, 114, 153, 154, 181, 203, 215, 230.
DECEMBER 1966:	RFs 29, 95, 98, 100, 101, 105, 106, 109, 111, 119, 129, 134, 166, 167, 169, 172, 219.
JANUARY 1967:	RFs 53, 54, 73, 78, 82, 94, 118, 120, 142, 144, 145, 156, 170, 178, 281.

(b) RF2/1 to RF2/4

JANUARY 1967:	RFs 76, 127, 176, 180.
FEBRUARY 1967:	RFs 35, 77, 88, 90, 102, 121, 122, 128, 135, 150, 168, 174, 178, 179, 186, 198, 200, 207, 259.
MARCH 1967:	RFs 91, 123, 125, 131, 139, 140, 148, 158, 162-165, 173, 182, 194, 205, 208, 209, 213, 223, 228.
APRIL 1967:	RFs 32, 34, 66, 80, 81, 84, 87, 101, 110, 112, 115, 124, 130, 141, 151, 155, 160, 171, 193.
MAY 1967:	RFs 143, 146, 218, 234, 241, 245, 246, 250, 253, 261, 267.
JUNE 1967:	RFs 27, 28, 31, 37, 38, 39, 43, 50, 68, 244, 248, 252, 263.
JULY 1967:	RF 63.

(c) RF2/1 to RF2/6

MARCH 1967:	RF 70.
APRIL 1967:	RF 89.
MAY 1967:	RFs 47, 79, 99, 138, 152, 175, 185, 195, 204.

GREEN LINE COACHES MODIFIED FOR ONE-MAN OPERATION
The following list shows the Green Line RFs which were modified for one-man operation, after the completion of the modernisation project.

JUNE 1967:	RFs 53, 54, 73, 78, 82, 144, 145, 170.
JULY 1967:	RFs 118, 120.
JANUARY 1968:	RFs 30, 45, 46, 49, 60, 75, 98, 100, 105, 106, 107, 109, 111, 129, 142, 156, 172, 178, 192, 281.
FEBRUARY 1968:	RFs 29, 44, 48, 57, 61, 62, 65, 67, 93, 94, 95, 103, 114, 119, 134, 136, 177, 181, 191, 201.
MARCH 1968:	RFs 26, 40, 74, 83, 104, 108, 157, 159, 167, 184, 196, 230, 235.
APRIL 1968:	RFs 56, 64, 85, 153, 154, 161, 166, 169, 183, 202, 203, 215, 219.

GREEN LINE COACHES DOWNGRADED TO BUSES

(a) by London Transport

SEPTEMBER 1965: RFs 36, 41 (reverted to coach August 1966), 116, 133, 199, 238, 249, 270, 271, 276, 279, 286.
OCTOBER 1965: RFs 33, 42, 59, 92, 113, 117, 149, 243, 269, 274, 277, 280.
NOVEMBER 1965: RFs 96, 188, 226, 278, 283, 285, 288.
MAY 1966: RFs 51, 52, 55, 58, 69, 71.
JUNE 1966: RF 72.
NOVEMBER 1966: RFs 187, 212, 214, 222, 229, 240, 242.
DECEMBER 1966: RFs 189, 197, 210, 216, 217, 225, 231, 233, 239, 247, 251, 255.
JANUARY 1967: RFs 220, 221, 232, 236, 254, 265.
FEBRUARY 1967: RF 86.
JULY 1967: RF 41 (second occasion).
MARCH 1968: RFs 26 (reverted to coach May 1968), 40, 74, 83, 157, 159, 167, 184, 196, 230.
APRIL 1968: RFs 54, 64, 85, 153, 154, 161, 166, 169, 183, 203, 215, 219.
MAY 1968: RFs 104, 108, 235.

(b) by London Country Bus Services Ltd

SEPTEMBER 1971: RFs 29, 34, 35, 57, 61, 62, 67, 103, 108.
OCTOBER 1971: RFs 30, 84.
NOVEMBER 1971: RF 44.
MARCH 1972: RFs 27, 50, 73, 77, 88, 90, 102, 107, 110, 114, 115, 118, 119 (reverted to coach May 1972), 120, 129, 150, 151, 177, 252, 267.
APRIL 1972: RFs 46, 48, 65, 68, 244.
MAY 1972: RF 45.
JUNE 1972: RFs 134, 135.
JULY 1972: RF 80.
OCTOBER 1972: RFs 39, 112, 165, 172.
JANUARY 1973: RF 173.
FEBRUARY 1973: RFs 81, 82, 201, 206, 213, 241, 245, 253, 259.
MARCH 1973: RFs 124, 155, 160, 246, 250.
AUGUST 1973: RF 263.
SEPTEMBER 1973: RF 93.
DECEMBER 1973: RFs 75, 127, 200, 209, 261.

The following coaches were downgraded at some time after 1973 but the exact dates are not known:
RFs 54, 127, 200, 209, 261.

All others officially remained coaches until they were withdrawn.

It was a long-established practice for Green Lines to do a spell of duty on a local bus service before setting out on their normal work. East Grinstead's modernised RF 261 is dressed ready for service on Green Line 708 but is first working a journey on bus route 424 in its home town. E. Shirras

RF 77 works a journey on bus route 489 prior to its day's work on the 701/702. The destination is the shortest ever displayed by an RF, taking up even less space than the route number. Both this RF and the one above ended their days demoted to buses. E. Shirras

APPENDIX 5
STARTING FLEETS — 1st JANUARY 1970
London Country Bus Services Ltd

(a) Coaches (modernised): RFs 27-35, 37-39, 43-50, 53, 54, 57, 60-70, 73, 75-82, 87-91, 93-95, 98-103, 105-107, 109-112, 114, 115, 118-125, 127-131, 134-136, 138-146, 148, 150-152, 155, 156, 158, 160, 162-165, 168, 170-182, 185, 186, 191-195, 198, 200-202, 204-209, 213, 218, 223, 228, 234, 241, 244-246, 248, 250, 252, 253, 259, 261, 263, 267, 281.

(b) Buses (modernised — formerly coaches): RFs 26, 40, 56, 74, 83, 85, 104, 108, 153, 154, 157, 159, 161, 166, 167, 169, 183, 184, 196, 215, 230, 235.

(c) Buses (including downgraded former coaches): RFs 36, 41, 42, 51, 52, 55, 58, 59, 69, 71, 72, 84, 86, 92, 96, 113, 116, 117, 133, 149, 187-189, 197, 199, 203, 210, 212, 214, 216, 217, 219-222, 225, 226, 229, 231-233, 236, 238-240, 242, 243, 247, 249, 251, 254, 255, 265, 269-271, 274, 276-280, 283, 285, 286, 288-313, 539-544, 546-562, 564-569, 571-579, 581-589, 591-597, 599-601, 604-607, 609-616, 618-626, 628-631, 633-684, 686-700.

London Transport Executive

RFs 314-377, 379-463, 465-475, 477-538, 545, 563, 570, 580, 590, 598, 602, 603, 608, 617, 627, 632, 685.

The following RFs were on temporary loan from LTE to LCBS: 325, 341, 374, 388, 393.

APPENDIX 6
FLEET REPLACEMENT PROGRAMME — 1951-1954

The following lists show the programme for the deployment of the RFs as originally planned by the Central and Country operating departments.

GREEN LINE COACH ROUTES

ORDER OF PRIORITY	ROUTE	NO. OF VEHICLES			ORDER OF PRIORITY	ROUTE	NO. OF VEHICLES		
		Service	Spare	Total			Service	Spare	Total
1.	704	15	2	17	9.	714	8	1	9
2.	711	14	2	16	10.	712/713	14	2	16
3.	709/710	15	3	18	11.	718	13	2	15
4.	715	21	2	23	12.	706/707	16	2	18
5.	708	13	2	15	13.	720	7	1	8
6.	716/717	15	3	18	14.	723†	14	1	15
7.	701/702	12	2	14	15.	705	13	2	15
8.	727*	7	1	8	16.	703	7	2	9
					Duplication and additional spares			29‡	29‡
					Totals		204	59	263

* Later incorporated with 714 and total reduced by one.
† Later amended to include 723ᴬ, total increased by four
‡ Later reduced to 26 as a result of above changes.

CENTRAL AREA BUSES

ORDER OF PRIORITY	ROUTE	NO. OF VEHICLES			ORDER OF PRIORITY	ROUTE	NO. OF VEHICLES		
		Service	Spare	Total			Service	Spare	Total
1.	210	14	1	15	8.	228	13	1	14
2.	208ᴬ	13	1	14	9.	202	7	–	7
3.	227	24	2	26	10.	233	22	–	22
4.	237	8	1	8	11.	208	13	–	13
5.	200	6	1	7	12.	212	30	1	31
6.	213	29	3	33	13.	241	29	1	30
7.	234ᴬ	5	–	5		TOTAL	213	12	225

COUNTRY AREA BUSES

ORDER OF PRIORITY	ROUTE & GARAGE	NO. OF VEHICLES			ORDER OF PRIORITY	ROUTE & GARAGE	NO. OF VEHICLES		
		Service	Spare	Total			Service	Spare	Total
1.	447 RG	12	1	13	25.	422 LH	2	–	2
2.	440/A RG	2	1	3	26.	435,462			
3.	406ᶜ RG	1	–	1		(LH allocation)	4	–	4
4.	430 RG	1	–	1	27.	419 LH	3	–	3
5.	RG duplicates	1	–	1	28.	LH duplicates	1	–	1
6.	365/391 SA	14	1	15	29.	462 WY	4	–	4
7.	355 SA	8	1	9	30.	427/437/456 WY	6	1	7
8.	304 SA	3	–	3	31.	322 HH	6	1	7
9.	382 SA	1	–	1	32.	337 HH	1	–	1
					33.	404 DG	1	–	1
10.	372 HG	4	1	5	34.	421 DG	2	1	3
11.	342 HG	4	1	5	35.	432 GF	2	–	2
12.	308/384/399				36.	425 GF/DS	8	3	11
	(HG allocation)	3	–	3	37.	GF duplicates	1	–	1
13.	390 HG	1	–	1	38.	DS duplicates	1	–	1
14.	308etc.				39.	424 EG	5	1	6
	(HN allocation)	3	1	4	40.	434/473 EG	1	–	1
15.	364 HN	2	–	2	41.	EG duplicates	1	–	1
16.	390 HN	1	–	1	42.	424 CY	1	–	1
17.	364 LS	1	–	1	43.	434/473 CY	6	1	7
18.	356/376 LS	4	1	5	44.	308/384/399			
19.	LS duplicates	1	–	1		(EP allocation)	2	1	3
20.	458 WR	8	1	9	45.	EP duplicates	1	–	1
21.	407ᴬ WR	2	–	2	46.	489/489ᴬ NF	3	1	4
22.	WR duplicates	1	–	1		Not yet allocated	3	–	3
23.	318/318ᴬ WT	10	2	12		Diverted to route 725	–	8	8
24.	363 HE	4	1	5		TOTAL	157	30	187

APPENDIX 7
SUMMARY OF OTHER VEHICLE TYPES MENTIONED IN THE TEXT

CLASS	CHASSIS and MODEL	BODY	YEAR NEW	REMARKS
1T1	AEC Regal 662*	LGOC* B30F	1929	
3T3	AEC Regal 662	Tilling B30F	1932	
7T7	AEC Regal 662	Weymann/Ransomes/Duple B30F	1930-31	
9T9	AEC Regal 0662	Weymann C30F	1936	7.7 litre engines
10T10	AEC Regal 0662	LPTB C30/34F	1938-39	8.8 litre engines
11T11	AEC Regal 0662	Weymann B30F	1930-31 (chassis); 1935 (bodies)	
14T12	AEC Regal 0662	Weymann B35F	1946	
15T13	AEC Regal 111 0962/9621E	Mann Egerton B31F	1948	
1LTL1‡	AEC Renown 664†	LGOC B35F	1931	
4Q4	AEC 'Q' 0762	Birmingham Railway Carriage & Wagon Co. B35C	1935/36	
5Q5	AEC 'Q' 0762	Park Royal B37F	1936	No doors
6Q6	AEC 'Q' 0762	Park Royal C32C	1936/37	
1LTC1	AEC Renown 663	Weymann C30F	1937/38	Diesel engines-1949
1TF1	Leyland FEC	LPTB C34F	1937	Prototype
2TF2	Leyland FEC	LPTB C34F	1939	
2TF3	Leyland FEC	Park Royal C33F	1939	Only survivor TF9
1TD1	Leyland Tiger PS1	Weymann B33F	1946/47	Later B32F
1/1TD2	Leyland Tiger PS1	Mann Egerton B31F	1948/49	

* 18 rebuilt by Marshalls of Cambridge 1949; 26 fitted with diesel engines in 1950.
† 59 rebuilt by Marshalls of Cambridge 1948/49; 98 fitted with diesel engines 1950.
‡ Numbered in the LT class.

APPENDIX 8
WITHDRAWAL DATES AND FINAL ALLOCATIONS
The following list shows the month in which each vehicle was delicensed as a passenger vehicle for the last time and the garage at which it last saw service. In most cases the date of final disposal was some time later.

MAY 1962:	RF 18 (EP).
JUNE 1962:	RF 19 (SA).
AUGUST 1962:	RFs 16 (LS), 20 (ST), 22 (GM), 23 (GR), 25 (GF).
OCTOBER 1962:	RFs 17 (DG), 21 (SA), 24 (R).
JANUARY 1963:	RF 464 (FW).
MAY 1963:	BEA: MLL742 (HB).
AUGUST 1963:	RFs 4 (AK), 7 (AK), 14 (WR), 15 (T).
SEPTEMBER 1963:	RFs 1 (J), 2 (J), 5 (CF), 6 (CF), 9 (RL), 10 (W), 11 (AL), 12 (WD), 13 (HH); RFWs 4 (GM), 5 (GM).
OCTOBER 1963:	RFs 3 (RL), 8 (WD), 126 (HE), 256 (ST), 273 (GD), 275 (SA); RFWs 2 (NX), 3 (AF); 7 (NX), 8 (GM), 9 (Q), 10 (Q), 12 (R), 13 (Q), 15 (GM), 224 (DG).
DECEMBER 1963:	RFs 227 (DG), 237 (CM), 260 (HF), 266 (WR), 268 (RG).
JANUARY 1964:	RF 190 (DS).
FEBRUARY 1964:	RF 272 (HE).
MARCH 1964:	RFs 211 (TW), 262 (HF), 284 (HF).
APRIL 1964:	RFs 257 (GM), 258 (LS).
MAY 1964:	RFs 132 (SJ), 264 (WR), 282 (NF), 287 (ST).
OCTOBER 1964:	RFs 97 (SA), 137 (NF), 147 (NF); RFWs 1, 6, 11, 14, (all RE).
OCTOBER 1965:	BEA: MLL743 (HB).
AUGUST 1966:	RF 347 (TC).
SEPTEMBER 1966:	BEA: MLL756 (CK).
NOVEMBER 1966:	BEA: MLL739, 741, 744 (CK).
DECEMBER 1966:	BEA: MLL713, 715, 716, 745, 748, 751, 752 (CK).
JANUARY 1967:	BEA: MLL714, 720, 723, 724, 735, 746, 747, 749, 750, 753, NLP648 (CK).
FEBRUARY 1967:	BEA: MLL718, 719, 722, 725-727, 754, 755, 757-762, NLP636, 642 (CK).
MARCH 1967:	BEA: MLL721, 728-733, NLP637-641, 643-647, 649, 650 (CK).
APRIL 1967:	BEA: MLL 717, 734, 736-738 (CK).
MAY 1967:	RF 475 (K).
AUGUST 1968:	RF 378 (TB).
SEPTEMBER 1968:	RFs 332 (TB), 357 (AR), 476 (NB).
OCTOBER 1968:	RFs 361 (NX), 397 (NX), 477 (TB).
JUNE 1969:	RF 430 (D).
JUNE 1970:	RF 376 (TB).
SEPTEMBER 1970:	RF 496 (TB), 590 (MH).
OCTOBER 1970:	RF 348 (TB).
NOVEMBER 1970:	RF 339 (AR).
JANUARY 1971:	RFs 318, 337, 344, 372, 377, 393, 493, 500 (all TB), 386 (AR).
FEBRUARY 1971:	RFs 207 (NF), 228 (DS), 434 (T).
MARCH 1971:	RFs 325 (SV), 341 (DG), 374 (DS), 388 (CY).
APRIL 1971:	RFs 158 (HA), 335, 410, 416, 433, 435, 447, 451, 467, 469, 494, 501 (all T), 373, 394, 395, 405, 413, 446, 466, 474, 484 (all D).
AUGUST 1971:	RFs 86, 600, 626, 628, 633 (all HG), 197 (DG), 232 (SA), 557 (WR), 572 (WR), 573 (WY), 575 (LH), 591 (DS), 595 (GF), 635 (DG), 657 (WY).
SEPTEMBER 1971:	RFs 306 (GY), 605, 654, 656 (all HG), 642 (HA), 643 (DS), 658 (DG), 660 (GR), 662 (SA).
OCTOBER 1971:	RFs 630 (HG), 644 (WY), 645 (HG), 661 (SA), 664 (SA).
JANUARY 1972:	RFs 669, 689, 693 (all SA), 672 (ST), 680 (HH).
FEBRUARY 1972:	RFs 116 (HG), 254 (CM), 539, 650, 675 (all LH).
MARCH 1972:	RFs 36, 199, 681 (all ST), 113, 117, 652, 686 (all DG), 133 (DS), 233 (GY), 271 (CY), 279 (NF), 280 (NF), 676 (WY), 677 (HH), 679 (WY).
APRIL 1972:	RFs 52 (SA), 270 (GR), 649 (DG), 699 (HH).
MAY 1972:	RF 131 (DS).

JUNE 1972:	RFs 269 (HG), 694 (RG).
JULY 1972:	RFs 96 (DS), 188 (ST), 665 (LH).
AUGUST 1972:	RFs 62 (SA), 274 (DG), 491 (TC).
SEPTEMBER 1972:	RFs 149 (GR), 691 (SV).
OCTOBER 1972:	RFs 283 (ST), 288 (DS), 514 (FW), 578 (HH), 631, 682, 683 (all WR), 695 (HH).
NOVEMBER 1972:	RFs 44 (HG), 552 (WR).
DECEMBER 1972:	RFs 308 (HE), 541 (GF), 556 (WR), 558 (WR).
JANUARY 1973:	RFs 204 (SA), 205 (GR), 309 (DG), 411 (R), 544 (GF), 549 (CY), 566 (HH), 579 (DG), 647 (LH).
FEBRUARY 1973:	RFs 29 (GF), 34, 35, 61 (all SA), 57, 298, 616 (all HG), 109 (RE), 305, 551, 555 (all MA), 315 (FW), 316 (L), 486 (NB), 562 (HH), 569 (CY), 577 (SV), 612 (HE), 629 (HH), 636, 637, 638 (all LH), 700 (GR).
MARCH 1973:	RFs 30 (SA), 90 (NF), 328 (L), 382 (K), 439 (A), 473 (TC), 497 (K), 553 (MA), 585, 622, 696 (all HH), 594 (WR).
APRIL 1973:	RFs 317 (A), 342 (EW).
MAY 1973:	RFs 58 (HG), 163 (GR), 313 (HG), 322 (EW), 327 (TC), 362 (EW), BEA: MLL740 (CK).
JUNE 1973:	RFs 71 (HG), 77 (CM), 112 (HG), 320 (L), 331, 438, 457, 482 (all A), 456 (K), 478 (K), 487 (NB).
JULY 1973:	RFs 31 (LS), 46 (SA), 60 (HH), 82 (LS), 110 (ST), 114 (ST), 138 (NF), 293 (HG), 687 (GY), 698 (DG).
AUGUST 1973:	RFs 118 (SA), 216 (HG), 290 (LS).
SEPTEMBER 1973:	RFs 291 (LH), 296 (MA), 297 (MA), 609 (HG).
OCTOBER 1973:	RFs 100 (ST), 101 (SA), 105 (SA), 139 (LS), 170 (GR), 607 (GR).
NOVEMBER 1973:	RFs 192 (TG), 570 (K), 580 (AD).
DECEMBER 1973:	RFs 128 (ST), 135 (RG), 136 (CM), 172 (HE), 203 (SA), 215 (SA), 249 (HG), 589 (DG), 668 (DG), 688 (HG).
JANUARY 1974:	RFs 63 (DS), 121 (CM), 124 (SA), 157 (WR), 162 (DS), 210 (HH), 234 (ST), 651 (HG).
FEBRUARY 1974:	RFs 159 (DS), 195 (NF), 208 (DS), 261 (DG), 265 (LS), 588 (HG), 646 (HH).
MARCH 1974:	RFs 83 (SA), 186 (TG), 259 (SA), 634 (HH), 666 (GR).
APRIL 1974:	RFs 38 (ST), 43 (SA), 143 (HH), 206 (SA), 574 (HG), 587 (HG), 606 (WR).
MAY 1974:	RFs 32 (NF), 37 (NF), 39 (HA), 56 (HA), 198 (WR), 230 (LH), 250 (LH), 286 (HG).
JUNE 1974:	RFs 142, 245, 581 (all HG), 155 (HH), 209 (DG), 241 (WR), 582 (DG).
JULY 1974:	RFs 47 (HH), 76 (WR), 87 (ST), 161 (HG), 167 (WR), 226 (LH), 229 (GF), 300 (GY), 639 (LH).
AUGUST 1974:	RFs 235 (HG), 253 (HG), 542 (CM), 659 (GR).
SEPTEMBER 1974:	RFs 78 (HG), 99 (ST), 144 (NF), 164 (GF), 182 (NF), 220 (HE), 240 (HG).
OCTOBER 1974:	RFs 104 (HG), 238 (LH), 565 (WR), 576 (LH), 593 (LS).
NOVEMBER:	RFs 41 (GF), 181 (CM), 219 (HG), 623 (RG).
DECEMBER 1974:	RFs 53 (HG), 653 (LH).
JANUARY 1975:	RFs 27 (GR), 72 (DS), 94, 130, 177 (all CM), 95 (HH), 115 (HH), 156 (WY), 165 (SV), 177 (CM), 178 (CY), 201 (DG), 244, 295, 619 (all GY), 582 (DG), 597 (SV), 599 (HG), 604 (HG), 610 (WR), 618 (MA), 624 (SJ), 625 (LH).
FEBRUARY 1975:	RFs 73 (SJ), 123 (WR), 151 (WR), 154 (CM), 179 (RG), 289 (GY), 294 (HG), 592 (DG), 648 (HG), 671 (DG), 674 (LH).
MARCH 1975:	RFs 80 (MA), 91 (HA), 127 (HE), 292 (GR), 301 (WR), 546 (GR), 571 (MA).
APRIL 1975:	RFs 33 (GY), 51 (ST), 66 (WY), 93 (HH), 160 (TW), 176 (DT), 184 (HH), 276 (DS), 311 (MA).
MAY 1975:	RFs 59 (SV), 92 (HH), 222 (ST), 243, (HG), 248 (SA), 267 (WR), 285 (HG), 299 (GY), 307 (MA), 398 (UX), 399 (NB), 586 (LS), 670 (HH).
JUNE 1975:	RFs 42 (WR), 81 (DG), 84 (WY), 107 (GR), 141 (SA), 169 (DG), 225 (WY), 246 (HH), 278 (GY), 463 (K), 560 (DT).
JULY 1975:	RFs 49 (HG), 50 (WR), 153 (CY), 217 (GY), 252 (HH), 277 (HA), 303 (DT), 312 (WY), 360 (UX), 547 (SV), 561 (MA), 621 (LH), 697 (HH).
AUGUST 1975:	RFs 65 (HG), 70 (TG), 173 (DT), 255 (LH), 611 (MA).
SEPTEMBER 1975:	RFs 75 (CM), 85 (GR), 122 (DS), 145 (HH), 564 (HH), 583 (WR), 663 (CM).
OCTOBER 1975:	RFs 213 (LH), 304 (GR), 675 (MA).
NOVEMBER 1975:	RFs 74 (GY), 119 (SJ), 194 (ST), 543 (SJ).
DECEMBER 1975:	RFs 26 (CY), 111 (HH), 353 (AV), 559 (WR).
JANUARY 1976:	RFs 68 (LS), 150, 171, 584 (all HH), 187 (DG), 189 (SV), 596 (DT), 667 (MA), 673 (HE).
FEBRUARY 1976:	RFs 48 (DG), 64 (GY), 174 (GR), 196 (GY), 302 (HA), 310 (GY), 321 (AV), 568 (WR), 598 (UX), 601 (HG), 620 (MA).
MARCH 1976:	RFs 152 (WY), 319 (K), 323 (FW), 614 (GR), 615 (GR), 640 (MA).
APRIL 1976:	RFs 40 (DG), 67 (ST), 108 (GY), 166 (WR), 326 (NB), 333, 375, 417 (all EW), 334, 338, 356, 468 (all A), 366, 408, 454 (all K), 367 (NS), 423 (NB), 450 (FW), 470 (AV), 608 (AD).
MAY 1976:	RFs 69 (CM), 98 (HH), 102 (SV), 134 (SJ), 336 (FW), 462, 488, 538 (all R), 548 (WR), 563 (K).
JUNE 1976:	RFs 89 (WY), 103 (TG), 329 (K), 330 (NB), 340 (A), 349, 370, 391, 403, 407, 409 (all UX), 365 (A), 436 (K), 540 (WR), 641 (GR).
JULY 1976:	RFs 45 (GR), 88 (GR), 129 (DG), 379 (UX), 390 (K), 402 (UX).
AUGUST 1976:	RFs 324 (AV), 350, 364, 396, 400, 406 (all UX), 363 (FW), 414 (K), 490 (K).
SEPTEMBER 1976:	RFs 223 (GY), 231 (SJ), 263 (TG), 343 (FW), 345, 380, 535 (all TC), 355 (E), 371, 383, 389, 401, 404, 426 (all K).
OCTOBER 1976:	RFs 191 (HH), 352, 358, 422, 445, 499, 632 (all EW), 368 (E), 418 (UX), 424 (NB), 449, 472, 515 (all K), 524 (UX).
NOVEMBER 1976:	RFs 106 (GR), 384 (UX), 385 (AV), 427 (UX), 431 (K), 523 (AV), 554 (HG).
DECEMBER 1976:	RFs 351, 461, 479, 509 (all AV), 359 (UX), 440 (K), 550 (GR).
JANUARY 1977:	RFs 28 (WR), 55, 185, 193 (HH), 140 (WR), 180 (DS), 236 (DG), 242 (DG), 412 (K), 420, 498, 503, 525, 526 (all EW), 460, 485, 529 (all TC), 617 (AV).
MARCH 1977:	RFs 146 (GR), 247 (HH), 419 (UX), 513 (AV), 567 (LH), 602 (AV), 613 (WR), 627 (K), 655 (LH).
APRIL 1977:	RFs 120 (WR), 214 (WR), 387, 432, 443, 448, 455, 508, 517 (all AV), 429, 444, 458, 459, 521, 534 (all K).
MAY 1977:	RFs 168 (GR), 200 (SA), 212 (HG), 442, 531, 685 (all K).
JUNE 1977:	RFs 239 (DT), 251 (WR), 527, 528, 537 (all K).
JULY 1977:	RFs 28 (WR), 453 (K), 530 (K).
AUGUST 1977:	RFs 218 (LH), 281 (WY), 346, 519, 532, 603 (all K).
SEPTEMBER 1977:	RFs 506 (K), 545 (K).
OCTOBER 1977:	RFs 54 (LH), 79 (LH), 533 (K).
NOVEMBER 1977:	RFs 421, 465, 489 (all K).
DECEMBER 1977:	RFs 354 (K), 480 (K).
JANUARY 1978:	RFs 125 (WR), 175 (WY), 392, 415, 425, 485 (all K).
FEBRUARY 1978:	RF 183 (ST).
MAY 1978:	RF 684 (GY).
JUNE 1978:	RF 690 (DT).
JULY 1978:	RF 518 (K).
MARCH 1979:	RFs 221 (CM), 314, 369, 381, 428, 437, 441, 452, 471, 481, 492, 502, 504, 505, 507, 510, 511, 512, 516, 520, 522, 536 (all K).
MAY 1979:	RF 495* (K).

*Not operated after March 1979 — to LT Museum in May.
NOTE: Not included above RF 202, shown as delicensed April 1977.

ROUTES OPERATED BY SINGLE-DECKERS: JANUARY 1951

This list shows all the routes which were operated by large saloons on Mondays to Fridays at the beginning of 1951 and which therefore formed the basis of the vehicle replacement programme. Reference to this list will help understanding of the main body of the book but for reasons of space it is not possible to include information about service changes during the whole twenty-eight years of operation of the RF class. The vehicle type shown is the one officially allocated to the route. In practice this would have been varied depending on the availability of particular vehicles. In the Country Area, a number of otherwise double-deck routes had small allocations of single-deckers; these are omitted from the list, as are double-deck allocations to otherwise single-deck routes.

ROUTE NO.	MAIN TERMINALS	GARAGES	VEHICLE TYPE	FIRST RF
200	Wimbledon Stn – Coombe Lane	Merton	5Q5	12/52
201	Feltham Stn – Kingston	Kingston	TD2	1/59
202	Canal Bridge – New Cross	Old Kent Road	5Q5	12/52
205	Chingford – Hammond Street	Enfield	TD2	to D/D
206	Hampton Court Stn – Claygate	Kingston	14T12	6/59
208	Clapton Pond – Bromley-by-Bow	Dalston	5Q5	2/53
208ᴬ	Clapton Pond – Maryland Stn	Dalston	LTsd	10/52
210	Finsbury Park – Golders Green	Muswell Hill	LTsd/someTD	9/52
211	Ealing Broadway – Ruislip High St	Southall	TD2	11/58
212	Finsbury Park – Muswell Hill Broadway	Muswell Hill	TD1	2/53
213	Kingston – Belmont	Kingston/Sutton	14T12/LTsd	12/52
215	Kingston – Ripley	Kingston	4Q4	5/62
216	Kingston – Sunbury – Staines	Kingston	TD2	7/60
218	Kingston – Laleham – Staines	Kingston	1T1	1/60
219	Kingston – Weybridge	Kingston	4Q4	1/60
221	North Harrow – Pinner	Harrow Weald	TD2	None
222	Uxbridge – Hounslow Central	Uxbridge	14T12	11/58
223	Uxbridge – West Drayton (Mill Rd)	Uxbridge	14T12	None
224	Uxbridge – Laleham	Uxbridge	11T11	6/59
227	Penge – Chislehurst	Elmers End	LTsd	11/52
228	Well Hall Stn – Chislehurst	Sidcup	14T12	1/53
233	Finsbury Pk – Northumberland Park	West Green	5Q5	1/53
234ᴬ	Hackbridge – Purley (Old Lodge Lane)	Croydon	LTsd	1/53
236	Leyton High Rd – Stroud Green	Leyton/Tottenham	TD2	11/58
237	Hounslow – Chertsey	Hounslow	LTsd	12/52
238	Emerson Park – Noak Hill	Hornchurch	TD2	to D/D
240 (part)	Edgware – Mill Hill East	Edgware	TD2	to D/D
240ᴬ	Edgware – Mill Hill East	Edgware	TD2	5/62
241	Sidcup Garage – Welling Stn	Sidcup	5Q5	3/53
242	Wake Arms – Potters Bar Garage	Enfield	TD2	to D/D
243	Upshire – Cheshunt	Enfield	TD2	None
244	Muswell Hill Broadway – Winchmore Hill	Muswell Hill	LTsd	to D/D
250	Hornchurch Garage – Epping Town	Hornchurch	TD2	7/59
251	Burnt Oak – Arnos Grove	Muswell Hill	TD2	12/56
252	Romford Stn – Birch Road	Hornchurch	9T9	to D/D
254	Buckhurst Hill Stn – Loughton Stn	Loughton	11T11	10/53
264	Sunbury (French Street) – Hersham Green	Kingston	1T1	6/59
304	Tyttenhanger – Whitwell	St Albans	10T10	4/53
307	Boxmoor – Harpenden	Hemel Hempstead	15T13	10/57
308/308ᴬ	Hertford – Newgate St/Little Berkhamsted	Hertford	10T10	5/53
309	Rickmansworth – Harefield – Uxbridge	Watford (Leavesden Rd)	4Q4/15T13	2/69
316	Chesham – Hemel Hempstead – Adeyfield	Hemel Hempstead	4Q4	8/54
317	Watford – Berkhamsted	Hemel Hempstead	15T13	7/56
318/A/B/C	Watford – Chipperfield/Two Waters	Watford (Leavesden Rd)	15T13/4Q4	10/58
319	Boxmoor – Little Gaddesden	Hemel Hempstead	15T13	10/58
320	Watford – Bedmond – Boxmoor	Hemel Hempstead	15T13	None
322	Watford – Hemel Hempstead	Hemel Hempstead	15T13	8/53
329	Hertford – Knebworth (Nup End)	Hertford	10T10	to GS
337	Hemel Hempstead – Dunstable	Hemel Hempstead	15T13	10/57
342	New Barnet – Broxbourne	Hertford	10T10	5/53
352	Berkhamsted – Dunstable	Hemel Hempstead	15T13	12/60
355	St Albans (Lancaster Rd) – Borehamwood	St Albans	6Q6	4/53
356	Luton – Flamstead	Luton	9T9	6/53
361	Rickmansworth – Chorleywood Gate	Watford (Leavesden Rd)	11T11	to GS
363	High Wycombe – Totteridge	High Wycombe	11T11	7/53
364	Luton – Hitchin	Luton/Hitchin	10T10	6/53
365	St Albans – Luton	St Albans	4Q4	4/53
372	Hertford – Welwyn Garden City	Hertford	10T10	5/53
373	Holtspur – Penn	Amersham	10T10	to GS
375	Rainham – Rainham Ferry	Grays	TF	5/59
376/376ᴬ	Luton/Dunstable – Kensworth	Luton	9T9	6/53
382	St Albans – Codicote	St Albans	4Q4	4/53
384/A	Hertford – Letchworth/Gt Munden	Hertford	10T10	5/53
386	Bishops Stortford – Hitchin	Hertford	10T10	5/53
387	Tring – Aldbury	Tring	4Q4	12/60
389	Hertford – Sawbridgeworth	Hertford	10T10	5/53
390	Hertford – Stevenage	Hertford/Hitchin	10T10	5/53
391/391ᴬ	Hill End – Harpenden/Townsend	St Albans	4Q4	4/53
394/A/B/C	Hyde Heath/Chesham Moor/Chesham – Gt Missenden	Amersham	10T10	7/56
399	Hertford – Coopersale Street	Hertford	10T10	5/53
404	Sevenoaks – Shoreham Village	Dunton Green	9T9	9/53
406ᶜ	Earlswood – Kingswood (Windmill Press)	Reigate	4Q4	3/53

Route	Description	Place	Code	Date
412	Dorking North – Holmbury St Mary	Dorking	TF	9/53
413/413ᴬ	Chipstead – Brasted/Four Elms	Dunton Green	9T9	7/54
419	West Ewell – Epsom – Langley Vale	Leatherhead	4Q4/10T10	8/53
421	Sevenoaks – Heverham	Dunton Green	9T9	9/53
422	Leatherhead – Boxhill (Holiday Camp)	Leatherhead	10T10	11/53
424	Reigate – East Grinstead / Horley – Horne/Outwood	East Grinstead/ Crawley	4Q4	9/53
425	Dorking North – Guildford	Dorking/Guildford	10T10	9/53
426	Crawley – Horley – Crawley	Crawley	4Q4	10/57
427	Weybridge – Byfleet – Pyrford – Woking	Addlestone	10T10	8/53
432	Guildford – Great Bookham	Guildford	6Q6	9/53
434	Horsham – Dormansland	Crawley/East Grinstead	4Q4	9/53
435	Leatherhead – Tadworth	Leatherhead	10T10	11/53
437	Weybridge – Byfleet – Woking	Addlestone	10T10	8/53
440/440ᴬ	Redhill – Salfords/Redstone Estate	Reigate	4Q4	3/53
445	Windsor – Datchet Common	Windsor	10T10	12/66
447	Redhill – Reigate – Woldingham	Reigate	4Q4	3/53
450	Dartford – Bean – Betsham – Gravesend	Northfleet	10T10	11/53
453	Warlingham – Caterham-on-the-Hill	Chelsham	4Q4	to D/D
456	Weybridge – Pyrford – Woking	Addlestone	10T10	8/53
458	Slough – Iver – Uxbridge	Windsor	10T10	6/53
459	Richings Park Estate – Uxbridge	Windsor	10T10	6/53
462	Chertsey – Leatherhead	Addlestone/Leatherhead	10T10	11/53
489/489ᴬ	Gravesend – Ash/Meopham (Hook Green)	Northfleet	4Q4	11/53
497	Gravesend – Dover Road Schools	Northfleet	4Q4	to D/D
701/702	Gravesend – Ascot/Sunningdale	Northfleet/Staines	10T10	2/52
703	Wrotham – Amersham	Swanley/Amersham	10T10	6/52
704	Tunbridge Wells – Windsor	Tunbridge Wells/Windsor	10T10	10/51
705	Sevenoaks – Westerham – Windsor	Dunton Green/Windsor	10T10	6/52
706/707	Westerham/Oxted – Aylesbury	Chelsham/Tring	10T10	4/52
708	East Grinstead – Hemel Hempstead	East Grinstead/Hemel Hempstead	10T10	2/52
709	Caterham-on-the-Hill – Chesham	Godstone/Amersham	10T10	12/51
710	Crawley – Amersham	Crawley/Amersham	10T10	12/51
711	Reigate – High Wycombe	Reigate/High Wycombe	10T10	12/51
712/713	Dorking – Luton/Dunstable	Dorking/St Albans	TF	3/52
714	Dorking – London (Baker St)	Dorking	TF	3/52
715	Hertford – Guildford	Guildford/Hertford	6Q6	12/51
716	Chertsey – Hitchin	Addlestone/Hitchin	10T10	2/52
717	Woking – Welwyn Garden City	Addlestone/Hatfield	10T10	2/52
718	Windsor – Epping	Windsor/Epping	10T10	3/52
720	Bishops Stortford – London (Aldgate)	Epping	TF	5/52
723	Tilbury – London (Aldgate)	Grays	TF	1/52
727	Luton – London (Kings Cross)	Luton	TF	None

NOTES:
1. The following single-deck routes were introduced (one taken over from another operator) between 1951 and the completion of the RF delivery programme:
   407/407ᴬ   Windsor – Slough Trading Estate via Slough or Chalvey respectively.
   473   Horsham – Edenbridge via Rowfant.
2. Routes shown as 'to D/D' were converted directly from the type shown, except for routes 244 and 252 which first went to TD.
3. Routes 309, 361, 373, 387 and 445 were initially converted to GS.
4. Routes 352, 394 (group) and 426 were initially converted to 15T13.
5. When double-decked, routes 221, 243 and 320 were absorbed into other services as part of route re-organisations.
6. The single-deck section of route 240 was absorbed into route 240ᴬ.
7. Route 727 was absorbed into extended route 714.

The route which had RFs allocated for the longest period of time was the 237, between December 1952 and April 1977. At the start of its career, RF 366 is seen at Hounslow. G.A. Rixon

Overleaf RF 198 in original Green Line style and RF 170 in the mid-sixties scheme, showing how well the class responded to the modernisation.
LT Museum H/4140
John Aldridge